GRAMMAR IN CONTEXT

GRAMMAR IN CONTEXT

SANDRA N. ELBAUM

SECOND EDITION

BOOK 3

◆ ◆ ◆

Heinle & Heinle Publishers
An International Thomson Publishing Company
Boston, Massachusetts, 02116, USA

The publication of *Grammar in Context,* Second Edition, was directed by members of the Newbury House Publishing Team at Heinle & Heinle:

Erik Gundersen, Editorial Director
John F. McHugh, Market Development Director
Kristin M. Thalheimer, Production Services Coordinator

Also participating in the publication of this program were:

Vice President and Publisher: Stanley J. Galek
Director of Production: Elizabeth Holthaus
Project Manager/Desktop Pagination: Thompson Steele Production Services
Manufacturing Coordinator: Mary Beth Hennebury
Photo Coordinator: Philippe Heckly
Associate Editor: Ken Pratt
Interior Designer: Sally Steele
Illustrator: Jim Roldan
Photo/video Specialist: Jonathan Stark
Cover Designer: Gina Petti, Rotunda Design

Photo Credits
p. 18 © Jonathan Stark; **p. 48** © Len Rubenstein/The Picture Cube, Inc.; **p. 84** © Michael Newman/PhotoEdit; **p. 104** © Donald Dietz/Stock, Boston; **p. 133** © Owen Franken/Stock, Boston; **p. 145** © UPI/Bettman; **p. 160** © J. Taposchaner/FPG International; **p. 191** © Emilio Mercado/The Picture Cube, Inc.; **p. 212** © Daemmrich/Stock, Boston; **p. 239** © Sarah Putnam/The Picture Cube, Inc.; **p. 270** © Jonathan Stark; **p. 301** © Michael Newman/PhotoEdit.

Heinle & Heinle Publishers is a division of International Thomson Publishing, Inc.

Manufactured in the United States of America

Library of Congress Cataloging-in-Publication Data

Elbaum, Sandra N.
        Grammar in context / Sandra Elbaum.
            p.   cm.
        ISBN 0-8384-4688-4 (bk. 1). —ISBN 0-8384-4689-2 (bk. 2). —ISBN
        0-8384-6651-6 (bk. 3)
            1. English language—Grammar—Problems, exercises, etc.
        2. English language—Textbooks for foreign speakers. I. Title.
        PE1112.E3641995
        428.2'4—dc20   95-49062
                                                            CIP

ISBN 0-8384-6651-6

    10 9 8 7 6 5 4 3 2

PREFACE

Grammar in Context, Book Three is the third part of a three-part grammar series for adult students of English as a Second Language. This series of work-texts is designed for the high beginning to low advanced instructional levels.

As ESL teachers know, presenting English in a meaningful context allows for a better understanding of the grammar point. *Grammar in Context* is unique among grammar texts in its use of culturally rich, informative readings to present and illustrate the target grammar, and to stimulate interest in the topic.

Grammar in Context is organized as follows:

Lesson Focus The lessons begin with an overview and brief explanation of the grammar points covered. The Lesson Focus also includes sentences which illustrate the grammar point(s) being addressed.

Pre-Reading Questions These questions stimulate student interest in the topic of the reading which follows.

Introductory Readings A short reading illustrates each new grammar point in a natural, authentic context. These high-interest readings about culturally rich topics engage the student's attention and help focus on the grammar points. The real-life subject matter provides practical information about American life and customs, stories about famous people and events, and contemporary issues that are of concern to Americans as well as to recently-arrived residents. These readings can be used as springboards for lively classroom discussions, as well as inspiration for out-of-class activities.

Since *Grammar in Context* is not a reader, the readings are written at a simple, accessible level, for their primary goal is to exemplify the target grammar. The practical vocabulary and idioms that are needed to understand the passage are anticipated and glossed in footnotes or illustrations.

The grammar explanations use simple language, illustrative example sentences, and charts with a clear graphic overview. Because *Grammar in Context* does not rely on a knowledge of linguistic jargon, fine points of grammar are often placed in a footnote so as not to overwhelm students who do not need so much detail.

The Language Notes provide the students with additional information on the functions of language, level of formality/informality, appropriate usage, spelling, and pronunciation. They often include information on the differences between American English and British English.

Grammar Boxes and Language Notes Special attention is given to trouble spots. This book anticipates difficulties that most students have—for example: *used to* vs. *be used to, stop* + gerund or infinitive, negatives of modals, and comparison of tenses. Also, a great deal of attention is given to word order.

Exercises There is a great variety of exercise types. The change of pace from one exercise to another reduces boredom in the classroom and offers challenges to different types of language learners as well as language teachers. Exercises include traditional fill-ins, cloze tasks, pair work, editing exercises, and combination exercises which review previous material in the context of the new or integrate several subskills from within the lesson. Many of the exercises allow students to personalize their remarks to reflect their own observations about American life, their opinions on cultural matters, and their feelings.

Expansion Activities These activities, grouped at the end of each lesson, allow students to use the grammar points covered in more communicative ways. Expansion Activities include pair work; group discussions; writing; poetry, proverbs, famous quotes and sayings; and outside activities. These activities give subjects for debate and discussion, topics for written reflection, and ideas for further research on the context of the lesson or on a related topic (including suggestions for interviewing Americans and bringing the findings back to share with the class). The poems, proverbs, famous quotes and sayings not only illustrate the grammar items, but also provide an opportunity for a rich cross-cultural interchange.

Because they are progressively more challenging, the Expansion Activities lead away from a mechanical manipulation of grammar toward situations in which students put their recently learned grammatical knowledge to immediate practical use.

The teacher may choose to have students do Expansion Activities after a related grammar point has been thoroughly studied, or may assign them after the lesson has been completed.

Editing Advice Potentially troublesome issues with the grammar points covered in the lesson are presented, showing students common errors, and ways to correct them.

Summary   The end-of-lesson summary encapsulates all of the grammar presented in the chapter in a simple graphic format.

Test/Review   Each lesson ends with a test/review section that allows both the teacher and the students to evaluate the mastery of concepts. Different formats—editing, fill-ins, and multiple choice questions—are used.

Appendices   This book includes appendices that provide useful information in list or chart form. The appendices are cross-referenced throughout the text.

Differences Between the First and Second Editions

There is now a third book in the series. Previous users of this text should note that the new Book One is easier than the original. Users of the former Book One would choose either Book One of the new series for a high beginning class or Book Two of the new series for an intermediate class. The original Book Two corresponds more closely to Book Three of the new series.

In the first edition, Book Two continued where Book One ended. In the new series, grammar points overlap. Since students rarely master a point after only one presentation and practice, there is a repetition at the next level, as well as added complexity. All tenses covered in Book One are also in Book Two. Also included in Books One and Two are singular and plural, pronouns and possessive forms, modals, count and noncount nouns, and comparative and superlative adjectives and adverbs. Included in Books Two and Three are modals, adjective clauses, gerunds, infinitives, and time clauses.

There is a higher degree of contextualization in both the readings and the grammar exercises.

Pre-reading questions have been added to stimulate interest and discussion. New readings contain many topics of a contemporary nature—for example, self-help groups, job rankings and personal ads. Older readings have been updated and extended.

Many of the exercises and exercise types are completely new. Older exercises have been updated and revised. More interactive, task-based activities are included, some to be done in class, asking students to work with a partner or small group. Outside activities encourage students to talk with Americans, note their responses, and report them to the class.

There are more visual aids, illustrations, and charts to support the vocabulary in the readings, and the context of the exercises. Maps of the United States and references to states, major cities, and regions familiarize the students with names they will frequently hear.

Most lessons include editing advice and an error correction or editing exercise. In addtion, a new and comprehensive testing program has been added.

Overall, the new edition of *Grammar in Context* provides thorough coverage of the grammar, a variety of exercise types, and an anticipation of student problems, thereby freeing the teacher from excessive class preparation. By providing grammar practice in the context of relevant and stimulating ideas, the *Grammar in Context* series eases the transition to American life, both linguistically and culturally.

Acknowledgments

I would like to thank my editor at Heinle and Heinle, Erik Gundersen, for his enthusiasm about this new edition, and for his gentle but firm way of pushing me in the direction that I needed to go.

I would also like to show my appreciation to the following teachers who reviewed my books: Kevin McClure, ELS Language Center, San Francisco; Kathi Jordan, Contra Costa College; Laurie Moody, Passaic County Community College; Sherry Trechter, George Mason University; Bettye Wheeler, El Paso Community College; Ethel Tiersky, Truman College; Colleen Weldele, Palomar College; Emily Strauss, De Anza College; Peggy Armstrong; Pat Ishill, Union County College; Tay Leslie, ELS Language Centers Central Office; Kiran Razzak, ELS Language Center @ Chapman University; Terry Pruett-Said, Kansas State University.

Thanks to Christine Meyers, Judi Peman, and Merle Weiss for their kindness and understanding in getting me through it all.

And last, but most certainly not least, many thanks to my students at Truman College. They have increased my understanding of my own language and taught me to see life from another point of view. By sharing their insights and life stories, they have enriched my life enormously.

I thought Russians were different from Americans and that was why life in Russia and America were so different. When I came to America, I gradually realized that any national character is nothing but an adaptive social behavior. The more I learned about America, the more I saw that there was no difference between Russians and Americans as individual human beings. I saw a familiar spectrum of personalities, intimate problems, emotions, complexes, virtues, and vices.

American social chemistry was based on the same periodic table as the Russian. Individual atoms of human nature were the same but Russian and American social molecules were arranged differently. The two cultures seemed to contrast as strongly as the lifestyles of birds and fish, although beautiful species could be found among both . . .

The chemistry of society is universal, and history is a record of most unexpected transformations.

(from Memoirs of 1984, *by Yuri Tarnopolsky, published by University Press of America, Maryland.)*

CONTENTS

GRAMMAR
IN CONTEXT

REVIEW LESSON

This is a review of *Grammar in Context, Book Two.* Read the grammar explanations and notice the edited examples. Then edit for mistakes in the exercises that follow.

Part 1   Verbs

1. Use the *-s* form of present tense verbs when the subject is a singular noun; *he, she, it;* or a gerund (verb + *ing*).

    He work$\overset{s}{.}$

    Learning another language take$\overset{s}{}$ time.

2. Do not use the *-s* form when the subject is plural; *I,* or *you.*

    People need$\cancel{s}$ love.

3. Use a singular verb after *every* or *no.*

    Every student $\overset{has}{\cancel{have}}$ homework.

    Nobody know$\overset{s}{}$ the answer.

4. Use *was* with *I, he, she, it,* or a singular noun. Use *were* with *we, you, they,* or a plural noun.

    They $\overset{were}{\cancel{was}}$ late.

5. Do not use *was* or *were* to form the simple past tense of a verb.

    He $\overset{went}{\cancel{was\ go}}$ home at 6:00.

6. For continuous forms, use *be* + verb-*ing.*

    He $\overset{is}{}$ sleeping now.

    They are eat$\overset{ing}{}$ now.

    He $\overset{was}{}$ sleeping when the phone rang.

7. For perfect forms, use *have/has/had* + third form of the verb (past participle).

    They $\overset{have}{}$ known each other for three years.

8. Use the simple form after *do, does, did.*

    He didn't $\overset{know}{\cancel{knew}}$ the answer.

    Does he speak$\cancel{s}$ English?

9. Use an infinitive after certain verbs.

 She wanted ^to^ go home.

 I need ^to^ talk with you.

10. Use the simple form after *to*.

 She wanted to ~~left~~ ^leave^.

 She wants to finish college and find~~ing~~ a job.

11. Use the simple form after a modal *(can, could, will, would, may, might, must, should)*. Do not use *to* after a modal.

 She can ~~to~~ speak French.

 She couldn't ~~went~~ ^go^ to the party.

12. After *will*, do not use *be* with another verb.

 She will ~~be~~ drive to the party.

13. Do not use the future tense in an *if* clause or time clause.

 When I ~~will~~ return to my country, I will visit my friends.

EXERCISE I   Find the mistakes with verb forms, and correct them. Not every sentence has a mistake. If the sentence is correct, write *C*.

EXAMPLES: He drink ^s^ coffee every day.

  Where were you yesterday?   *C*

1. She going to buy a new car.

2. I'm go to the library once a week.

3. Where does your brother lives?

4. She didn't go home.

5. He have a new car.

6. He lives in New York.

7. I watching TV last night when the telephone rang.

8. He likes dogs. He doesn't likes cats.

9. Last year I was buy a new car.

10. I'll be talk to you later.

11. He speaks Russian. He doesn't speaks Polish.

12. She will take a vacation next week.

13. He been a doctor since 1992.

14. Nobody know how I feel.

15. I had have a lot of experience at my job.

16. He driving to work when he had a flat tire.

17. I've work in a hotel for three years.

18. I want eat lunch now.

19. She forgot to turned off the oven.

20. If we will have time next week, we will go to the zoo.

21. You should to buy a new car.

22. Every student need a textbook.

Part 2   Adjectives, Adverbs, and Noun Modifiers

1. A descriptive adjective has no plural form.

They have two beautiful daughters.

2. *This* and *that* are singular. *These* and *those* are plural.

These
~~This~~ apples are delicious.

3. *Another* is singular. *Other(s)* is plural.

Other
Some students come from Japan. ~~Another~~ students come from Korea.

4. Use an adjective after *be* or other linking verbs *(seem, look, smell, sound, taste, feel).*

He is very carefully.

The coffee smells freshly.

5. Use an adverb of manner (usually adjective + *ly*) to describe a verb phrase.

He speaks English fluent~~.~~ *ly*

She cooks ~~good~~ *well*.

6. Use *too* before adjectives and adverbs. Use *too **much*** before nouns.

That car is too ~~much~~ expensive.

7. Use *too* only if there is a problem. If there's no problem, use *very*.

I found a wonderful job. I'm ~~too~~ *very* happy.

8. Put *enough* after adjectives and adverbs.

He is (enough) old *'* to drive.

9. *Very* cannot come before a verb. Use *very **much*** after a verb phrase.

I ~~very~~ like your dress *very much*.

10. The adjective comes before the noun.

She has ~~a job interesting~~ *an interesting job*.

11. A noun can describe another noun. Put the specific noun before the general noun.

He works as a ~~driver truck~~ *truck driver*.

12. When a noun describes a noun, the first noun is always singular.

He put the books on the book~~s~~ shelf.

He has a five-year~~s~~-old son.

EXERCISE 2 Find and correct the mistakes with adjectives, adverbs, and noun modifiers. Not every sentence has a mistake. If the sentence is correct, write *C*.

EXAMPLES: **He drives very careful~~.~~ *ly*.**

He speaks English well.   *C*

1. Her daughters are very intelligents.

2. He is very proudly because his daughter graduated from college.

3. This coffee smells freshly.

4. This is fresh coffee.

5. I'm too much busy today. I don't have time for you.

6. She very likes her new job.

7. She got her license driver's last month.

8. This books are mine.

9. If you don't like this course, you can take another one.

10. Some students prefer morning classes. Another students prefer evening classes.

11. That box is enough big for your shoes.

12. He has enough time to help you.

13. She had a two weeks vacation.

Part 3   Comparatives, Superlatives, and Equatives

1. Use *-er* and *-est* for short adjectives and adverbs. Use *more* and *most* with long adjectives and *-ly* adverbs.

   He is the ~~most tall~~ *tallest* person in his family.

   He walks ~~quicklier~~ *more quickly* than his wife.

2. Do not use *more* and *-er* together.

   He speaks English ~~more~~ better than you.

3. Use *as . . . as* with adjectives and adverbs. Use *the same . . . as* with nouns.

   She is ~~the same~~ *as* tall as her husband.

   She is the same height as her husband. — *correct*

4. Use *look like* for a physical similarity. Use *be like* for a character similarity.

   She ~~is~~ look*s* like her sister. They both have curly blond hair and blue eyes.

   She is ~~look~~ like her sister. They are both very intelligent.

5. Use *don't* or *doesn't* to make the negative of sense perception verbs.

          doesn't
   She ~~isn't~~ look like her mother.

6. Use *than* before the second item of comparison.

                 than
   New York is bigger ∧ Philadelphia.

7. Use *the* before a superlative form.

           the
   New York is ∧ biggest city in the U.S.

8. Put the comparative word before the noun.

   She has money (more) than I do.

9. Put the comparative adverb after the verb phrase.

   She (better) speaks English than her husband.

EXERCISE 3 Find the mistakes with comparatives, superlatives, and equatives, and correct them. Not every sentence has a mistake. If the sentence is correct, write *C*.

   EXAMPLES: **She (better) drives than her husband.**

              I have more free time than you do. *C*

1. He's taller than his brother.

2. He speaks English more better than his brother.

3. He's as smart as his brother.

4. He earns more money his wife.

5. New York is the biggest city in the U.S.

6. January is the colder month of the year.

7. San Francisco is one of the most interesting cities in the U.S.

8. She is funniest girl in the class.

9. He's not as old as his wife. His wife is older.

10. He's not the same tall as his son. His son is taller.

11. He and his wife are the same age.

12. Coca-Cola tastes like Pepsi.

13. She looks like her mother.

Part 4   Count and Noncount Nouns[1]

1. Use *much* and *a little* with noncount nouns. Use *many* and *a few* with count nouns.

   He has a ~~little~~ *few* friends in the U.S.

   He has ~~much~~ *many* friends in his country.

2. Use *much* in negatives and questions. Use *a lot of* in affirmative statements.

   He has ~~much~~ *a lot of* time.

3. Use *too much/too many* only if there is a problem. Use *many* or *a lot of* if there is no problem.

   He has ~~too~~ many good friends.

4. Use *a few* and *a little* to emphasize a positive quantity. Use *few* and *little* to emphasize a negative quantity. Often, *very* helps emphasize the negative.

   He's a lucky man. He has ∧*a* few good friends.

   I can't help you today. I have ∧*very* a little time.

5. Use *of* with a unit of measure.

   He bought five pounds ∧*of* meat.

EXERCISE 4   Find the mistakes with count and noncount nouns and quantity words, and correct them. Not every sentence has a mistake. If the sentence is correct, write *C*.

   EXAMPLES: My counselor gave me a lot of advices.

                     The teacher gave a lot of homework.   *C*

1. He has many money.

2. He has many credit cards.

3. He has too much money. He can buy whatever he wants.

4. There were a lot of people at the party.

---

[1]See Appendix A for a list of noncount nouns.

5. I can't talk to you now. I have very little time.

6. She drank three waters today.

7. She drank some water today.

8. She put a little sugar in her coffee.

9. There's no elevator in this building.

10. I bought two cans of soup.

11. He has a lot of mistakes on his test, but he doesn't have a lot on his composition.

12. I have any friends.

13. He has much time to do his job.

14. She uses a little of milk in her coffee.

15. There was a lot of snow last winter.

Part 5   Nouns and Pronouns

1. Use '*s* for possession of singular nouns and irregular plural nouns. Use just an apostrophe for regular plural nouns. Put the possessive form before the noun.

   My sister's house
   ~~House my sister~~ is big.

   The children's toys are on the floor.

   My parents' house is in a suburb.

2. Do not use an apostrophe (') for a plural ending.

   girls
   I saw two ~~girl's~~ in the park.

3. Use the plural form to talk about more than one thing.

   A lot of my friends speak Greek.

4. Some nouns have irregular plurals. Do not use the -*s* ending with these nouns: *people, men, women, children, feet, teeth.*

   They have five children.

5. Do not use *a* or *an* before a plural form.

   She has ~~a~~ pretty eyes.

6. Use the plural form of the noun after phrases of quantity such as *one of my . . ., some of the. . . .*

   One of my friend^(s) lives in New York.

7. Do not repeat the subject with a pronoun.

   My parents ~~they~~ have a big house.

8. After some verbs, you must use an object (noun or pronoun).

   My teacher told ^(me) to finish the homework.

9. After *want, need, expect, like,* etc., use object + infinitive.

   I want ~~that he~~ ^(him to) leave.

   He expected ~~that I worked~~ ^(me to work).

10. Use *there* + a form of *be* to introduce a new noun.

    There are trees in the park.
    ~~In the park are trees.~~

    ^(There) ~~It~~ is a table in the kitchen.

11. Use the correct pronoun (subject, object, possessive, reflexive). See Appendix L for a list of pronouns and possessive forms.

    My parents need ~~they~~ ^(their) car.

    My brother loves ~~her~~ ^(his) wife.

EXERCISE 5 Find the mistakes with pronouns and possessive forms, and correct them. Not every sentence has a mistake. If the sentence is correct, write *C.*

EXAMPLES: Three ~~woman~~ ^(women) came to the meeting.

My sister's son lives in Los Angeles. *C*

1. They have four childrens.

2. Twenty men came to the party.

3. Do you like dogs? I like its very much.

4. Are a lot of flowers in front of my house.

5. One of my friend lives in New York.

6. My parents they live in Montreal.

7. I want to talk to she.

8. They parents don't live in the U.S.

9. My parents' house is not very big.

10. You didn't bring your dictionary. You can use mine.

11. Mine car is in the shop now.

12. He didn't wash him hands before dinner.

13. She wrote a letter to hers sisters.

14. I didn't see my cousins at school, but I saw they at the library.

15. Car of my father is not very good.

16. What is name your sister?

17. Mary speaks English well, but his husband doesn't.

18. I have two cats, I got them from my sister.

19. They lost there suitcases at the airport.

20. Do you have any brother's? What are theirs names?

21. Do you like your teachers? Yes, we like them very much.

22. William and Henry are men's names.

23. My sister husband works as a computer programmer.

24. I want he leave.

25. They expect me to answer their questions.

26. Who's book is this?

27. We lost ours books.

28. They looked at themself in the mirror.

Part 6   Sentences and Word Order

1. Every sentence must have a verb.

   My teacher ∧ very nice.
   is (inserted above ∧)

2. Every verb must have a subject.

   It is
   I̶s̶ important to speak English well.

                                                              it
   He didn't understand the lesson because ∧ was too hard.

   There are
   A̶r̶e̶ a lot of Asian students at this college.

3. The basic sentence word order is subject + verb + complement. Put the subject before the verb in all clauses.

   The workers left when was finished (the meeting.)

   Everything that said (the teacher) is true.

4. Do not start with a pronoun and put the subject at the end. Start with the subject noun.

   The movie
   I̶t̶ was very interesting t̶h̶e̶ ̶m̶o̶v̶i̶e̶.

5. Don't repeat the subject with a pronoun.

   My sister s̶h̶e̶ lives in Boston.

6. An adverbial phrase or clause (of time, place, reason) can come before the subject or at the end of the verb phrase. Do not put a phrase between the subject and the verb.

   She (once in a while) takes the bus to work.

7. Put the adverb of frequency between the subject and simple verb; after the verb *be;* and between the auxiliary verb and the main verb.[1]

   I wash (always) my hands before dinner.

   She (always) is late to class.

   I have wanted (always) to visit Paris.

   He doesn't know (always) the correct answer.

---

[2]Exception: *Sometimes* usually precedes the subject in a sentence with *don't/doesn't/didn't.*
   Sometimes I don't do the homework.

8. Most frequency words can come at the beginning of the sentence. However, *always* and *never* rarely come at the beginning of the sentence.

   We never
   ~~Never we~~ eat lunch in a restaurant.

9. The word *maybe* can come at the beginning of the sentence. You can also use *may* as a modal verb with about the same meaning.

   Maybe it
   ~~It maybe~~ will rain. OR *It may rain.*

10. One-word adverbs *(probably, even, only, just, especially, also)* usually come between the subject and the simple verb; between the auxiliary verb and the main verb; and after the verb *be*.[3]

    I liked the desserts you prepared. I liked (especially) the cake.

    He has had (probably) a lot of problems.

    He's sick (probably) today.

11. Do not separate the verb from the object.

    She speaks (fluently) English.

    She likes (very much) her apartment.

    He needs (all the time) to wear a watch.

12. If a compound subject includes *I*, put *I* at the end.[4]

    My brother and I
    ~~I and my brother~~ went to Miami.

13. Don't use a double negative.

    any
    I don't understand ~~nothing~~.

    any
    I don't have ~~no~~ time.

---

[3]If you put the adverb before the subject, the meaning of the sentence changes.
COMPARE:

   He only has $10. means He doesn't have more money.
   Only he has $10. means Nobody else has $10.

   The teacher doesn't know the answer. He doesn't *even* understand the question.
   Nobody knows the answer. *Even* the teacher doesn't know the answer.

[4]You sometimes hear people say "My friend and me" or "Me and my friend." These are common but not correct.

14. Put *together* after the complement.

    They (together) ate lunch.

15. We can use an adjective complement after *make* and *spell*. Note the word order:

    S   V   O   Adjective Complement
    She made   her children happy.
    She spelled the word   wrong.
    She made   the situation better.

    He made (better) the situation.

EXERCISE 6   Find the mistakes with sentences and word order, and correct them. Not every sentence has a mistake. If the sentence is correct, write *C*.

    EXAMPLES: We did (at night) the homework.

               On Monday and Wednesday, the teacher is usually in her office.   *C*

1. Came in late the student and took a seat in the back.

2. She all the time has problems with spelling.

3. My biology teacher I don't like very much.

4. Because she has a full-time job, she always doesn't have time to study.

5. Is very important to know your rights.

6. I have always wanted to learn to speak English fluently.

7. Began registration on August 18.

8. I don't like very much my biology class.

9. I found on the desk a dictionary.

10. Whenever I have a problem, I talk to my father.

11. She doesn't know anything about your problem.

12. There's in my class a Japanese woman.

13. She can't always come to class.

14. He usually eats cereal for breakfast.

15. He usually is sleepy in the afternoon.

16. Never he eats eggs for breakfast.

17. San Francisco a very beautiful city.

18. Are a lot of newspapers on the desk.

19. There isn't no milk in the refrigerator.

20. Just she finished her homework. Now she can relax.

21. She opened carefully the package.

22. Once in a while, Mary and Bob eat dinner together in a restaurant.

23. I don't have enough money to buy the book. Only I have ten dollars on me.

24. The counselor maybe can help you later.

25. After arrived the teacher, the lesson began.

26. After my brother found a job, bought a car.

27. He doesn't want to eat for dinner anything.

28. She spelled wrong six words on her composition. Even she spelled wrong her name.

29. Came to the U.S. my father last year.

30. My husband last month found a job.

31. I and my friend together went to Toronto.

32. She left angrily the room.

33. At nine o'clock starts the second part of the movie.

34. It's very good the novel you wrote.

35. He made more interesting his composition by adding very specific examples.

36. Sometimes I make the situation worse by saying too much.

37. I may go to a movie this weekend.

38. I maybe will go to a movie this weekend.

39. Maybe you should ask the teacher for help.

40. He will probably go to Mexico for Christmas vacation.

41. He made his house bigger by adding a second floor.

42. I will be probably absent next week.

Part 7 Question Word Order

1. The word order with a main verb is: (*Wh-* word +) *do/does/did (n't)* + subject + main verb + complement.

   Where *do* you live?

   Why ~~they didn't~~ *didn't they* stay?

   How *do* you spell "occasion"?

   What ~~means~~ *does* "occasion" *mean*?

2. The word order with *be* is: (*Wh-* word) + *be* + subject + complement.

   Where ~~they are~~ *are they*?

3. The word order with an auxiliary verb is: (*Wh-* word) + auxiliary verb (n't) + subject + main verb + complement.

   When ~~they will~~ *will they* come back?

   Why ~~you haven't~~ *haven't you* seen the movie?

4. Do not use *do/does/did* with questions about the subject.

   Who ~~did come~~ *came* to the party?

   Who ~~does have~~ *has* a computer?

   How many students ~~do~~ need help?

EXERCISE 7 Find the mistakes with question formation, and correct them. Not every sentence has a mistake. If the sentence is correct, write *C*.

> EXAMPLES: Why (you) didn't call me last night?
>
> Who called you last night?   *C*

1. What means "invent"?

2. Who lives in the White House?

3. How do you spell your name?

4. Where I can buy a good stereo?

5. How many languages speaks your father?

6. How is tall your son?

7. How old your son is?

8. Does the Vice President live in the White House?

9. What should I take to the party?

10. How much costs a new car?

11. How say "car" in your language?

12. When was Columbus discovered America?

13. What kind of car he bought?

14. How much do you have money?

15. Where does live your teacher?

16. What time you go to bed every night?

17. Why did you afraid of that man?

18. Do you ever drink coffee at night?

19. Why don't you buy a new car?

20. How many states has the U.S.?

21. How many states have a sales tax?

LESSON ONE

GRAMMAR

The Present Perfect
The Present Perfect
Continuous

CONTEXT

A Job Résumé and Cover Letter

Lesson Focus Present Perfect Tense; Present Perfect Continuous Tense

- We form the present perfect tense with the auxiliary verb *have* or *has* and the past participle. We use the present perfect tense when the action of the sentence is during a period of time that began in the past and includes the present. We also use the present perfect to refer to an action that occurred at an indefinite time in the past.

  I *have studied* English for six months.

  They *have visited* us many times.

  I *have known* my best friend since we were in high school.

  Have you *seen* any good movies lately?

- We form the present perfect continuous tense with *have* or *has* + *been* + verb + *-ing*. We use the present perfect continuous tense with actions that began in the past and continue to the present. The present perfect continuous tense emphasizes the length of time.

  She *has been working* with me for three years.

  I *have been studying* English for two years.

. . . .

R
E
A
D
I
N
G

Before you read:

1. Did you have a job in your country? What did you do? How did you find your job?

2. What are you majoring in? What kind of job do you hope to find after you graduate?

Read the job résumé[1] and the cover letter that follows on the next two pages.

_____

[1]A *résumé* is a paper that lists one's job experience and educational background. When applying for a professional job, people send out a résumé and a cover letter to employers. (The résumé on the next page is a very simple one that lists schools and jobs. A more complex résumé would give a list of the responsibilities of each job.)

Daniel Mendoza
6965 North Troy Avenue
Chicago, Illinois 60659
(312) 555–1946

EDUCATION

1980–1984   National University of Mexico
                 Mexico City, Mexico
                 Degree in Hotel Management

1984–1988   University of Illinois
                 Urbana, Illinois
                 Bachelor of Science Degree: Business
                    Administration

1988–1990   Northwestern University
                 Evanston, Illinois
                 Master of Science Degree: Business
                    Administration

EMPLOYMENT

1990–present   Town and Country Hotel
                 Chicago, Illinois
                 Front office manager

1988–1990   Mid-Town Hotel
                 Evanston, Illinois
                 Auditor (part-time)

1984–1988   Travel Time Hotel
                 Champaign, Illinois
                 Front desk clerk (part-time)

1974–1984   Hotel Mendoza
                 Mexico City, Mexico
                 Variety of duties

Pay special attention to the present perfect verbs in the cover letter.

6965 North Troy Avenue
Chicago, Illinois 60659
June 4, 1996

Mr. Ray Johnson, General Manager
Paradise Hotel
226 West Jackson Boulevard
Chicago, Illinois 60606

Dear Mr. Johnson:

I would like to apply for the job of hotel office manager at the Paradise Hotel.

I come from Mexico City, where my family owns a hotel. I worked in the family business part-time when I was in high school. After high school, I studied hotel and restaurant management at the National University of Mexico. I came to the U.S. in 1984 because I wanted to improve my English, continue my education, and learn about managing larger hotels. Since I came to the U.S., I **have worked** in several American hotels. Over the years my English **has improved,** and I now consider myself bilingual, fluent in both Spanish and English, which is a plus in the hotel business. I **have** also **studied** French and can speak it fairly well. I **have been** a U.S. citizen for the past two years.

I received my bachelor's degree from the University of Illinois in 1988 and my master's degree from Northwestern University in 1990. For the past few years, I **have been working** at the Town and Country Hotel. As you can see from my résumé, I **have had** a lot of experience in the hotel business. Now that I have my degree in business administration, I am ready to assume[2] more responsibilities.

If you **have** already **filled** the manager's position, I would like you to consider me for any other position at your hotel. I **have** always **loved** the hotel business, and I know I can be an asset[3] to your hotel.

Thank you for considering my application. I look forward to meeting with you soon.

Sincerely,

Daniel Mendoza

Daniel Mendoza

---

[2]*Assume* means *take on* or *accept.*

[3]To be an *asset* to a company means to have a talent or ability that will help the company.

1.1 The Past Participle

The past participle is a form of the verb. It is not a tense. We use the past participle after the auxiliary verb *have* to form the present perfect tense.

> He *has studied.*
> They *have left.*

The past participle for regular verbs ends in *-ed.*

Base Form	Past Form	Past Participle
work	worked	worked
look	looked	looked
listen	listened	listened

Some irregular verbs have the same form for the past and the past participle.

Base Form	Past Form	Past Participle
send	sent	sent
understand	understood	understood
cut	cut	cut

The verbs below have a past participle that is different from the past tense. They are grouped according to the type of change. For an alphabetical listing of irregular past tenses and past participles, see Appendix H.

Base Form	Past Form	Past Participle
become	became	become
come	came	come
run	ran	run
blow	blew	blown
draw	drew	drawn
fly	flew	flown
grow	grew	grown
know	knew	known
throw	threw	thrown
swear	swore	sworn
tear	tore	torn
wear	wore	worn

Base Form	Past Form	Past Participle
break	broke	broken
choose	chose	chosen
freeze	froze	frozen
speak	spoke	spoken
steal	stole	stolen
begin	began	begun
drink	drank	drunk
ring	rang	rung
sing	sang	sung
sink	sank	sunk
swim	swam	swum
arise	arose	arisen
bite	bit	bitten
drive	drove	driven
ride	rode	ridden
rise	rose	risen
write	wrote	written
eat	ate	eaten
fall	fell	fallen
forgive	forgave	forgiven
give	gave	given
mistake	mistook	mistaken
shake	shook	shaken
take	took	taken

Miscellaneous Changes		
be	was/were	been
do	did	done
forget	forgot	forgotten
get	got	gotten
go	went	gone
lie	lay	lain
prove	proved	proven (or proved)
see	saw	seen
show	showed	shown (or showed)

1.2 The Present Perfect Tense

We form the present perfect tense by using the auxiliary verb *have* or *has* + a past participle.

Subject	*Have/Has*	Past Participle
I		worked.
You		eaten.
We	have	forgotten.
They		understood.
		known.
He		left.
She	has	known.
It		begun.
There	has	been a mistake.
There	have	been some problems.

Compare statements, questions, and short answers that use the present perfect.

Wh- Word	*Have*	Subject	*Have*	Main Verb	Complement	Short Answer
		He	has	been	in the hotel business.	
		He	hasn't	been	in the restaurant business.	
	Has	he		been	in the hotel business for long?	Yes, he has.* No, he hasn't.
How long	has	he		been	in the hotel business?	
		Who	has		been	in the hotel business?	

*NOTE: Don't use a contraction for a short *yes* answer.

Language Notes

1. We can make contractions with subject pronouns:

I have = I've	He has = He's[4]
You have = You've	She has = She's
We have = We've	It has = It's
They have = They've	There has = There's

2. We can put an adverb of time (*always, never, recently, often,* and so on) between the auxiliary verb and the main verb.

He has *never* worked in a store.
He has *recently* sent out résumés.

---

[4]*He's* is the contraction for both *he has* and *he is.*

The word following *he's* will tell you what the contraction means:
    He's leaving. = He *is* leaving.
    He's left. = He *has* left.

EXERCISE 1   Fill in each blank with the correct form of the verb in parentheses ( ) to form the present perfect tense.

EXAMPLE: Daniel ____*has sent*____ three résumés this week.
          (send)

1. He _____ in the U.S. for a few years.
        (live)

2. You _____ his résumé.
         (see)

3. He _____ several interviews.
        (have)

4. Mr. Johnson _____ a letter from Daniel.
                 (get)

5. There _____ many applicants for the job.
          (be)

6. Daniel's parents _____ in the hotel business.
                     (always/be)

7. Daniel _____ from college.
          (recently/graduate)

8. I _____ Daniel's résumé.
      (read)

9. Daniel _____ his age on his résumé.
           (not/include)

10. _____ the general manager already _____ the
                                                      (fill)
    position?

11. How many people _____ for this job?
                        (apply)

Language Notes

1. We use the present perfect tense when the action of the sentence began in the past and continues into the present.

   Daniel *has worked* in the U.S. since 1984.
   He *has worked* in the hotel business for many years.
   He *has* always *loved* the hotel business.
   He *has* never *worked* in a large hotel.

2. We also use the present perfect to refer to an action that happened at an indefinite time in the past.

   Mr. Johnson *has received* Daniel's letter.
   He *hasn't answered* the letter yet.
   Has he already *filled* the position?
   Has Daniel ever *worked* in a restaurant?

1.3 Continuation from Past to Present

- We use the present perfect tense when the action of the sentence began in the past and continues into the present.

  Daniel *has worked* in the U.S. since 1984.
  He *has worked* in the hotel business for many years.

- A sentence with the present perfect tense sometimes has another clause telling the time the action began in the past.

Main Clause (Present Perfect)	*Since* Clause (Simple Past)
Daniel has worked in a hotel	since he was in high school.
He has been a front office manager	since he graduated from college.

Notice that the verb in the *since* clause is in the simple past tense because it shows when the action began.

Language Notes

For and *Since*

1. We use *since* or *ever since* with the time the action began.

   He has worked in a hotel *since 1974.*
   He has wanted to manage hotels *ever since he was a teenager.*

   We use *for* with the amount of time.

   He has been a U.S. citizen *for 8 years.*

2. Omit *for* with an expression beginning with *all.*

   You've been in the U.S. *all your life.*

3. We can use *ever since* at the end of a sentence.

   Daniel went to Chicago in 1988. He's been there *ever since.*

4. We can use the following expressions with the present perfect:

   for the past ____ (years)
   for ____ (years) now
   He has been a citizen *for the past few years.*
   He's been in the U.S. *for ten years now.*

5. We can ask an information question with "How long . . .?" The answer to this question usually contains *for* or *since.*

   A. *How long* have you lived in this city?
   B. *Since* 1992.
   A. *How long* have you been a student at this college?
   B. *For* three years.

EXERCISE 2   Fill in each blank with the missing word. (Not every sentence needs a word.)

> EXAMPLE: I _have_ been in the U.S. for three years.

1. He has been in the U.S. _____ 1992.

2. How _____ have you been married?

3. She found a good job in 1990. She has worked at the same job ever

    _____.

4. He has worked at a hotel ever since he _____ to the U.S.

5. They have lived in the U.S. _____ all their lives.

6. She has lived in the U.S. for the _____ ten years.

7. _____ you lived in the U.S. all your life?

8. I've been at this college for three years. _____ have you been at this college?

9. He'_____ been sick _____ Monday.

10. We'_____ known each other for many years.

EXERCISE 3   Write **true** sentences using the present perfect with the words given and *for* or *since*. Share your answers with the class.

> EXAMPLES: know _I've known the teacher for three years._
>
> be _We've been in the classroom for fifteen minutes._

1. have _____

2. be _____

3. want _____

4. know _____

The Simple Present vs. the Present Perfect

Contrast the simple present with the present perfect.

> I *have* a car. (simple present)
> I*'ve had* my car for two years. (present perfect)
> I*'m* married. (simple present)
> I*'ve been* married since January. (present perfect)

The simple present refers only to the present. The present perfect with *for* or *since* shows continuation from past to present.

EXERCISE 4   The following statements refer to the present only. Show when the action began by changing the tense to the present perfect and adding *for* or *since*. Fill in each blank to make **true** statements about yourself.

> EXAMPLE: **I'm interested in** _American history._
>
> **I've been interested in American history ever since I was in high school (OR for the past 10 years).**

1. I'm interested in _____.

2. I'm at school now.

3. I own a _____.

4. I like (to) _____.

5. I have a _____.

EXERCISE 5   Fill in each blank to complete the following conversations.

> EXAMPLE: **A. Do you have a computer?**
>
> **B. Yes, I do.**
>
> **A. How long** _have you_ **had your computer?**
>
> **B. I** _have had_ **my computer for three years.**

1. A. Do you have a car?

   B. Yes, I do.

   A. How long _____ your car?

   B. I _____ my car for six months.

2. A. Are you married?

   B. Yes, I am.

   A. How long _____ married?

   B. I _____ since 1985.

3. A. Where _____ your sister live?

   B. She lives in New York.

   A. How _____ in New York?

   B. She _____ for _____.

4. A. Do you want to learn English?

   B. Of course, I do.

   A. _____ long _____ to learn English?

   B. I _____ to learn English ever since I _____ to the U.S.

5. A. Does your mother have a driver's license?

   B. Yes, she _____.

   A. How _____ her driver's license?

   B. She _____ driver's license since _____.

6. A. _____ Ms. Foster your teacher?

   B. Yes, she is.

   A. How long _____ your teacher?

   B. For _____.

7. A. Does your school have a computer lab?

   B. Yes, it _____.

   A. _____ long _____ a computer lab?

   B. It _____ a computer lab since _____.

8. A. Do you know your friend Mark very well?

   B. Yes, I _____.

   A. How long _____ each other?

   B. We _____ each other ever _____ we _____
      in elementary school.

Language Notes

For and *Since* with Negative Statements

1. Notice the use of *for* and *since* in negative statements.
   Daniel hasn't worked in Mexico *since* 1984.
   (He worked in Mexico before 1984. He stopped in 1984.)
   Daniel hasn't seen his parents *for* three years.
   (He saw his parents three years ago. That was the last time.)

2. In negative sentences, you can use either *for* or *in*.
   He hasn't seen his family *for* a long time.
   He hasn't seen his family *in* a long time.

EXERCISE 6   Name something.

> EXAMPLE: **Name something you haven't eaten for a long time.**
> **I haven't eaten fish for a long time.**

1. Name someone you haven't seen in a long time.
2. Name a place you haven't visited for a long time.
3. Name a food you haven't eaten in a long time.
4. Name a subject you haven't studied since you were in high school.
5. Name a game you haven't played since you were a child.
6. Name something you haven't had time to do since you started to study English.

EXERCISE 7   Fill in the blank. Discuss your answer in a small group or with the entire class.

   I haven't _____ in a long, long time.

Language Notes

Always and *Never*

1. We use the present perfect with *always* to show that an action or state began in the past and continues to the present.
   Daniel has *always* loved the hotel business.

2. We use the present perfect with *never* to show that an action or state has not happened from the past to the present.
   He has *never* worked in a factory.

3. We often use *before* in a *never* statement. We mean "before now."
   Daniel is writing to Mr. Johnson. Daniel has never written to him *before*.

EXERCISE 8   Make statements with *always.*

> EXAMPLE: **Name something you've always thought about.**
>   **I've always thought about my future.**

1. Name something you've always disliked.
2. Name something you've always liked.
3. Name something you've always wanted to own.
4. Name something you've always wanted to do.
5. Name something you've always believed in.

EXERCISE 9   Make statements with *never.*

> EXAMPLE: **Name a machine you've never used.**
>   **I've never used a fax machine.**

1. Name a food you've never tried.
2. Name something you've never drunk.
3. Name something you've never owned.
4. Name something you've never done.
5. Name something the teacher has never done in class.

EXERCISE 10   Write four **true** sentences telling about things you've always done or ways you've always been. Share your answers with the class.

> EXAMPLES: *I've always gone to church on Sundays.*
>
> *I've always been very religious.*

1. _____
2. _____
3. _____
4. _____

EXERCISE 11   Write four **true** sentences telling about things you've never done or ways you've never been but would like to. Share your answers with the class.

> EXAMPLES: *I've never gone to Paris, but I'd like to.*
>
> *I've never flown in a helicopter, but I'd like to.*

1. _____
2. _____

3. _____

4. _____

1.4 The Present Perfect Continuous

Study the formation of the present perfect continuous tense.

Subject	*Have/Has*	*Been*	Verb + *-ing*
He	has	been	talking.
I	have	been	working.
They	have	been	studying.

Compare statements, questions, and short answers that use the present perfect continuous.

Wh- Word	*Have*	Subject	*Have*	*Been*	Verb + *-ing*	Complement	Short Answer
		He	has	been	living	in Chicago since 1984.	
		He	hasn't	been	living	with his parents.	
	Has	he		been	living	alone?	Yes, he has.
How long	has	he		been	living	alone?	
		Who	has	been	living	in Mexico?	

Language Notes

1. With some verbs *(live, work, study, teach, wear)*, we can use either the present perfect or the present perfect continuous tense with actions that began in the past and continue to the present. There is very little difference in meaning.

   Daniel *has been working* in the hotel business for many years.
   Daniel *has worked* in the hotel business for many years.

2. We do not use the continuous form with nonaction verbs.

   He *has had* a lot of hotel experience since he came to the U.S. (NOT: He *has been having* a lot of experience.)

Nonaction verbs are the following:

believe	know	need	seem
care	like	own	think*
cost	love	prefer	understand
have*	matter	remember	want
hear	mean	see	

*NOTE: *Have* and *think* are sometimes action verbs.

EXERCISE 12 Write **true** sentences using the present perfect continuous with the words given and *for* or *since*. Share your answers with the class.

>   EXAMPLE: study *My sister has been studying at the University of California for three years.*

>   1. study English _____

>   2. work _____

>   3. live _____

>   4. use _____

>   5. try _____

>   6. _____ [5]

EXERCISE 13   Ask the teacher questions by using "How long . . .?" and the words given. The teacher will answer your questions.

>   EXAMPLE: speak English

>>   **A. How long have you been speaking English?**

>>   **B. I've been speaking English all my life.**

>   1. teach English   4. use this book
>   2. work at this college   5. _____
>   3. live in this city

EXERCISE 14   Fill in each blank in the following conversations.

>   EXAMPLE: A. Do you *play*_____ a musical instrument?

>>   B. Yes. I play the guitar.

>>   A. How long *have*_____ you *been playing*____ the guitar?

>>   B. I*'ve been playing*____ the guitar since I *was*_____ ten years old.

>   1. A. Do you work with computers?

>>   B. Yes, I do.

>>   A. How long _____ you _____ with computers?

>>   B. I _____ with computers since 1988.

---

[5]Where you see blank spaces in this book, you can add your own items to the list.

2. A. _____ your father smoke?

   B. Yes, he does.

   A. How long _____ he been _____?

   B. He _____ since he _____ eighteen years old.

3. A. Does your teacher have a lot of experience?

   B. Yes, she _____.

   A. How long _____ teaching English?

   B. She _____ English for twenty years.

4. A. Do you wear glasses?

   B. Yes, I _____.

   A. How _____ glasses?

   B. I _____ glasses since I _____ in high school.

5. A. _____ your parents live in this city?

   B. Yes, they _____.

   A. How _____ in this city?

   B. For _____.

6. A. Is your roommate preparing to take the TOEFL[6] test?

   B. Yes, he _____.

   A. How long _____ to take this test?

   B. Since _____.

7. A. Let's go to a movie tonight.

   B. I can't. I'm studying for my chemistry test. I _____ for a week.

---

[6]The *TOEFL* is the Test of English as a Foreign Language. Many U.S. colleges and universities require foreign students to take this test.

1.5   The Present Perfect with Repeated Past Actions

When we talk about the repetition of an action in a time period that includes the present, we can use the present perfect. The present perfect shows that the action can happen again in this time period.

Daniel *has had* three interviews this month. (It is possible that he will have more interviews this month.)

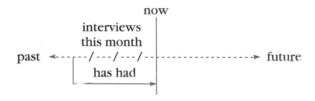

Language Notes

1. We sometimes use *so far*, *up to now*, or a time expression that includes the present moment (*today*, *this week*, *this semester*, *this year*).

   Daniel has sent out four résumés *up to now*.
   He has had many interviews *this year*.
   So far, he hasn't found a job.

2. We can use *several*, *many*, or *a lot* to show repetition from the past to the present

   I've worked overtime *a lot* this month.
   I've missed *several* classes this semester.
   I've had *many* problems since the semester began.

3. We can ask a *yes/no* question about repetition, or a question with "How many/much . . .?"

   A. Have you spent any money today?
   B. Yes, I have.
   A. *How much money* have you spent today?
   B. I've spent $30 today.

   A. Have you written any letters this week?
   B. Yes, I have.
   A. *How many letters* have you written?
   B. I've written four letters this week.

4. If we use a past time expression, such as *last week*, *last month*, or *yesterday*, we use the past tense. The present is not included.

   COMPARE:

   I've *seen* two movies *this month*.
   I *saw* four movies *last month*.
   He's *been* absent twice *this semester*.
   He *was* absent four times *last semester*.

EXERCISE 15   Ask a question with "How much . . .?" or "How many . . .?" and the words given. Talk about today. Another student will answer.

    EXAMPLES: coffee/have
              A. How much coffee have you had today?
              B. I've had three cups of coffee today.

              glasses of water/drink
              A. How many glasses of water have you drunk today?
              B. I haven't drunk any water at all today.

1. tea/have	5. cigarettes/smoke
2. glasses of beer/have	6. miles/walk or drive
3. cookies/eat	7. money/spend
4. glasses of cola/have	8. _____

EXERCISE 16   Write a statement to tell how many times you have done something in this city. Find a partner, and ask about his/her experience in this city.

    EXAMPLES: live in/apartment(s)
          I've lived in one apartment in this city.
          How many apartments have you lived in?

          get lost/time(s)
          I've gotten lost two times in this city.
          How many times have you gotten lost in this city?

1. have/job(s)

    _____

2. have/job interview(s)

    _____

3. have/traffic ticket(s)

    _____

4. buy/car(s)

    _____

5. attend/school(s)

    _____

6. live in/apartment(s)

_____

7. go downtown/time(s)

_____

8. _____

_____

EXERCISE 17   Write four questions to ask another student or your teacher about repetition from the past to the present. Use *how much* or *how many*. Report an interesting answer to the class.

EXAMPLE: *How many times have you gone to Europe?*

1. _____

2. _____

3. _____

4. _____

1.6   The Present Perfect with an Unspecified Time

We use the present perfect to talk about an action that occurred at an unspecified time in the past. This action still has relevance to the present.

Daniel *has worked* in Evanston, Illinois.
Has he ever *worked* in Chicago?

Certain words refer to the past without being specific: *lately, recently, ever, yet, already, just.*

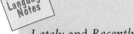

Lately and *Recently*

1. *Lately* and *recently* refer to an unspecified time in the near past.

   A. Have you seen any good movies *recently*?
   B. No, I haven't. I haven't had time to go to the movies. I've been busy looking for a job.

2. A present perfect question is often answered with a specific time. If so, the simple past tense is used in the answer.

   A. *Have* you *seen* any good movies lately?
   B. Yes. I *saw* a great movie last weekend.

3. We can use the present perfect continuous with *lately* and *recently* to show that an activity has repeated in the near past.

   Daniel *has been sending* out a lot of résumés lately.
   He's *been going* on a lot of interviews recently.

EXERCISE 18   Ask a *yes/no* question with the words given. Another student will answer. A past-tense statement may be added to a *yes* answer.

     EXAMPLE: **go swimming recently**
          A. Have you gone swimming recently?
          B. Yes, I have. I went swimming yesterday.

1. write to your family lately
2. go to the library recently
3. go to the zoo lately
4. see any good movies lately
5. receive any letters lately
6. be absent lately
7. have a job interview lately
8. read any good books recently
9. make any long-distance calls lately
10. _____

EXERCISE 19   Work with a partner. Write four questions to ask your teacher about what he or she has done lately. Your teacher will answer.

     EXAMPLE: *Have you taken a vacation lately (or recently)?*

    1. _____

    2. _____

    3. _____

    4. _____

Ever

1. A present perfect question with *ever* asks about any time in a person's life. We put *ever* between the subject and the main verb.

   Have you *ever* worked in a hotel?

2. We can answer an *ever* question with a frequency response: *a few times, many times, often, never.*

   A. Have you ever worked in a hotel?
   B. Yes, I've worked in *a few* hotels.
   A. Have you ever worked in a restaurant?
   B. No, I've *never* worked in a restaurant.

3. We can answer an *ever* question with no reference to time.

   Have you *ever* studied French?
   Yes, I've studied French.

4. We can answer an *ever* question with a specific time. Use the simple past tense with a specific time.

   A. *Have* you ever *been* a desk clerk?
   B. Yes, I *was* a desk clerk from 1984 to 1988.

EXERCISE 20   Ask a question with "Have you ever . . .?" and the words given. Another student will answer. With a specific time, use the simple past tense. With a frequency response, use the present perfect tense.

EXAMPLES: go to the zoo
            A. Have you ever gone to the zoo?
            B. Yes, I've gone there many times.

            be in jail
            A. Have you ever been in jail?
            B. No, I've never been in jail.

            go to Disneyland
            A. Have you ever gone to Disneyland?
            B. Yes, I went there last summer.

1. find money on the street
2. go to a garage sale
3. meet a famous person
4. study art history
5. get a ticket for speeding
6. be on television
7. win a contest
8. lend money to a friend
9. lose your keys
10. break an arm or a leg
11. get lost in this city
12. go to court
13. hear of[7] Martin Luther King, Jr.
14. _____

_____

[7]*Hear of* means to recognize a name.

EXERCISE 21   Find a partner. Ask your partner a question with *Have you ever . . .?* and the words given. If the answer is *yes,* ask for more specific information. Report something interesting about your partner to the class.

>   EXAMPLE: eat a hotdog
>   A. Have you ever eaten a hotdog?
>   B. Yes, I have.
>   A. When did you eat a hotdog?
>   B. I ate one at a picnic last summer.

>   1. go to a football game
>   2. tell a lie
>   3. go to Canada
>   4. travel by train
>   5. eat pizza
>   6. bet on the horses
>   7. be on a roller coaster
>   8. see a play in this city
>   9. eat Chinese food
>   10. use a fax machine
>   11. buy a lottery ticket
>   12. go camping

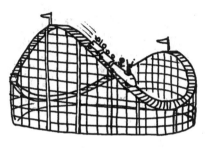

roller coaster

EXERCISE 22   Work with a partner. Use *ever* to write four questions to ask your teacher. Your teacher will answer.

>   EXAMPLES: *Have you ever eaten raw fish?*
>
>   *Have you ever written a poem?*

>   1. _____
>   2. _____
>   3. _____
>   4. _____

Yet, Already, and Just

1. *Yet* and *already* refer to an indefinite time in the near past.

    Have you found a job *yet*?
    Yes. I've found a job *already*.

2. We use *yet* in a question to ask if an expected activity took place a short time ago. We use *yet* in a negative answer.

    A. Have you found a job *yet*?
    B. No, I haven't found a job *yet*.
       OR
    I haven't *yet* found a job.
       OR
    No, *not yet*.

3. For an affirmative statement, we use *already*.

    I've found a job *already*.
       OR
    I've *already* found a job.

4. We can answer a *yet* question with the simple past tense and a specific time.

    A. *Have* you *taken* the TOEFL test yet?
    B. Yes. I *took* it three months ago.

5. We sometimes use *already* in a question.
    Have you found a job *already*?

6. We often use *just* to show that the action happened immediately before the sentence was said.

    We've *just* eaten dinner.
    He's *just* taken a shower.

We can also use the simple past tense with *just*.

    We just *ate* dinner.
    He just *took* a shower.

EXERCISE 23   Ask a student who is a recent immigrant questions with the words given and *yet* or *already*. The student who answers should use the simple past tense if the answer has a specific time.

    EXAMPLE: go downtown
        A. Have you gone downtown yet?
        B. Yes, I went downtown three weeks ago.

1. buy a car
2. find an apartment
3. get a Social Security number
4. get your green card
5. visit any museums
6. _____

EXERCISE 24   Ask a question with the words given and *yet* or *already*. The student who answers should use the simple past tense if the answer has a specific time.

    EXAMPLES: the teacher/take attendance
        A. Has the teacher taken attendance yet (already)?
        B. Yes, he has. He took attendance at the beginning of the class.

        the teacher/return the homework
        A. Has the teacher returned the homework yet?
        B. No, he hasn't. OR No, not yet.

1. we/have an exam
2. we/study modals

3. you/learn the irregular past tenses
4. the teacher/learn the students' names
5. you/learn the other students' names
6. the teacher/teach the past perfect

Language Notes

1. Sometimes we use the present perfect to talk about the past without any reference to time.

   I've decided to become a doctor.
   I've applied to medical school.
   My family *has helped* me financially.

2. The time is not important or not known. Or the action took place gradually over a period of time.

   Over the years, *I've met* many interesting people.

EXERCISE 25   Name something. Remember to use the present perfect tense when the time that this thing happened is not important.

> EXAMPLE: **Name something you've done in the U.S.**
>   **I've gotten my driver's license.**

1. Name an American food you've eaten.
2. Name some places you've visited in the U.S.
3. Name two American movies you've seen.
4. Name something the teacher has done or said.
5. Name something interesting you've done in this city.

EXERCISE 26   Fill in each blank in the conversations with the simple past, the present perfect, or the present perfect continuous tense of the verb in parentheses ( ).

Conversation 1

A. _____*Have*_____ you _____*eaten*_____ dinner yet?
                              (eat)

B. No, I _____. I _____ lunch at 2:30, so I'm not hungry now.
              (1)   (2 eat)

A. Do you want to eat dinner with me?

B. Sorry. I _____ other plans.
              (3 already/make)

Conversation 2

A. I _____ my mother to the doctor yesterday. She _____ a lot of
        (1 take)   (2 have)
problems with her back lately.

B. How long _____ she _____ bad?
(3 feel)

A. Ever since she _____ down last month and _____ her back.
(4 fall)   (5 hurt)

B. Why _____ she _____ to the doctor when it _____?
(6 not/go)   (7 happen)

A. At that time, she _____ her back would get better. But it
(8 think)

_____ worse.
(9 get)

EXPANSION ACTIVITIES

WRITING

1. Write about how your life has changed since you came to the U.S.

2. Write about two or three things that your life experience in the U.S. has taught you.

OUTSIDE ACTIVITIES

1. *What Color Is Your Parachute?* by Richard Bolles is a popular book for job hunters. Go to the library. Find a recent copy of this book. Find information about job hunting skills. Report something interesting to the class.

2. You can find many books about how to write a professional résumé in the career section of the library or bookstore. Find a guide to résumé writing. Write your own résumé and cover letter. In class, exchange résumés with another student. Take turns interviewing each other for a job.

3. Use the ideas in Exercises 20 and 21 to interview an American about his or her experiences. Invite the American to interview you. Tell the class something interesting you found out about the American. Tell the class an interesting question that the American asked you.

EDITING ADVICE

1. Don't confuse the *-ing* form and the past participle.

   taking
   I've been ~~taken~~ English courses for several years.

   been
   Have you ever ~~being~~ in Texas?

2. Use the past, not the present perfect, with a specific past time and in questions with *when*.

   wrote
   He ~~has written~~ a book five years ago.

   She ~~has~~ bought a car when she ~~has~~ found a job.

   did he get
   When ~~has he gotten~~ his driver's license?

3. Use the simple past in a *since* clause.

   came
   He's had three jobs since he ~~has come~~ to the U.S.

4. Use correct word order.

   never been
   He has ~~been never~~ in New York.

   ever eaten
   Have you ~~eaten ever~~ Chinese food?

5. Use *yet* in negative statements. Use *already* in affirmative statements.

   yet
   I haven't finished the book ~~already~~.

   already
   I've finished the book ~~yet~~.

6. Use *how long* for a question about length of time.

   How long ~~time~~ have they been working in a restaurant?

7. If the main verb is *have*, be sure to include the auxiliary verb *have* for the present perfect.

   has
   He ˄ had his job since March.

Comparison of Tenses

We use the simple past with:

1. An action or state that is completely past

   He *worked* in Mexico from 1974 to 1984.
   He *found* a job in 1990.
   He *bought* his car when he came to the U.S.
   When *did* he *come* to the U.S.?

2. A repeated past action that took place in a completed time period (yesterday, last month)

   He *sent* out three résumés last month.

3. An action that occurred at a specific time in the past

   He *came* to the U.S. in 1984.

We use the present perfect with:

1. An action or state that continues from past to present

   He *has worked* in the U.S. since 1984.

   He *has had* his present job since 1990.
   He *has had* his car since he came to the U.S.
   How long *has* he *been* in the U.S.?

2. A repeated past action that takes place in a time period that includes the present (today, this month)

   He *has had* three interviews this month.

3. A past action that does not mention a specific time

   He *has* already *become* an American citizen.

We use the present perfect with:

1. A continuous state (nonaction verbs)

   Daniel *has been* in the U.S. for ten years.

2. A repeated action

   His father *has visited* the U.S. two times.
   How many times *has* his mother *visited* the U.S.?

We use the present perfect continuous with:

1. A continuous action (action verbs)

   Daniel *has been living* in the U.S. for ten years.

2. A nonstop activity

   His friend *has been visiting* him for the past two weeks.
   How long *has* he *been living* in Chicago?

LESSON ONE TEST/REVIEW

Part 1 Find the mistakes in the following sentences, and correct them. Not every sentence has a mistake. If the sentence is correct, write *C*.

EXAMPLES: How many times have you ~~seeing~~ *seen* the movie?

Have you ever traveled by train?   *C*

1. How long time have you known your husband?

2. Has your mother been sick lately?

3. She's worked in a restaurant since five months.

4. Have you gone ever to the art museum?

5. How long does she work as a doctor?

6. I'm studying English for three years.

7. How long you've been living in the U.S.?

8. He's had three jobs since he's come to the U.S.

9. How many times have you calling your country this month?

10. When have you come to the U.S.?

11. She bought a car when she has won the lottery.

12. Have you ever giving your sister a present?

13. She bought a car when she graduated.

14. She has her car since she graduated.

Part 2 Fill in each blank with the simple present, simple past, present perfect, or present perfect continuous tense of the verb in parentheses ( ).

I _____*am*_____ in the U.S. now. I _____ here for one year. My life
    (be)   (1 live)

_____ a lot since I _____ to the U.S. For example, in my country
 (2 change)   (3 come)

I _____, but I _____ a job now. This month I _____
  (4 work)   (5 not/have)   (6 look)

for a job, but I _____ one yet.
      (7 not/find)

In my country, I _____ a lot of friends, but here I am alone. So far I
                         (8 have)

_____ several nice people, but I don't consider any of them my friends.
      (9 meet)

It takes time to make friends. I suppose I _____ these people long
                                                (10 not/know)

enough.

Here everybody has a car. I _____ to own a car. I _____ a car
                                (11 always/want)   (12 not/buy)

yet because I don't have enough money, but I plan to. I _____ my
                                                            (13 have)

driver's license for two months.

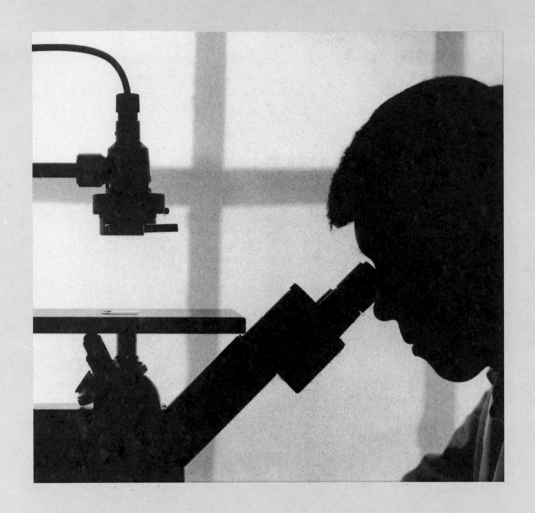

LESSON TWO

GRAMMAR

Passive and Active Voice
Participles Used as
   Adjectives

CONTEXT

The FDA
Movie Ratings
Day Care

Lesson Focus   Passive and Active Voice; Participles as Adjectives

- The verb in some sentences is in the active voice. The verb in other sentences is in the passive voice. We form the passive voice by using a form of *be* + the past participle.

    ACTIVE: Columbus *discovered* America.
    PASSIVE: America *was discovered* by Columbus.

- We can use participles as adjectives:
    Don't touch the *broken* glass. (past participle)
    She is a *loving* mother. (present participle)

R
E
A
D
I
N
G

Before you read

Do you use a prescription drug? In your country, do you need a prescription for this drug?

Read the following article. Pay special attention to the passive-voice verbs.

THE FDA

The Food and Drug Administration (FDA) is a federal agency that decides if foods and drugs are safe. When a new food or drug **is developed**, the FDA conducts tests. If the new product **is found** to be safe, the manufacturer **is allowed** to sell it.

Changes **are** constantly **being made** by the FDA as it learns more about a food or drug. Saccharin is a sugar substitute that **is used** by dieters and others who can't eat sugar. However, after saccharin **was sold** for many years, the FDA found that it might not be safe. Experiments **were conducted** on rats. Rats that **were fed** large amounts of saccharin developed cancer. A danger to humans **has not been proved** and saccharin continues **to be sold,** but manufacturers **have been required** to put a warning label on products that contain saccharin. Sometimes after a food or drug has been on the market for years, it **is recalled** by the FDA because new evidence shows that it may be harmful. Not long ago, a birth-control device **was taken** off the market because some women had serious side effects[1] from it. In some cases, this device even caused death.

warning label

The FDA also decides if a medicine **can be sold** without a prescription. For many drugs, a prescription **is required** because the FDA believes that the user **needs to be supervised** by his or her doctor. Some drugs **must be controlled** by the pharmacy because they **might be abused.**[2]

---

[1]A *side effect* is a secondary effect of a drug. Often it is a bad effect.

[2]When a drug is *abused,* it is used for something other than a medical purpose.

Drugs that **are sold** without a prescription are called "over-the-counter" drugs. Aspirin, which **is used** to treat pain, is one of the most common over-the-counter drugs. Sometimes the FDA decides that a prescription drug is safe enough **to be sold** over the counter. Over the past 15 years, about 45 drugs that were originally prescription drugs **have been approved** for over-the-counter sale.

New drugs **are being developed** and **tested** all the time. Drugs **have to be tested** for years before they **can be sold** to the public.

2.1 Tense and Passive Voice

Compare sentences that use the active voice and the passive voice in the different tenses.

Tense	Active	Passive (*be* + past participle)
Simple Present	They speak English.	English is spoken (by them).
Present Continuous	They are speaking English.	English is being spoken.
Future	They will speak English.	English will be spoken.
	They are going to speak English.	English is going to be spoken.
Simple Past	They spoke English.	English was spoken.
Past Continuous	They were speaking English.	English was being spoken.
Present Perfect	They have spoken English.	English has been spoken.
Modal	They should speak English.	English should be spoken.
Infinitive	They need to speak English.	English needs to be spoken.

Language Notes

1. An adverb can be placed between the auxiliary verb and the main verb or between two auxiliaries.
   An aspirin is *often* taken for a headache.
   Medicine should *always* be taken with caution.
2. Study the negative forms for active and passive.
   ACTIVE: They *don't use* aspirin.   ACTIVE: We *didn't see* the doctor.
   PASSIVE: Aspirin *isn't used.*   PASSIVE: The doctor *wasn't seen.*
3. Study the question forms for active and passive.
   ACTIVE: *Do* they *use* aspirin?   ACTIVE: *Did* you *see* the doctor?
   PASSIVE: *Is* aspirin *used?*   PASSIVE: *Was* the doctor *seen?*

EXERCISE 1   Fill in each blank with the tense and verb indicated to form a passive sentence.

>   EXAMPLE: (simple present: *use*)
>
>   Aspirin _is_____ _used_____ for pain.

   1. (simple present: *sell*)

      Many drugs _____ _____ without a prescription.

   2. (present continuous: *make*)

      New drugs _____ _____ _____ all the time.

   3. (future: *take*)

      If the FDA finds a problem with a drug, the drug _____ _____

      _____ off the market.

   4. (simple past: *give*)

      In an experiment, rats _____ _____ large amounts of saccharin.

   5. (present perfect: *approve*)

      About 45 prescription drugs _____ _____ _____ for over-the-counter sale.

   6. (modal: *can/sell*)

      The FDA decides if a medicine _____ _____ _____ without a prescription.

   7. (infinitive: *to use*)

      Aspirin is safe enough _____ _____ _____ without a prescription.

   8. (past continuous: *take*)

      The patient died while she _____ _____ _____ to the hospital in an ambulance.

   9. (simple present: *not/sell*)

      Penicillin _____ _____ _____ without a prescription.

10. (simple past: *not/give*)

Saccharin _____ _____ _____ to people in the laboratory test.

11. (simple present: *often/do*)

Tests _____ _____ _____ on animals.

2.2 Using the Passive Voice

The verb in active voice shows that the subject performs the action of the verb. The verb in passive voice shows that the subject receives the action; the subject does not perform the action of the verb.

(1) The patient *took* a pill.
(2) The patient *was taken* to the hospital.

In sentence 1, the patient took something. In sentence 2, the patient did not take anything. Somebody took him to the hospital.

We form the passive voice by using a form of *be* + the past participle.

Subject	*Be* (*Not*)	(Adverb)	Past Participle	
Aspirin	is	often	taken	for a headache.
Some drugs	aren't		sold	without a prescription.

Language Notes

The passive voice is used without a performer in the following cases:

1. We do not know who performed the action or if it is not important to say who performed the action.

> My watch *was made* in Switzerland. (The person who made the watch is not important.)
> Her purse *was stolen* while she was shopping. (We do not know who stole the purse.)

2. The performer of the action is obvious.

> Drugs *are made* and *tested* in a laboratory. (We all know that scientists make drugs.)
> The thief *was arrested* and *taken* to jail. (We all understand that the performer of this action was a police officer.)

3. We make a general statement.

> Aspirin *is used* for pain.
> Aspirin *can be bought* in a drugstore.
> Spanish *is spoken* in Mexico.

> NOTE: In conversation, the active voice is often used with the subject *they* or *you* to give the same meaning.

> You *can buy* aspirin in a drugstore.
> They *speak* Spanish in Mexico.

4. We want to avoid mentioning the performer.

> We *were told* not to say anything more about the new drug.
> The reporter *was given* some information about the new drug.

5. We want to give an impersonal tone, especially in scientific and technical writing.

> New drugs *are being developed.*
> An experiment *was conducted.*

Language Notes

Active and Passive with The Simple Present Tense

ACTIVE: People *use* aspirin for a headache.   PASSIVE: Aspirin *is used* for a headache.
ACTIVE: Pharmacies *sell* drugs.   PASSIVE: Drugs *are sold* at pharmacies.

EXERCISE 2   Fill in each blank with the passive voice of the verb in parentheses ( ). Use the simple present tense.

> EXAMPLE: A textbook _____*is used*_____ in this course.
>   (use)
>
> 1. The students _____ to bring the book to class.
>   (tell)
>
> 2. The homework _____ every day.
>   (collect)

3. The papers _____ and _____.
              (correct)   (return)[3]

4. Corrections _____ in red ink.
              (make)

5. The students _____ a test at the end of the lesson.
              (give)[4]

6. The students _____ to use the book during the exam.
          (not/permit)

EXERCISE 3   Change to the passive voice to tell about Christmas in the U.S. Do not mention the performer. Be sure to make the verb agree with the new subject.

    EXAMPLE: **People celebrate Christmas on December 25.**

        Christmas is celebrated on December 25.

1. People decorate a Christmas tree.

    _____

2. People hang ornaments on the tree. (Begin: Ornaments . . .)

    _____

3. The post office reminds us to send our Christmas cards early. (Begin: We . . .)

    _____

4. The post office doesn't deliver the mail on Christmas day. (Begin: The mail . . .)

    _____

5. People leave presents under the Christmas tree. (Begin: Presents . . .)

    _____

---

[3]Do not repeat the verb *be* after *and*. Use only the past participle.

[4]When there is a test in class, we say that the teacher *gives* (administers) the test. The students *take* (write) the test.

6. People wrap presents with brightly colored paper. (Begin: Presents . . .)

_____

7. People tell small children about Santa Claus. (Begin: Small children . . .)

_____

8. People usually open presents on Christmas morning.

_____

9. People prepare special food for the holiday.

_____

10. People hear Christmas music on the radio in December.

_____

EXERCISE 4   Fill in each blank with the active or passive voice of the verb in parentheses ( ). Use the simple present tense.

EXAMPLES: A textbook _____*is used*_____ in this course.
                           (use)

           The students _____*use*_____ a textbook in this course.
                           (use)

1. The students _____ to bring their homework on time.
                  (tell)

2. Sometimes the students _____ the teacher to repeat a word or
                           (tell)

   sentence.

3. The homework _____ every day.
                 (collect)

4. The teacher _____ the homework and _____ it to the students.
               (correct)   (return)

5. The teacher usually _____ comments in red ink.
                       (write)

6. The comments _____ in the margins and between the lines.
                (find)

7. The students _____ a test at the end of the lesson.
                (usually/give)

8. The test _____ to determine the student's grade and to help the
            (use)

   student understand what he or she _____ to review.
                                     (need)

EXERCISE 5   Write a few sentences telling about school, tests, homework, teachers, etc. in your country. (Not all sentences need to be passive.) Share your sentences in a small group or with the entire class.

EXAMPLE: *Tests are given once a year, in December.*

The teacher is called "professor." The teacher is never called by his or her first name.

Students stand up when the teacher enters the room.

1. _____

2. _____

3. _____

4. _____

Active and Passive with The Present Continuous Tense

ACTIVE: Scientists *are testing* a new drug.   PASSIVE: A new drug *is being tested*.
ACTIVE: Scientists *are developing* new drugs.   PASSIVE: New drugs *are being developed*.

EXERCISE 6   Fill in each blank with the passive voice of the verb in parentheses ( ). Use the present continuous tense.

EXAMPLE: **Progress** _____*is being made*_____ **in the field of science.**
                                     (make)

1. Research _____ to find a cure for diseases.
                    (do)

2. Studies _____.
               (conduct)

3. Reports _____.
               (write)

4. Animals _____ in experiments.
               (use)

5. We _____ of medical advances.
          (inform)

EXERCISE 7   Change these sentences from the active to the passive voice.

EXAMPLE: **They are offering many new courses this semester.**

Many new courses are being offered this semester.

1. We are using the textbook for this exercise.

   _____

2. We're practicing the passive voice.

   _____

3. We're changing the sentences from active to passive.

   _____

4. We are correcting the mistakes.

   _____

5. Someone is asking the teacher a question.

   _____

EXERCISE 8   Fill in each blank with the active or the passive voice of the verb in parentheses ( ). Use the present continuous tense.

EXAMPLES: **The blackboard** ___is not being used___ **now.**
(not/use)

The teacher ___is helping___ **the students with this exercise.**
(help)

1. The students _____ to the teacher.
(listen)

2. The students _____ by the teacher to use the passive voice.
(instruct)

3. The students _____ in the blanks with passive or active verbs.
(fill)

4. A passive verb _____ in some of these sentences.
(use)

5. We _____ the textbook for this exercise.
(use)

6. The teacher _____ the students' mistakes.
(correct)

7. The answers _____.
(discuss)

8. The students _____ the passive and the active voice.
                        (practice)

9. Modal verbs _____ at this time.
                    (not/study)

2.3 The Passive Voice with a Performer

We, you, they, or *people,* when they mean people in general, are weak subjects and are often omitted. The passive voice is used instead.

> People use aspirin for pain.
> Aspirin *is used* for pain.
> They speak English in Australia.
> English *is spoken* in Australia.

However, sometimes there is a strong performer, and it can't be omitted. We have a choice between active voice and passive voice. Choosing the passive voice gives more emphasis to the event than to the performer. Compare:

Active	Passive
The FDA *approved* the new drug.	The new drug *was approved* by the FDA.
Fleming *developed* penicillin.	Penicillin *was developed* by Fleming.
Edison *invented* the phonograph.	The phonograph *was invented* by Edison.

Language Notes

1. Notice the difference in pronouns in an active sentence and a passive sentence. After *by,* the object pronoun is used.[5]

   ACTIVE: *She* saw *him.*   PASSIVE: *He* was seen by *her.*
   ACTIVE: They *helped* us.   PASSIVE: *We* were helped by *them.*

2. We often use the passive voice when the performer *made, discovered, invented, built, wrote,* or *composed* something.

---

[5]When an active sentence has a direct object (D.O.) and an indirect object (I.O.), either object can be the subject of a passive sentence. (*To* is used before the indirect object.)

                    I.O.   D.O.
ACTIVE: The doctor gave the patient a pill.
PASSIVE: The patient was given a pill (by the doctor).
PASSIVE: A pill was given to the patient (by the doctor).

Active and Passive with the Simple Past

ACTIVE: The patient *took* the medicine.
PASSIVE: The medicine *was taken* by the patient.

EXERCISE 9   Fill in each blank with the passive voice of the verb in parentheses ( ). Use the past tense.

EXAMPLE: A British colony __*was started*__ in America in the 1600s.
                                          (start)

1. America _____ by Great Britain until the eighteenth century.
                 (rule)

2. Americans wanted to be independent. A war of independence _____
   against the British.   (fight)

3. Many people _____ during the war.
                    (kill)

4. The war _____ by the Americans.
                (win)

5. The Constitution _____ in 1787.
                        (write)

6. Americans _____ many freedoms by the Constitution.
                  (give)

7. George Washington _____ to be the first American President.
                         (choose)

8. The first capital of the U.S. was New York. Later the capital _____ to
   Washington, D.C.   (move)

EXERCISE 10   Change from active to passive voice. Mention the performer because the performer is an important person.

EXAMPLE: Bell invented the telephone.

The telephone was invented by Bell.

1. Shakespeare wrote *Romeo and Juliet.*

   _____

2. Mozart composed *The Magic Flute.*

   _____

3. Columbus discovered America.

   _____

4. President Lincoln ended slavery.

   _____

5. DaVinci painted *The Mona Lisa*.

   _____

Language Notes

<u>Active and Passive with the Past Continuous</u>

ACTIVE: The woman had a baby while the ambulance *was taking* her to the hospital.
PASSIVE: The woman had a baby while she *was being taken* to the hospital.
REMEMBER: A past continuous action is often interrupted by a past action.

EXERCISE 11   Change the underlined words to the passive voice. Do not mention the performer.

    EXAMPLE: **The thief fell while <u>the police were chasing him.</u>**

           The thief fell while _he was being chased._

1. The doctor's phone rang while <u>she was examining me</u>.

   The doctor's phone rang while _____.

2. While <u>the ambulance was taking the patient to the hospital</u>, he died.

   While _____, he died.

3. While <u>the wife was cleaning the house</u>, <u>the husband was preparing the dinner</u>.

   While _____, _____.

4. While <u>the beautician was cutting her hair</u>, <u>the manicurist was giving her a manicure</u>.

   While _____, _____.

5. <u>A neighbor was watching the house</u> while the family was on vacation.

_____ while the family was on vacation.

Language Notes

<u>The Passive with the Present Perfect</u>

ACTIVE: Someone *has driven* the car.
PASSIVE: The car *has been driven*.

EXERCISE 12   Fill in each blank with the passive voice of the verb in parentheses ( ). Use the present perfect tense.

> EXAMPLE: **Cancer-causing substances** _____*have been found*_____ **in saccharin.**
>   (find)

1. Experiments _____ on rats.
                        (do)

2. A danger to humans _____.
                              (not/prove)

3. Manufacturers _____ to put a warning label on products that

   contain saccharin.
                        (require)

4. In the last 15 years, about 45 drugs _____ for sale over the
                                                  (approve)

   counter.

5. A cure for cancer _____ yet.
                            (not/find)

EXERCISE 13   Change to the passive voice. Do not mention the performer.

> EXAMPLE: **They have found harmful substances in some foods and drugs.**
>
>   *Harmful substances have been found in some foods and drugs.* _____

1. They have ordered manufacturers to label products. (Begin: Manufacturers . . .)

   _____

2. They have not permitted some drugs to go on the market. (Begin: Some drugs . . .)

   _____

3. They have informed consumers by radio and TV.

_____

4. They have found cancer-causing substances in cigarettes.

_____

5. They have put warnings on cigarette packages.

_____

6. They have taken a birth-control device off the market.

_____

EXERCISE 14 Fill in each blank with the active or passive voice of the verb in parentheses ( ). Use the present perfect tense.

> EXAMPLES: **Foods and drugs** _have been controlled_ **for many years.**
> (control)
>
> **People** _have taken_ **more interest in good health and**
> (take)
> **nutrition in recent years.**

1. In recent years, Americans _____ more concerned about their
   (become)

   health.

2. People _____ about the possible dangers of some products.
   (warn)

3. Manufacturers _____ warning labels on certain products.
   (put)

4. Some foods and drugs _____ off the market.
   (take)

5. Many restaurant managers _____ nonsmoking sections.
   (add)

6. Smoking _____ on domestic airline flights.
   (prohibit)

7. People _____ about the dangers of smoking, and some people
   (tell)

   _____.
   (quit)

• •

R
E
A
D
I
N
G

Before you read:

1. What kind of movies do you like?
2. Did you see American movies in your country? Which ones?

Read the following article. Pay special attention to the passive voice used with infinitives and modals.

MOVIE RATINGS

Movies in the U.S. are rated according to their appropriateness for children. Many movies contain sex, violence, or bad language.

G means that the movie **can be seen** by a general audience. This rating **is given** to children's movies, even though the movie **might** also **be enjoyed** by an adult. PG means that parental guidance is suggested. PG movies may not be good for some children. PG-13

MOVIE RATING GUIDE

A Service of
Film-makers and Theaters
Under the motion picture
Code of Self-Regulation

G - Suggested for
General audiences

PG - Parental Guidance Suggested: Some
material may not be suitable for children

PG-13 Parents Strongly Cautioned -
Some material may be inappropriate for
children under 13

R - Restricted
Persons under 17 will not be admitted
unless accompanied by parent or adult
guardian

NC-17 - No Children under 17 will be
admitted

means that parental guidance is recommended, especially for children under 13. The age and maturity of the child **need to be considered.** R means restricted. Children under 17 **must be accompanied** in the theater by an adult. NC means that children under 17 **will not be admitted** to the theater.

Movie ratings **can be found** in the movie section of the newspaper. They **can** also **be found** on the box of a rental video.

• •

Active and Passive with Modals and Infinitives

ACTIVE: Children *can see* a G movie.
PASSIVE: A G movie *can be seen* by children.

ACTIVE: Parents *need to guide* their children.
PASSIVE: Children *need to be guided* by their parents.

EXERCISE 15   Fill in each blank with the passive voice of the verb in parentheses ( ).

EXAMPLE: **Movie ratings** _____*can be found*_____ **in the movie section of a**
                                            (can/find)
          newspaper.

1. G means general. A G movie _____ by the whole family.
                                          (can/enjoy)

2. PG means parental guidance. Children _____ by their
                                                      (should/advise)
    parents.

3. PG-13 means that parents should guide young children. A PG-13 movie

    _____ by some children under 13.
        (should/not/see)

4. R means restricted. Persons under seventeen _____ by a
                                                              (must/accompany)
    parent.

5. NC-17 means children under seventeen _____ to enter the
                                                      (will/not/permit)
    theater.

6. Children _____ guidance by their parents.
   (need to/give)

7. Teenagers don't _____ which movies to see.
   (like to/tell)

EXERCISE 16   Change from active to passive voice. Do not mention the performer.

> EXAMPLE: **You must accompany children to an R movie.**
>
>   *Children must be accompanied to an R movie.*
>   _____

1. We will see most current movies on TV in a few years.

   _____

2. They will cut out some parts of these movies for television.

   _____

3. They might remove bad language.

   _____

4. The program might offend some viewers.

   _____

5. We shouldn't allow children to watch some programs.

   _____

6. You can find information about the programs in the newspaper.

   _____

7. You need to consider the age of the child.

   _____

EXERCISE 17   Write the active or passive voice of the verbs in parentheses ( ).

> EXAMPLES: **The children** _____*will watch*_____ **a movie tonight.**
>   (will/watch)
>
>   **The movie** _*should not be seen*_ **by small children.**
>   (should/not/see)

1. Children _____ some movies.
   (should/not/see)

2. Some children _____ by some movies.
   (might/frighten)

3. Information about movies _____ in the movie section of the
   (can/find)

   newspaper.

4. You _____ for cable TV.
   (have/to pay)

5. People under 17 _____ to enter some movies.
   (may/not/permit)

6. Parents _____ if a movie is good for their children.
   (need to/decide)

7. Movies _____ at a video store.
   (can/rent)

8. Parents _____ rental videos for their small children.
   (should/choose)

EXERCISE 18   Fill in each blank with the active or passive voice of the verb in parentheses ( ). Choose an appropriate tense.

   I __*have used*__ the same medication for ten years. Every day I _____ two
       (use)   (1 take)

pills. Usually when I _____ a refill, I call my doctor, and my doctor
                      (2 need)

_____ the pharmacy.
   (3 call)

   Last week I _____ to the drugstore to get a refill on my medication. I
               (4 go)

_____ the prescription number to the pharmacist. I _____ by the
   (5 give)   (6 tell)

pharmacist to come back in half an hour. While I _____ in the store, my
                                                   (7 shop)

name _____ over the loudspeaker. I _____ to the pharmacy, and I
      (8 call)   (9 go)

_____ that the prescription couldn't _____ because it was more than
   (10 tell)   (11 refill)

six months old. I _____ the pharmacist that I _____ this medication
                   (12 tell)   (13 use)

for a long time. She said that this medication _____ carefully and that the
                                                (14 control)

refill had to _____ by the doctor. She _____ to call the doctor for me.
              (15 approve)   (16 offer)

The doctor _____ her permission to refill the prescription. Finally, I
            (17 give)

_____ my medication and _____ to use the medication carefully. This
   (18 give)   (19 tell)

medication shouldn't _____ when drinking alcohol and should _____
                      (20 use)   (21 take)

after meals.

Language Notes

Using the Active Voice Only

1. A verb that is followed by an object is called a **transitive** verb. A verb that has no object is called an **intransitive** verb. Only a transitive active verb can be passive. Verbs such as *happen, go, fall, seem, sleep, live,* and *die* are intransitive and cannot be made passive.

The following sentence does not have an object. It cannot be changed to the passive voice.

Subject Verb Prepositional Phrase
They   went to the drugstore.

2. Even though *have* is followed by an object, it is not usually used in the passive voice:

The patient has a prescription.

NOT: A prescription is had by the patient.

3. We do not use the passive voice with actions that happen by themselves. Circumstances caused them to happen, not a specific performer. COMPARE:

I *changed* as I grew up.
I *was changed* by the death of my father.
The leaves on the trees *moved* in the wind.
The dead leaves *were moved* by the janitor.

4. Some verbs are used in the active voice even though the subject is not the performer. COMPARE:

The car *stopped* at the corner.
The car *was stopped* by the police.
The store *opens* at 8 A.M.
The store *is opened* by the manager.

5. Notice that we say *was/were born*. (This is a passive construction.) However, *die* is always an active verb.

She *was born* in 1930. She *died* in 1992.

EXERCISE 19   Which of the following sentences can be changed to passive voice? Change them. If the sentence cannot be changed, write *No Change*.

EXAMPLES: **My grandfather died in 1982.**

No change

Someone found my wallet.

My wallet was found.

1. The janitor closed the windows.

_____

2. The supermarket closes at 9 o'clock.

_____

3. His experiences in the war changed him.

_____

4. Children change as they grow up.

   _____

5. Edison invented the phonograph.

   _____

6. She has a good job.

   _____

7. Someone opened my letter.

   _____

8. Something happened to my credit card.

   _____

9. The clock stopped.

   _____

10. The police stopped me for driving too fast.

    _____

• •

R
E
A
D
I
N
G

Before you read:

1. In your country, who takes care of the children of working parents?
2. In your country, do mothers of newborn babies get time off from their jobs to take care of their babies? Do they get paid?

Read the following article. Pay special attention to participles used as adjectives.

DAY CARE

In the U.S., where 58% of American women work outside the home, there is an **increasing** demand for good, low-cost day care. Twenty percent of American children under the age of three are in day care. Presently, day-care centers are privately **owned** institutions. They are not owned by the state, and the cost is not **controlled.** Often parents spend a large part of their salaries on day care. They are **worried** that day care is only a babysitting service and that their children are not provided with **interesting** activities.

In most industrialized societies, mothers are given more generous maternity leave than in the U.S. In Germany, for example, a mother can take a 14-week leave at full pay. In countries where a **growing** number of women work, publicly **funded** day-care centers allow women to receive quality care for their children. In some cases, the day-care center may even be **located** at the workplace. **Working** women can visit their children during their breaks.

Most people agree that day care is a **needed** service. More and more Americans want the government to provide **working** parents with quality, low-cost care for their children.

● ●

2.4 Participles Used as Adjectives

A present participle (verb + *-ing*) or a past participle (verb + *-ed/-en*) can be used as an adjective.

Present Participle as Adjective	
The child is sleeping.	Don't disturb the *sleeping* child.
The parents work.	They are *working* parents.
The need for day care is increasing.	There is an *increasing* need for day care.

Past Participle as Adjective	
Parents need day care.	Day care is a *needed* service.
Someone broke the dish.	Don't touch the *broken* dish.
Someone closed the door.	The door is *closed*.

1. A present-participle adjective shows that the noun it describes actively performs an action (as in the active voice).

A *sleeping* child is a child who is sleeping.

2. A past-participle adjective shows that the noun it describes passively receives an action (as in the passive voice).

A *needed* service is a service that is needed by parents.
A *closed* door is a door that was closed by somebody.

a closed
door

Language Notes

1. Some present participles that are often used as adjectives are found in phrases such as these:

a trusting child	a sleeping dog	a flashing light
a working parent	a lasting relationship	an understanding friend
a moving car	a growing problem	changing times
a winding road	the leading cause	opening remarks
a speeding car	a moving train	a living relative
a charming woman	a flying object	the following words

2. Some common past participles that are used as adjectives are the following:

accustomed to	crowded	made (in Japan)
air-conditioned	deserted	made (of cotton)
allowed	divorced	married
broken	injured	permitted
carpeted	insured	scared
closed	known	be used to
concerned	locked	worried
		wounded

3. The following past participles are used as adjectives even though they have no passive form: *gone, lost, located, drunk, done.*

> The child is *lost*. His mother is *gone*.
> The day-care center is *located* downtown.

4. A present participle used as an adjective can also show that an action is still in progress, whereas a past participle can show that an action is finished.

> *Growing* children need their parents.
> (Growing children are children who are still growing.)
> *Grown* children often leave home when they finish college.
> (Grown children have finished growing. They are adults.)

EXERCISE 20   Fill in each blank with the present participle or the past participle of the verb in parentheses ( ).

EXAMPLES: I drove a   *rented*   car to California.
                             (rent)

               Drive carefully on a   *winding*   road.
                                   (wind)

1. It's dangerous to jump from a _____ car.
                                  (move)

2. The police watch out for _____ cars.
                                 (speed)

3. Be careful of _____ drivers.
              (drink)

winding road

4. The police try to locate _____ cars.
   (steal)

5. Drivers must stop at a _____ red light.
   (flash)

6. It is a _____ fact that drunk drivers are the _____ cause of many
   (know)   (lead)

   serious traffic accidents.

7. Drunk drivers are a _____ problem.
   (grow)

8. _____ men are better drivers than single men.
   (marry)

9. Is your car _____?
   (insure)

10. There is a lot of traffic in the morning. The streets are _____.
    (crowd)

11. I'm _____. I need to stop at a gas station and ask for directions.
    (lose)

2.5 Emotions: Present Participle vs. Past Participle

Sometimes both a present participle and a past participle can result from the same verb, especially from a verb that shows emotion or feeling.

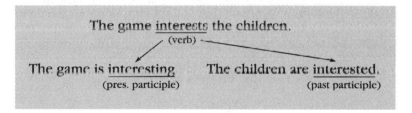

The game <u>interests</u> the children.
(verb)

The game is <u>interesting</u>   The children are <u>interested</u>.
(pres. participle)   (past participle)

Language Notes

- The present participle *(-ing)* shows that the noun described (the game) actively causes a feeling of interest.

  The game is *interesting*. = The game causes the children to have interest.
- The past participle *(-ed/-en)* shows that the noun described (the children) passively receives a feeling.[6]

  The children are *interested*. = The children receive interest from the game.

---

[6]Since a thing can't receive a feeling, the past participle cannot be used to describe a thing. A person can be interested or interesting. A game can be *interesting* but never *interested*.

1. Common participles of this type are the following:

amazing	amazed	exhausting	exhausted
amusing	amused	frightening	frightened
annoying	annoyed	frustrating	frustrated
boring	bored	interesting	interested
convincing	convinced	puzzling	puzzled
depressing	depressed	relaxing	relaxed
disappointing	disappointed	satisfying	satisfied
embarrassing	embarrassed	surprising	surprised
exciting	excited	terrifying	terrified
		tiring	tired

2. The following pictures show you the difference between *frightening* and *frightened*.

   A. The man is frightening the children. = He's a *frightening* man.

   B. The man is frightened by the robber. = He's a *frightened* man.

EXERCISE 21   Use the verb in each sentence to make two new sentences. In one sentence, use the present participle. In the other, use the past participle.

> EXAMPLE: **The game entertains children.**
>   **1. The game is entertaining.**
>   **2. The children are entertained.**

1. The movie frightened the children.
2. The book interests the children.
3. The children are amusing the adults.
4. The trip tired the children.
5. The game excited the children.
6. The vacation exhausted the adults.
7. The movie bored the adults.

EXERCISE 22   This is a composition written by a married woman. Fill in each blank with the correct participle of the verb in parentheses ( ) to complete the story.

My children are _____*grown*_____ and _____. When my youngest child
(grow)   (1 marry)

got married, I was all alone at home for the first time, and I felt _____.
(2 bore)

I wasn't _____ to having no one to take care of. Then I decided to find
(3 accustom)

some _____ activities to keep me busy. I enrolled in an adult education
(4 interest)

class.[7] I'm taking a home repair class. I used to think that only men could fix

things. But these are _____ times. My husband is _____ at how
(5 change)   (6 amaze)

well I can repair things around the house.

I'm thinking about taking more classes next semester. I'm even thinking about

starting a career. An _____ woman has many opportunities today. After
(7 educate)

so many years of being a housewife, I might like to be a _____ woman.
(8 work)

I would like to find a _____ career. My husband is a little _____,
(9 reward)   (10 surprise)

but he's very _____.
(11 understand)

2.6 Past Participles and Adjectives with *Get*[8]

We often use *get* before a past participle or other adjective.

Subject	*Get*	Past Participle or Adjective
He	got	shot.
He	got	married.
He	got	angry.

---

[7]An *adult education class* is not for college credit. It is for self-improvement or to learn a new skill.

[8]For more uses of *get*, see Appendix C.

Language Notes

1. In conversation, *get* with a past participle is often used instead of *be*. However, a performer is rarely used with *get*. COMPARE:

He got shot.
He was shot by the robber.

Get can be used with *killed, wounded, paid, hired, fired,*[9] *laid off.*[10]

2. In some cases, we can use *get* + past participle to show the beginning of an action. *Get* means "become."

get accustomed to	get divorced	get hurt	get tired
get acquainted	get dressed	get lost	get used to
get bored	get drunk	get married	get worried
get confused	get engaged	get scared	

COMPARE:

He *is* married to a wonderful woman. He *got* married in 1988.
This child *is* lost. He *got* lost when he left his mother's side.
He *got* drunk at the party. He couldn't drive home because he *was* too drunk.
I'*m* accustomed to speaking English now. It took me a long time to *get* accustomed to it.

3. We can also use *get* with many other adjectives to mean *become*.

get angry	get hungry	get rich	get well
get dark	get nervous	get sleepy	
get fat	get old	get upset	

COMPARE:

My uncle *is* a rich man.   He *got* rich in the oil business.
She'*s* a nervous person.   She *got* nervous when the teacher asked her to read a paragraph aloud.

EXERCISE 23   Fill in the blank with *get* or *be* + the adjective or past participle of the verb in parentheses ( ). Choose an appropriate tense.

EXAMPLES: I __*am worried*__ about my grades.
                              (worry)

The mother __*got worried*__ when her son didn't come home
                                  (worry)

from school.

1. I _____. I don't understand the lesson at all.
        (confuse)

2. He understood the explanation about the passive voice, but he _____
                                                                                                        (confuse)

   when the teacher explained the difference between "interested" and "interesting."

3. When did you _____?
                          (marry)

_____

[9]When a worker is *fired,* he loses his job because the boss is not happy with his work.

[10]When a worker is *laid off,* he loses his job because his company doesn't have enough work for him.

4. Bob and Sue _____ for five years.
　　　　　　　　　(marry)

5. I like waking up at 6:00 A.M. I _____ to it because I've been doing it
　　　　　　　　　　　　　　　　　　(accustom)
all my life.

6. I can't _____ to the climate in this city.
　　　　　　(use)

7. Don't pay any attention to what he is saying. He _____.
　　　　　　　　　　　　　　　　　　　　　　　　　　　(drink)

8. Be careful. If you drink too much, you're going to _____.
　　　　　　　　　　　　　　　　　　　　　　　　　(drink)

9. How's your mother? She _____, thank you.
　　　　　　　　　　　　　(well)

10. I heard your brother is sick. I hope he _____ very soon.
　　　　　　　　　　　　　　　　　　　　(well)

11. When she heard the bad news, she _____ and started to cry.
　　　　　　　　　　　　　　　　　(upset)

12. The old woman _____ because her children never visit her.
　　　　　　　　　　　(upset)

EXPANSION ACTIVITIES

PROVERBS

1. The following proverbs use participles as adjectives. Discuss the meaning of each proverb. Do you have a similar proverb in your language?

   Let sleeping dogs lie.
   A rolling stone gathers no moss.
   A watched pot never boils.
   A penny saved is a penny earned.

2. The following proverbs use the passive voice. Discuss the meaning of each proverb. Do you have a similar proverb in your language?

   Children should be seen and not heard.
   Rome wasn't built in a day.

DISCUSSIONS In a small group or with the entire class, discuss the following topics:

1. In your country, do you need a prescription to buy drugs? Are the laws stricter in the U.S. or in your country? Are pharmacies, doctors, and medicines in your country different from in the U.S.?

2. Compare food in your country to food in the U.S. Are chemical or artificial ingredients used much in your country? Does the government in your country tell you about the dangers of certain foods?

3. Are movies rated in your country?

4. Fill in each blank in the following sentences. Discuss your answers in a small group or with the entire class.

EXAMPLE: **I'm interested in** *learning how to ski.*

a. I'm interested in learning more about _____ because

_____.

b. I think that _____ is an interesting person. I'd like to

learn more about him or her because _____.

c. _____ is confusing for me.

d. When I came to the U.S., I was surprised to find that

_____.

e. When I came to the U.S., I was disappointed to find that

_____

f. _____ is/are not very interesting for me.

g. I feel bored when _____.

h. _____ is a boring school subject for me.

i. I was very excited when _____.

WRITING

1. Write a paragraph or short composition about a person whom you're interested in. This can be a famous person or a friend or member of your family. The person can be living or dead. Describe the person and tell why he or she is interesting to you. Some famous people to choose from:

Madonna	The president or leader	Napoleon
Michael Jackson	of your country	Mohammed Ali
Princess Diana	Josef Stalin	Elizabeth Taylor
The U.S. President	Albert Einstein	Elvis Presley

2. Write about how a holiday is celebrated in your country. Use both passive and active voice.

3. Write a paragraph about an important event in your country. Begin with a passive sentence, if possible. Then write more information about this event. Read your paragraph to the class.

EXAMPLE: **Indira Ghandi was assassinated in 1984. . . .**
Parts of Mexico City were destroyed by an earthquake in 1986. . . .

OUTSIDE
ACTIVITIES

1. Look at the movie section of a newspaper. Notice the ratings for movies that interest you. The next time you rent a movie, notice how the movie is rated. Do you agree with the rating?

2. Look for signs on streets or in buildings. Look for passive constructions. Copy these sentences and bring them to class to discuss their meanings. (Sometimes the verb *be* is omitted from a sign to save space.)

EXAMPLES: **Smoking (is) not permitted in this section.**
Bus tokens (are) sold here.
No one will be admitted without an ID.

EDITING ADVICE
. . . .

1. Use a form of *be* + *not* to make a negative with the passive voice.
   wasn't
   This watch ~~didn't~~ made in Japan.

2. Don't use the passive voice with intransitive verbs (verbs that have no object).

   The accident ~~was~~ happened at 10:30 P.M.

   My grandfather ~~was~~ died fifteen years ago.

3. Don't confuse the *-ing* form and the past participle.
   eaten
   The candy was ~~eating~~ by the child.

4. Don't forget the *-ed* ending for a regular past participle.
   ed
   The floor was wash⌄by the janitor.
   d
   Are you tire⌄after work?

5. Use an object pronoun after *by*.
   her
   The meal was prepared by ~~she~~.

6. Don't forget the *-d* in *used to*.
   d
   Are you use⌄to cold weather?

SUMMARY OF LESSON TWO

1. Active and Passive

Active			Passive		
Subject +	Active Verb +	Object	Subject +	Passive Verb +	(By Performer)
The dog	bit	the man.	The man	was bitten	by the dog.
She	will write	the book.	The book	will be written	by her.
No one	has driven	the car.	The car	has not been driven.	

2. Uses of the Passive

   A. Without a performer

      • When the performer is not known or is not important:
        My watch was made in Japan.

      • When the performer is obvious:
        The man was arrested.

      • When the performer is everybody or people in general:
        English is spoken in the U.S.

      • When we want to avoid mentioning the performer:
        I was told that you found a job.

   B. With a performer

      When we want to emphasize the action more than the performer.

      The telephone was invented by Alexander Graham Bell. (The telephone is the
      focus of attention, not Bell.)

      The dish was broken by the child. (The dish is the focus of attention, not the
      child.)

3. Present and Past Participles Used as Adjectives

   A. A present participle shows that the noun it describes performs an action:
      A *loving* mother is a mother who loves her child.

   B. A past participle shows that the noun it describes receives an action:
      A *broken* window is a window that was broken by someone.

   C. We can use participles to describe emotions. The present participle describes the
      activity that produces the emotion; the past participle describes a person's
      emotional reaction to the activity:
      The movie was *boring.* I was *bored.*
      The trip is *exciting.* I am *excited.*

LESSON TWO TEST/REVIEW

Part 1   Find the mistakes with participles and passive voice, and correct them. Not every sentence has a mistake. If the sentence is correct, write *C.*

> EXAMPLES: He was born in 1922, and he ~~was~~ died in 1990.
>
> A great movie was shown at the theater.   *C*

1. The composition didn't written by Jim.

2. The criminal was taking to the police station.

3. A dictionary left on the floor of the classroom.

4. Where was the accident happened?

5. I wasn't told about the party.

6. I had a tired day at work yesterday.

7. I'm worried about my children.

8. It is a well know fact that women live longer than men.

9. Married people live longer than single people.

10. Everyone should have insurance. Is your car insure?

11. I'm very tire. I can't do this exercise now.

12. I come from a warm country. I'm not use to cold weather.

13. Last week we saw a very boring movie.

14. She has an interesting job.

15. I was surprised to find out that you are marry.

Part 2   Change the following sentences to the passive voice. No performer is necessary. Use the same tense as in the original sentence.

> EXAMPLE: People use aspirin for pain.
>
> _Aspirin is used for pain._

1. Someone has taken my dictionary.

_____

2. They are washing the windows now.

_____

3. They were testing a new drug.

_____

4. They must drive us to the hospital soon.

_____

5. They didn't write the letter carefully.

_____

6. Someone has to tell her.

_____

7. They will not sell new drugs if the government doesn't approve them. (Change both verbs.)

_____

Part 3   Change the following sentences to the active voice. Use the same tense as in the original sentence.

   EXAMPLE: **Children are often left alone by their parents.**

   Parents often leave their children alone.
   _____

1. The video was rented by him.

_____

2. Corrections should be made by the teacher.

_____

3. The homework has been done by the child.

_____

4. Children have to be taught by their parents.

_____

5. A story was being read by her.

_____

6. Our dictionaries can be used during the test.

_____

7. A movie is being shown by the teacher.

_____

Part 4   Some of the sentences below are active. Change them to passive. Some are passive. Change them to active. Omit the performer in passive sentences if it is not necessary. Use the same tense as in the original sentence.

EXAMPLE: **They sell some drugs without a prescription.**

Some drugs are sold without a prescription.
_____

1. We call a videocassette recorder a "VCR."

_____

2. A prescription is not needed by the patient.

_____

3. They don't speak English in Cuba.

_____

4. Someone has found my ring.

_____

5. The pizza is being eaten by them.

_____

6. The children will be taken to the zoo by the teacher.

_____

7. This drug is taken by people with cancer.

_____

8. They can't sell this drug without a prescription.

_____

9. She has been taken to the doctor by him.

_____

10. We have to use drugs carefully.

_____

11. Your doctor should be told about the problem.

_____

12. You should read the directions.

_____

Part 5   Fill in each blank with the passive or the active voice of the verb in parentheses
( ). Use an appropriate tense.

EXAMPLE: The teacher _____*usually gives*_____ homework.
                                    (usually/give)

1. A lot of corrections _____ on my last composition.
                                    (make)

2. The composition _____ at the end of the day.
                                    (collect)

3. The teacher _____ the homework.
                                    (return)

4. The students _____ their answers in the book.
                                    (write)

5. Your name _____ at the top of the page.
                                    (should/write)

6. The students _____ to use their textbook during the
                                    (not/permit)

exam.

7. The teacher _____ the students during the test.
                                    (watch)

8. The test _____ the next day.
                                    (return)

9. The students _____ before a test.
                                    (should/study)

Part 6   Fill in each blank with the present participle or the past participle of the verb in parentheses ( ).

EXAMPLES: The ___*following*___ sentences contain a participle.
                               (follow)

Many women are ___*interested*___ in a career.
                               (interest)

1. There are many _____ mothers in the U.S.
                          (work)

2. Some women have _____ careers.
                          (interest)

3. Some women wait until their children are _____ before starting a
                                                    (grow)

   career.

4. _____ children need someone to take care of them.
       (grow)

5. All children need _____ parents.
                          (love)

6. Many women are _____ with housework.
                          (bore)

7. Housework is usually _____.
                               (bore)

8. Where is your day care center _____?
                                       (locate)

9. When did you get _____?
                          (marry)

10. It's not easy to get _____ to a new life.
                               (accustom)

LESSON THREE

GRAMMAR
The Past Perfect
The Past Perfect Continuous
Contrast of Past Tenses

CONTEXT
A Terrible Mistake

Lesson Focus   **The Past Perfect; The Past Perfect Continuous; Contrast of Past Tenses**

- The past perfect is formed with *had* + a past participle.
  He *had eaten* lunch.
  There *had been* a problem.

- The past perfect continuous is formed with *had* + *been* + verb *-ing*.
  They *had been working*.
  I *had been studying*.

- The past perfect (continuous) is often used in a sentence with the simple past tense to show the time relationship of the two verbs. The verb in the past perfect (continuous) happened first.
  I didn't understand the teacher's explanation because I *hadn't read* the assignment.
  When I got permission to come to the U.S., I *had been waiting* for three years.
  I returned the sweater that I *had bought*.

- The simple past is often used with the past continuous to show a time relationship.
  I *was sleeping* when the baby *started* to cry.

R
E
A
D
I
N
G

Before you read

Sometimes doctors or hospitals make mistakes. Have you heard of any cases in the U.S. or in your country about a mistake that a hospital made?

Read the following article. Pay special attention to past perfect (continuous) verbs.

A TERRIBLE MISTAKE

In December 1978, Arlena Twigg was born in a Florida hospital. Arlena was very sick; she had a malformed heart. By the time Arlena was nine and a half years old, she **had been suffering** most of her life. Finally, her doctors recommended that she have heart surgery. In preparation for the surgery, Arlena was given a blood test, and it was discovered that she could not possibly be the genetic daughter of Mr. and Mrs. Twigg. It was believed that Arlena **had been switched**[1] with another baby soon after her birth. Arlena died while in surgery. Her parents, the Twiggs, felt that they **had lost** two daughters—their natural daughter, who **had been taken** away from them at birth, and Arlena, whom they **had loved** and **raised** since she was an infant.

After investigating hospital records, the Twiggs found that their real daughter was a healthy nine-year-old girl named Kimberly Mays, who was born in the same hospital around the same date as Arlena. How or why the babies were switched is not known.

---

[1]*Switched* means *changed* or *exchanged*.

The Twiggs sued[2] the Florida hospital that **had made** this mistake. Mr. and Mrs. Twigg were allowed to meet with their daughter Kimberly, whom they **had never known.** However, the court decided that Kimberly should stay with the father who **had raised** her since birth. (Mr. Mays's wife, Barbara Mays, died when Kimberly was a baby.)

3.1 The Past Perfect and Past Perfect Continuous

The Past Perfect				
Subject	*Had*	*(Not)*	Past Participle	Complement
The Twiggs	had		lost	two daughters.
The Twiggs	had	not	known	Kimberly before 1988.
There	had		been	a mistake at the hospital.

The Past Perfect Continuous					
Subject	*Had*	*(Not)*	Been	Present Participle	Complement
Arlena	had		been	suffering	most of her life.
Kimberly	had	not	been	living	with the Twiggs.

Past Perfect with Passive					
Subject	*Had*	*(Not)*	Been	Past Participle	Complement
The babies	had		been	switched.	
Kimberly	had	not	been	raised	by her natural parents.

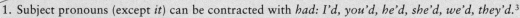

Language Notes

1. Subject pronouns (except *it*) can be contracted with *had*: I'd, you'd, he'd, she'd, we'd, they'd.[3]
2. Study these questions:

   Had he *lived* in the U.S. before?   *Had* he *been studying* English?
   When *had* he *lived* in the U.S.?   Where *had* he *been studying* English?
   How long *had* he *lived* in the U.S.?   How long *had* he *been studying* English?

---

[2]To *sue* means to take someone to court to try to prove that you were wronged.
[3]Apostrophe + *d* can be a contraction for both *would* and *had.* The word following *'d* will tell you what the contraction means:

   I'*d* rather drink coffee than tea. (*'d = would*)
   I'*d* done the homework before coming to class. (*'d = had*)

3.2   The Past Perfect Tense and the Simple Past

The simple past tense and the past perfect tense can be used in the same sentence to show a clear time relationship between two past events. The action of the past perfect verb occurred before the action of the simple past verb. Notice the types of clauses that result.

Time clause:

MORE RECENT PAST EVENT: Mrs. Twigg left the hospital.
EARLIER PAST EVENT: The babies were switched soon after birth.

   By the time Mrs. Twigg *left* the hospital, the babies *had* already *been switched.*

```
                                      now
       past  ◄-----1----------2----|----------------► future
              (switch)   (leave)  |
```

Reason clause:

MORE RECENT PAST EVENT: The Twiggs sued the hospital.
EARLIER PAST EVENT: The babies were switched.

   The Twiggs *sued* the hospital because the babies *had been switched.*

```
                                      now
       past  ◄-----1----------2----|----------------► future
              (switch)    (sue)   |
```

Noun clause:

MORE RECENT PAST EVENT: The Twiggs found out.
EARLIER PAST EVENT: They took the wrong girl home from the hospital.

   The Twiggs *found out* much later that they *had taken* the wrong girl home from the hospital.

```
                                      now
       past  ◄-----1----------2----|----------------► future
              (take)    (find out)|
```

Adjective clause:

MORE RECENT PAST EVENT: Kimberly stayed with the father.
EARLIER PAST EVENT: The father raised her.

   Kimberly *stayed* with the father *who had raised* her.

```
                                      now
       past  ◄-----1----------2----|----------------► future
              (raise)    (stay)   |
```

1. The past perfect can be used in a sentence with *before, after,* or *until.* However, the past tense is more common, especially in conversation, because these time words make the time relationship clear. There is no difference in meaning between the past and the past perfect in the following sentences.

> Mrs. Twigg *didn't know* Arlena's blood type before Arlena *had* the operation.
> Mrs. Twigg *hadn't known* Arlena's blood type before Arlena *had* the operation.
> Mrs. Twigg *sued* the hospital after Arlena *died*.
> Mrs. Twigg *sued* the hospital after Arlena *had died*.

2. The following time words are often used in sentences that contain the past perfect.

Just:

> By the time he arrived, his wife had *just* left.

Already:

> When Sarah got to class, class had *already* begun.

Yet:

> When the bell rang, we hadn't finished the test *yet.*

Never/not ever . . . before:

> When she left for college, she had *never* been away from home *before.*

For + a period of time:

> John Kennedy had been president *for* less than three years when he was assassinated.

By + exact time:

> *By* 10:00, everyone at the party had gone home.

EXERCISE 1   Fill in each blank with the simple past tense for the more recent past action and the past perfect tense for the earlier past action.

> **EXAMPLE:** **When I** _____*got up*_____**, my wife** _____*had already walked*_____ **the dog, so**
>   (get up)   (already/walk)
> **I didn't have to do it.**

1. When I _____, the sun _____.
                  (get up)   (already/rise)

2. I was going to make a pot of coffee, but my wife _____ a pot
                                                          (already/make)

   before she left.

3. I _____ several phone calls by the time I _____ the
        (make)   (leave)

   house.

4. I _____ take the subway to work because my wife
        (have to)

   _____ the car.
        (take)

5. When I _____ to work, my boss _____ .
               (get)   (not arrive/yet)

6. By the time I _____ out to lunch, I _____ to ten
                         (go)   (speak)

   clients.

7. I took an aspirin before I went home because I _____ a headache
                                                      (have)

   all day.

8. My children _____ to bed by the time I _____ home
                       (already/go)   (get)

   from work.

9. I _____ asleep right away because I _____ a very
              (fall)   (have)

   hard day at work.

EXERCISE 2   Tell if the following had already happened or hadn't happened yet by the
time you got to class.

> EXAMPLE: **The teacher/collect the homework**
>   **By the time I got to class, the teacher had already collected the
>   homework.**
>   OR
>   **When I got to class, the teacher hadn't collected the homework yet.**

1. the teacher/arrive
2. most of the students/arrive
3. the class/begin
4. the teacher/take attendance
5. I/do the homework
6. the teacher/hand back the last homework
7. _____

EXERCISE 3   Tell if the following had already happened, hadn't happened yet, or had
never happened before you came to the U.S.

> EXAMPLE: **study English**
>   **When I came to the U.S., I had already studied English.**
>   OR
>   **When I came to the U.S., I hadn't studied English yet.**
>   OR
>   **When I came to the U.S., I had never studied English before.**

1. eat American food
2. finish high school
3. start college
4. get a college degree
5. study English
6. visit another country
7. know a lot about the U.S.
8. buy an English dictionary
9. _____

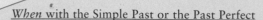

Language Notes

<u>*When* with the Simple Past or the Past Perfect</u>

The tense of the main clause (simple past or past perfect) tells you the meaning of *when*. Study the following pairs of sentences:

(1) When Arlena died, she *had* never *met* her real parents.
(2) When Arlena died, the Twiggs *sued* the hospital where she was born.

(1) When the Twiggs sued the hospital, Arlena *had* already *died*.
(2) When the Twiggs sued the hospital, they *won* millions of dollars.

In the first sentence of each pair, *when* means "before"; in the second sentence, *when* means "after."

EXERCISE 4   Write numbers to show which action happened first.

                             1   *2*

EXAMPLE: **When she got home, she took an aspirin.**

                             2   *1*

EXAMPLE: **When she got home, she had already taken an aspirin.**

1. When they came into the room, their son left.

2. When they came into the room, their son had just left.

3. When I got home from school, I did my homework.

4. When I got home from school, I had already done my homework.

5. When she got to my house, she had eaten dinner.

6. When she got to my house, she ate dinner.

7. The teacher gave a test when Linda arrived.

8. The teacher had already given a test when Linda arrived.

3.3 The Past Perfect Continuous Tense

The past perfect continuous tense is used to emphasize the duration of a continuous action that was completed before another past event.

Arlena *had been living* with the Twiggs for nine and a half years when she died.

By the time Arlena was nine and a half years old, she *had been suffering* most of her life.

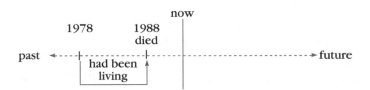

REMEMBER: Do not use the continuous form with a nonaction verb.

When she died, Arlena *had* never *seen* her real mother.

EXERCISE 5   Fill in each blank with the simple past tense or the past perfect continuous tense of the verb in parentheses ( ).

EXAMPLE: When I _____*came*_____ to the U.S., I __*had been studying*__ English
(come)   (study)
for three years.

1. I _____ for two years when I _____ a chance to leave my country.
   (wait)   (get)

2. I _____ in the same house all my life when I _____ my city.
   (live)   (leave)

3. I _____ very sad when I left my job because I _____ with the
   (feel)   (work)
   same people for ten years.

4. I _____ to be a nurse for six months when a war _____ in my
   (study)   (break out)
   country.

5. When I _____ my country, the war _____ for three years.
   (leave)   (go on)

6. My family _____ in a refugee camp for three months before we
   (wait)
   _____ permission to come to the U.S.
   (get)

7. By the time I _____ to the U.S., I _____ for four days.
   (get)   (travel)

EXERCISE 6   Fill in each blank with the simple past or the past perfect (continuous) of the verb in parentheses ( ).

SITUATION: Two friends are talking about jobs.

A. I heard you found a job last week.

B. Yes. I'm so happy.

A. How long _____*had*_____ you ___*been looking*___ when you found this job?

                                     (look)

B. For six months. By the time I found this job, I _____.

                                                                              (1 almost/give up)

A. _____ you _____ unemployment compensation?

               (2 get)

B. No. In order to get unemployment compensation, you have to get laid off. I quit my last job.

A. How long _____ you _____ there when you _____?

                        (3 work)   (4 quit)

B. For two years.

A. Why _____ you _____?

               (5 quit)

B. I quit because I couldn't make enough money. I started that job at minimum

wage,[4] and I thought I would get raises. But by the time I _____,

                                                                                                    (6 quit)

I _____ just a little more than minimum wage.

         (7 make)

EXERCISE 7   Fill in each blank with the simple past tense or the past perfect (continuous) tense of the verb in parentheses ( ).

1. Arlena Twigg _____ sick for a long time when she _____.

                                   (be)   (die)

2. Mr. Mays _____ to give up his daughter Kimberly because he

                       (not/want)

   _____ her from the time she was a baby.

                (raise)

3. It _____ that Arlena and Kimberly _____ at birth.

         (*passive*: discover)   (switch)

4. Arlena _____ with the Twigg family for nine years when she

                     (live)

   _____.

          (die)

5. When Arlena _____, she _____ her real mother.

                          (die)   (never/meet)

_____

[4]The government decides on the lowest salary an employer can pay an employee. This is called the *minimum wage.*

3.4 Past Perfect (Continuous) vs. Present Perfect (Continuous)

The past perfect and the present perfect cannot be used interchangeably.

- A past perfect (continuous) verb is used to show that one past action occurred before another past action.

    When he retired two years ago, he *had worked* (or *had been working*) at his job for twenty years.

    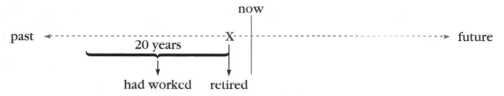

    By the time he died, he *had been married* five times.

- A present perfect (continuous) verb is used to show that an action occurred before the present time.

    She's working now. She *has worked* (or *has been working*) at this job for three years.

    She *has gone* to Paris five times.

EXERCISE 8   Fill in each blank with the present perfect (continuous) tense or the past perfect (continuous) tense of the verb in parentheses ( ).

> EXAMPLES: I live in the U.S. now. I ___*have been living*___ here for five years.
> (live)
>
> OR
>
> I lived in Canada until 1990. I ___*had been living*___ in Canada for
> (live)
>
> three years when I decided to come to the U.S.

1. My sister quit smoking last week. She _____ for five years when
   (smoke)

   she decided to quit.

2. I still smoke. I _____ since I was a teenager.
   (smoke)

3. He couldn't pay his rent last month because he _____ all his
   (spend)

   money at the racetrack.

4. This month I _____ $150 on groceries so far.
   (spend)

5. She was born in New York. Her cousins were born in Moscow. She

   _____ her cousins.
   (never/see)

6. Her father lived in Moscow until he died last year. When he died, he

   _____ his grandchildren in the U.S.
   (never/see)

7. He drank champagne when he got married. He _____ champagne
   (never/drink)

   before.

8. He likes beer. He _____ beer many times.
   (drink)

3.5 Simple Past vs. Past Continuous

1. We use the simple past tense for a completed past action that occurred at a specific time. The simple past does not show the relationship of one past action to another.

   Arlena Twigg *died* in 1988.

   ```
                                          now
   past  ◄-------X---------------------|---------------► future
                 died
   ```

   She *lived* with the Twiggs for 9 years.

   ```
                                          now
   past  ◄------ ▓▓▓▓----------------|---------------► future
                 lived
   ```

2. We use the past continuous tense for a continuous action. We use the past continuous in the following cases:

   A. To show what was happening at a specific time:

   Arlena *was living* with the Twiggs in 1980.

   ```
                    1980            now
   past  ◄---▓▓X▓▓-----------|---------------► future
                was living
   ```

   B. To show that two past actions occurred for the same general time:

   While the Twiggs *were taking* care of a sick child, the Mays *were raising* a healthy child.

   ```
                  were talking    now
   past  ◄---- ▓▓▓▓▓▓-------|---------------► future
                were raising
   ```

   C. To show the relationship of a longer action to a shorter action, use the simple past for the shorter action and the past continuous for the longer action:

   Arlena *was living* with the Twiggs when she *died.*

   ```
                  died            now
   past  ◄-- ▓▓X▓▓-----------|---------------► future
                was living
   ```

Other uses of the past continuous:
1. To emphasize the length of a past action:
   I *was working* hard all morning.
2. When telling a story, to describe the scene before the main event occurred:
   It *was raining*. Everyone in the house *was sleeping*. Suddenly, we heard a loud noise in the basement.
3. *Was/were going to* can be used to show that a past intention was not carried out:
   I *was going to* call you, but I lost your phone number.
   He *was going to* cook dinner, but he didn't have time.

EXERCISE 9   Fill in each blank with the simple past tense or the past continuous tense of the verb in parentheses ( ).

A. I'm really upset. My phone bill is so high this month.

B. Why? _____Did_____ you _____make_____ a lot of long-distance calls last month?
                    (make)

A. No. That's not the problem. While I _____, my 12-year-old son was
                                            (1 work)

   home alone. He _____ a 900 number. He _____ TV when
                        (2 call)   (3 watch)

   he _____ an offer by a psychic. She _____ that she could
         (4 see)   (5 say)

   read your fortune. My son _____ about 900 numbers. He
                                  (6 not/understand)

   _____ that they aren't free.
        (7 not/know)

B. How much do you have to pay for his call?

A. Sixty dollars. The call was four dollars a minute. He _____ for about
                                                              (8 talk)

   fifteen minutes.

B. I thought your wife is usually at home when he comes home from school.
   Wasn't she home at the time?

A. She _____ in the garden, and she thought that our son _____
             (9 work)   (10 do)
   his homework.

B. When _____ about the call?
           (11 you/find out)

A. I _____ when I _____ my phone bill. I was shocked.
         (12 find out)   (13 get)

B. Didn't he tell you that he made the call?

A. No. When I _____ home that day, he _____ his homework.
              (14 come)   (15 do)

    So I didn't know about the call until the bill _____.
                                          (16 arrive)

B. What _____ when you _____? Did you punish your son?
             (17 you/do)   (18 find out)

A. I _____ punish him, but then I _____ that he didn't
        (19 go)   (20 realize)

    understand that he had done anything wrong. So I just _____ to him
                                                 (21 explain)

    about 900 numbers, and he _____ never to do it again.
                              (22 promise)

3.6   More Than One Tense Can Sometimes Be Used

In some cases, two tenses are possible. There is very little difference in meaning.

- Present perfect or present perfect continuous:
  > I *have been working* as a machinist for three years.
  > I *have worked* as a machinist for three years.

- Past continuous or past perfect continuous:
  > Arlena *was living* with the Twiggs when she died.
  > Arlena *had been living* with the Twiggs when she died.

- Past continuous or simple past:
  > While I *was driving,* I *was listening* to the radio.
  > While I *drove,* I *listened* to the radio.

- Present perfect or simple past (with *yet, already, ever, lately,* or no time mentioned):
  > *Has* Kimberly ever *met* Mrs. Twigg?
  > *Did* Kimberly ever *meet* Mrs. Twigg?
  > *Have* you *eaten* dinner yet?
  > *Did* you *eat* dinner yet?

- Simple past or past perfect:
  > Arlena *didn't see* her real mother before she died.
  > Arlena *hadn't seen* her real mother before she died.

EXERCISE 10   Fill in each blank with the correct past tense of the verb in parentheses ( ).
In some cases, more than one answer may be possible.

I ___*was*___ born in Vietnam in 1960. I _____ there until 1975, when
     (be)   (1 live)

the government _____ and the communists _____ over. I will never
             (2 fall)   (3 take)

forget that moment. I _____ in high school at that time. I _____ a
             (4 study)   (5 take)

math test when the director of our school _____ into the class to announce
                             (6 come)

that the government _____. Everyone in my class _____ silent. The
             (7 fall)   (8 become)

teacher _____ our test and _____ us to go home. By the time I
      (9 stop)   (10 tell)

_____ home from school, my father _____ arrangements to leave
(11 get)   (12 already/make)

the country. Our lives _____ in great danger because my father _____
          (13 be)   (14 work)

for the U.S. military for ten years. We _____ in a hurry. We _____
                   (15 leave)   (16 have)

no time to say good-bye to our friends or pack our belongings. We _____
                            (17 take)

with us only the most necessary things. We _____ behind many things that
                     (18 leave)

_____ my family years to acquire.
(19 take)

After we _____ Vietnam, we _____ to Thailand, where we
       (20 leave)   (21 go)

_____ for three years. While we _____ for permission to come to the
(22 stay)   (23 wait)

U.S., we _____ English. We _____ to be prepared for our life in the
     (24 study)   (25 want)

U.S. I'll never forget December 5, 1978, one of the happiest days of my life. It

was three o'clock, and I _____ my brother practice his English lesson
            (26 help)

when my father _____ into the room with a letter in his hand. The U.S.
        (27 run)

government _____ us permission to go to America. We _____ so
      (28 give)   (29 be)

excited when my father _____ us the news.
        (30 tell)

When we _____ at the Los Angeles airport on February 6, 1979, our
                (31 arrive)

sponsor _____ for us. He _____ a sign that said, "Welcome to the
            (32 wait)   (33 hold)

U.S., Mr. Ly Tran and family." We _____ so happy and excited. My mother
                                        (34 be)

_____ to cry.
  (35 start)

Now we _____ in the U.S. for about fifteen years. At first it _____
            (36 be)   (37 be)

difficult for me to learn English. My little brother and sisters _____ it
                                                                  (38 learn)

quickly, but it _____ me much longer. I _____ classes at a
                 (39 take)   (40 attend)

community college from 1979 to 1983. I think I _____ to speak English
                                                  (41 learn)

pretty well. But my mother didn't learn English at that time because she

_____ to stay home to take care of the little ones. When the little ones
 (42 have)

_____ high school, my mother _____ to study English. About two
 (43 enter)   (44 start)

years ago, she _____ at City College. She _____ a lot of English
                 (45 enroll)   (46 learn)

lately. All of us _____ her. My younger brother and sisters _____ how
                   (47 help)   (48 forget)

to speak Vietnamese already, but I _____.
                                     (49 not/forget)

We _____ a hard life since we came to the U.S., but we _____ the
     (50 have)   (51 make)

right decision to leave when we did.

EXPANSION ACTIVITIES

DISCUSSIONS   1. In a small group or with the entire class, discuss your experiences with leaving your country, coming to the U.S., and learning English. Talk about the members of your family as well as yourself.

2. Fill in the blanks and discuss your answers in a small group.

   a. When I came to the U.S., I had never _____ before.

   b. By the time I came to the U.S., I had already _____.

DISCUSSION AND WRITING

In the case of the baby switch, do you think the judge did the right thing when he decided to leave Kimberly with the father who had raised her? Discuss your opinion with your classmates. Then write a composition. State your point of view, and then give your reason(s).

WRITING

Choose one of the topics below and write a short essay. Edit your essay for mistakes with past tense verbs.

1. The events that led up to your leaving your country. You may include your first experiences in the U.S.

2. An accident or unusual experience that happened to you or to a friend

3. How you met your spouse or a new friend, or how your parents met and married

4. A frightening experience you had

5. An important event in the history of your country

OUTSIDE ACTIVITY

Go to the reference section of the library. Ask the librarian to teach you how to do a topic search in periodicals. Look for the latest information on the case of Kimberly Mays. Report this information to the class.

SUMMARY OF LESSON THREE

1. We use the past perfect to show that one past action occurred before another past action.

> By the time Mrs. Twigg left the hospital, the babies *had been switched*.
> The Twiggs finally met the daughter whom they *had* never *known*.
> Arlena *had been hospitalized* several times by the time she died.

2. We use the past perfect continuous to show that a continuous past action occurred for a period of time before another past action.

> I *had been studying* English for five years when I came to the U.S.
> By the time he got permission to come to the U.S., he *had been living* in a refugee camp for three years.

3. Compare the past tenses.

SIMPLE PAST:	Arlena *died* in 1988.
PAST CONTINUOUS:	She *was living* with the Twiggs when she died.
PAST CONTINUOUS:	While Arlena *was living* with the Twiggs, Kimberly *was living* with the Mays.
PRESENT PERFECT:	Because of these problems, Kimberly Mays *has* always *had* a difficult life.
PRESENT PERFECT CONTINUOUS:	We *have been studying* the case of Kimberly Mays.
PAST PERFECT:	When Arlena died, she *had* never *met* her real mother.
PAST PERFECT CONTINUOUS:	By the time Arlena had her operation, she *had been suffering* most of her life.

LESSON THREE TEST/REVIEW

Part 1   Fill in each blank with one of the past tenses: simple past, past continuous, present perfect (continuous), or past perfect (continuous). In some cases, more than one answer is possible.

A. What ___*happened*___ to your car?
          (happen)

B. I _____ an accident yesterday.
      (1 have)

A. How _____ it _____?
        (2 happen)

B. I _____ to work when a dog _____ in front of my car. I
      (3 drive)   (4 run)

_____ my car suddenly, and the car behind me _____ my car
   (5 stop)   (6 hit)

because the driver _____ me too closely.
                    (7 follow)

A. _____ a ticket?
    (8 you/get)

B. No, but the driver who hit me did.

A. Who will pay to have your car fixed?

B. The other driver. He _____ me his insurance card. He's a new driver.
                       (9 give)

He _____ his driver's license for two months.
   (10 only/have)

A. You're a new driver too, aren't you?

B. Oh, no. I _____ for twenty years.
            (11 drive)

A. I thought you _____ your driver's license a few months ago.
                 (12 get)

B. In this state, I have a new license. But I _____ a driver's license for
                                             (13 have)

many years before I _____ to the U.S.
                    (14 come)

A. _____ you ever _____ a ticket?
    (15 get)

B. One time. I _____ about 65 miles an hour on the highway when a
              (16 drive)

police officer _____ me. She said that the speed limit was only 55. She
               (17 stop)

_____ me a ticket for speeding. She also gave me a ticket because I
    (18 give)

_____ my seat belt.
   (19 not/wear)

Part 2   Find the mistakes with past tense verbs, and correct them. Not every sentence
has a mistake. If the sentence is correct, write *C*.

        study
    EXAMPLES: I wanted to go to New York and ~~studied~~ art.

        Where was he born?   *C*

1. When was he died?

2. I was work when the fire started.

3. He didn't gave me the money.

4. Why you didn't come to class yesterday?

5. How long do you live in this city?

6. The accident was happened at 6:45 this morning.

7. They were getting married five years ago.

8. When he came to the U.S., he had never studied English before.

9. Have you ever seeing the mayor of this city?

10. He has been married for ten years. He got divorced two years ago.

11. She left her dictionary in the library yesterday.

12. When I came to the U.S., I have never spoken with an American before.

13. He has wanted to be a doctor ever since he has been a little boy.

14. They were watching TV at 9:30 last night.

15. They were living in Germany when the war was starting.

16. While they were living in Thailand, they were studying English.

17. I been studying English for five years.

18. I'm a nurse now. I had been a nurse for ten years.

LESSON FOUR

GRAMMAR
Modals
Related Expressions

CONTEXT
Medicine
Social Customs

Lesson Focus Modals; Related Expressions

The modal auxiliaries are *can, could, shall, should, will, would, may, might,* and *must.*
The base form is used after a modal. A modal never has a verb ending (*-s, -ing, -ed*).

    I *can* swim   He *can* swim.
    I *am able to* swim.
    He *is supposed to* help you.

• •

R
E
A
D
I
N
G

Before you read:

How is an American pharmacy different from a pharmacy in your country?

Read the following article and conversations. Pay special attention to modals and related words.

MEDICINE

Sometimes when you feel sick, you try to treat the illness yourself. You **can** buy over-the-counter drugs, such as aspirin, without a prescription. However, you **should** always use medications with caution. You **should** read the information on the package. For example, some medicines **shouldn't** be given to young children. Other medications **could** be harmful to pregnant women. In many cases, prolonged use[1] **could** be harmful; if the illness persists, you **should** see a doctor.

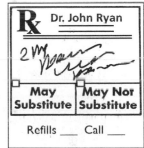

prescription

A pharmacist **cannot** sell prescription drugs without permission from a doctor. When you need a prescription drug, you **must** get a prescription from a doctor. Most people **can't** read a doctor's prescription because it is written in Latin. But a pharmacist **can** read the prescription.

The prescription form that the doctor uses has a place for the doctor to check:

   ❐ **May** substitute   ❐ **May** not substitute

If the doctor has checked the first box, this means that the pharmacist **can** give you a generic drug, which is cheaper than the name-brand equivalent. Tell the pharmacist which kind of drug you **would rather** have. If the doctor has checked the second box, the pharmacist **must** give you exactly what the doctor has ordered. Pharmacists **must** obey the law; otherwise, they **can** lose their license.

When you visit your doctor, you **should** always tell him or her about any other medications you are taking. The combination of some medications **could** be dangerous. Pharmacists often put warning labels on drugs: "This medication **may** cause drowsiness,"

---

[1]*Prolonged use* is use over a long period of time.

"Alcohol **can** intensify this effect," or "This medication **should** be taken after a meal."

A doctor's prescription also has a place to indicate refills. This tells the pharmacist how many times he or she **may** fill the same prescription. The medicine container tells you how many refills you **can** have. If the container says "call," this means that you **can't** get a refill without first calling or visiting the doctor. In many cases, you **don't have to** visit the doctor again. You **can** simply call your doctor and discuss your need for more of the same medication, or you **can** ask the pharmacist to call the doctor.

4.1 Modals—An Overview

Observe these seven patterns with a modal:

AFFIRMATIVE:	He *can* speak French.
NEGATIVE:	He *can't* speak German.
YES/NO QUESTION:	*Can* he speak English?
SHORT ANSWERS:	No, he *can't.*/Yes, he *can.*
Wh- QUESTION:	What languages *can* he speak?
NEGATIVE QUESTION:	Why *can't* he speak German?
SUBJECT QUESTION:	Who *can* speak German?

A modal can be made passive with *be* + the past participle.

Subject	Modal	*Be*	Past Participle	Complement
Aspirin	can	be	bought	without a prescription.
Some medicines	shouldn't	be	given	to children.

Language Notes

1. A modal is not used after another auxiliary.

    I should *be able* to help you later. (NOT: *should can*)
    She might *have to* leave early. (NOT: *might must*)
    I will *have to* appear in court. (NOT: *will must*)
    She has *had to* quit her job. (NOT: *has must*)

2. One use of modals is to make a request more polite.

    Open the door.
    MORE POLITE: *Would* you open the door, please?

3. *Shall* is more common in British English than in American English.

    BRITISH: We *shall* study verbs.
    AMERICAN: We *will* study verbs.

    Americans sometimes use *shall* in a question pattern for suggestions or invitations.

    Shall we leave now?
    Shall we dance?

• •

R
E
A   **Before you read:**
D
I   Did you use a medication in your country? Did you need a prescription for it?
N   Read the following conversation. Pay attention to modals and related words.
G

CALLING FOR A PRESCRIPTION

Part One: Wrong Number

   A. Hello?
   B. Hello. **I'd like** a refill on my prescription.
   A. You **must*** have the wrong number. This is Bill's Toy World, a toy store.
   B. Sorry.

Part Two: Talking to the Pharmacist

   A. Hello. Taylor's Pharmacy. How **can** I help you?
   B. I need a refill.
   A. **May** I have the prescription number, please?
   B. I don't have the bottle in front of me. **Could** you look it up on your computer?
   A. Sure. Your name please?
   B. Feingold.
   A. **Would you mind** spelling it?
   B. F-E-I-N-G-O-L-D.
   A. I'm sorry, Mr. Feingold, but I **can't** refill it.
   B. Why not? **I'm supposed to** get two refills.
   A. But the prescription is over one year old. I **can't** refill it without permission
      from the doctor.
   B. **Could** you call her for me?
   A. Of course. **Can** you give me her number?
   B. It's 555-9231.
   A. **Why don't you** check back with me in about an hour? If we **can** reach your
      doctor, we **should*** have it ready in about an hour.

Part Three: In the Pharmacy

   B. **I'd like** to pick up my prescription.
   A. I'm sorry. I **couldn't** reach your doctor. There was no answer. It's late. The
      office **must*** be closed. I'll try tomorrow.
   B. **Could** you give me just a few pills for now?
   A. I'm sorry. I **can't**. It's against the law.
   B. But **I've got to** have this medication now. What **can** I do?
   A. Your doctor **must*** have an emergency number. **Why don't you** call that num-
      ber? It **might** take a little while, but I'm sure someone will call you back.

_____

*NOTE: The meanings of these modals will be discussed in the next lesson. See if you can guess their
meaning for now.

B. **Would you mind if** I used your phone?

A. **I'm not supposed to** let you use our phone. There's a pay phone near the door. **Would** you use that one, please?

B. OK.

4.2 Polite Requests

Modals can be used to make a statement more polite. Observe the different ways to express the same idea.

- To ask permission:

Questions	Responses
May Can } I use your phone, please? Could	Yes, you may./No, you may not. Yes, you can./No, you can't.* No, I'm sorry.

*NOTE: Don't answer with *could*.

Questions	Responses

Would you *mind** if I *used* your phone?
   (past verb)
Do you *mind* if I *use* your phone?
   (present verb)
	To give permission:
	   No, I don't mind.
	   Not at all.
	   Of course not.
	To refuse permission:
	   I'm sorry. It's not for private use.

- To request that another person do something:

Request	Responses
Can *Could** *Will* } you spell your name for me? *Would**	Of course. Certainly. Sure.
Would you mind *spelling* your name for me? Gerund[2]	Not at all. I'd be glad to.

*NOTE: *Could* and *would* are softer than *can* and *will*.

---

[2]A *gerund* is verb + *-ing* that is used as a noun. See Lesson Eight for more on gerunds.

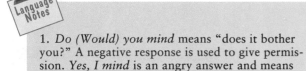

1. *Do (Would) you mind* means "does it bother you?" A negative response is used to give permission. *Yes, I mind* is an angry answer and means "no."

2. To express what you want, use *would like*:
   Would you *like* to talk to the doctor?
   Yes, I'*d like* to get a new prescription.

3. To make a suggestion, you can use a question:
   Call the doctor. = *Why don't you call* the doctor?
   Let's ask the pharmacist. = *Why don't we ask* the pharmacist?

4. To offer help, salespeople often say these words to a customer:
   May/Can I help you? How *may/can* I help you?

EXERCISE I   Make this conversation more polite by using modals and other related expressions in place of the underlined sentences.

How may I help you?

A. Belmont Clinic. This is Barb speaking. <u>What do you want?</u>

B. Hello. <u>I want to talk to Dr. Brown.</u>
                          (1)

A. The doctor is with a patient now. <u>I'll put you on hold.</u>
                                              (2)

(Two minutes later)

A. The doctor is still busy. <u>Give me your phone number.</u> I'll tell the doctor to
                                              (3)

   call you back.

B. It's 679-0098. <u>Tell him to call me before 5 P.M.</u> I have to leave at that time.
                          (4)

A. <u>Tell me your name.</u>
         (5)

B. It's John Wosniak.

A. <u>Spell that.</u>
         (6)

B. W-O-S-N-I-A-K.

A. I'll tell the doctor that you called.

B. Thanks. Bye.

4.3 Preference

Would rather is used to talk about preference.

Would	Subject	*Rather*	Base Form	*Or*	Second Choice
Would	you	rather	buy a generic drug	or	a name brand drug?

Subject	*Would*	*Rather*	Base Form	*(Than*	Second Choice)
I	would	rather	buy a generic drug	than	a name brand drug.

1. *Or* is used in a question between the choices. *Than* is used in a statement between the choices.

2. *Would* is contracted to *'d*.

   I*'d* rather buy a name brand.

3. In answer to a question about preference, the second part of the sentence is usually omitted.

   Would you *rather* use a credit card or cash?
   I*'d rather* use a credit card.

4. *Would prefer* can also be used. An infinitive is used after *would prefer*.

   A. Would you like us to deliver your prescription?
   B. I*'d prefer to pick* it up.

5. We can use a noun or an infinitive after *prefer*. After *would rather*, we always use the base form of the verb.

   I prefer *generics*.
   I (would) prefer *to buy* generics.
   I'd rather *buy* generics.

EXERCISE 2   Make a statement of preference.

> **EXAMPLE: work days/nights**
>   **I'd rather work days than nights.**

1. take a bath/a shower
2. drink coffee/tea (in the morning)
3. have a lot of kids/just a few
4. buy a generic drug/a name-brand drug
5. live in a cold climate/a warm climate
6. study math/history
7. _____

EXERCISE 3   Find a partner. Ask your partner questions of preference by using the words given. Report something interesting about your partner to the class.

> EXAMPLE: eat Chinese food/Italian food
> **A. Would you rather eat Chinese food or Italian food?**
> **B. I'd rather eat Chinese food.**

1. go to an American doctor/a doctor from your country
2. see a woman doctor/a male doctor
3. work for someone/be self-employed
4. eat food from your country/try food from other countries
5. own a dog/a cat
6. read a newspaper/watch the news on TV
7. _____

4.4   Ability/Possibility

Study the different ways to talk about ability and possibility.

Present	Future	Past
He *can* go	He *can* go later.	He *could* go yesterday.
He *is able to* swim.	He *will be able to* swim.	He *was able to* swim
He *knows how to* drive.	He *will know how to* drive.	He *knew how to* drive.

Language Notes

1. *Can* and *be able to* are used to show natural ability, learned ability, or possibility. For learned ability, *know how to* is also used.

Children *can* learn languages easily. = Children *are able to* learn languages easily.
The pharmacist *can* read Latin. =
The pharmacist *is able to* read Latin. =
The pharmacist *knows how to* read Latin.

2. *Can* is used for present or future. To emphasize the future, we use *will be able to*.

The doctor *can* call you later. = The doctor *will be able to* call you later.

3. Some idioms with *can* are:
  • *can afford*: He doesn't have enough money. He *can't afford* a new car.
  • *can tell*: Can you *tell* the difference between a generic drug and a name-brand drug?

4. *Can* is usually not stressed in affirmative sentences. Sometimes it is hard to hear the final *t*, so we must pay attention to the vowel sound to hear the difference. Listen to your teacher say these sentences:

I can gó. /kIn/
I cán't go. /kænt/

In a short answer, we pronounce *can* /kæn/.

Can you help me later? /kIn/
Yes, I can. /kæn/

EXERCISE 4   Ask another student about his or her abilities. Change the question so that
it uses the word in parentheses ( ).

> EXAMPLES: **Can you speak Arabic? (know)**
> **A. Do you know how to speak Arabic?**
> **B. No, I don't.**
>
> **Are you able to speak French? (can)**
> **A. Can you speak French?**
> **B. Yes, I can.**

1. Can you understand Americans when they talk fast? (able)
2. Are you able to study with the TV on? (can)
3. Can you drive a stick-shift car? (know)
4. Do you know how to cook Chinese food? (can)
5. Do you know how to play the piano? (can)
6. Can you do the homework later? (able: *future*)
7. Can you tell the difference between Americans and Canadians? (able)

4.5 Past Ability

Subject	Past Ability Word	Verb Phrase
My sister	could was able to knew how to	speak Polish when she was a child.
I	could was able to	run fast when I was a child.
I	was able to	reach the pharmacist immediately.

Language Notes

1. In affirmative statements, *could* and related expressions show that a person used to have an ability in the past over an extended period. However, when you want to express success in doing something at a specific time, not over an extended period of time, use *was/were able to*, not *could*.

> I *was able to* get an appointment with the doctor last Monday.

2. In negative sentences, *could* and *was/were able to* have the same meaning.

> I *couldn't* reach the doctor yesterday.
> I *wasn't able to* reach the doctor yesterday.

EXERCISE 5   Fill in each blank to express present or past ability.

A. You speak English very well.

B. Thank you. I _____*can*_____ speak it pretty well now, but I haven't always

been _____*able to*_____ to speak it.

A. _____n't you speak English before you came to the U.S.?
           (1)

B. I _____ how to read English, but I wasn't _____ speak it very
           (2)   (3)
well. And I _____n't understand Americans when they spoke fast.
               (4)
How about you?

A. When my sponsor met me at the airport, I _____ say, "Hello. My name
                                                    (5)
is Lee." But I _____n't understand a word he said to me. When I was a
                  (6)
child, I studied French, not English.

B _____ you speak French well?
       (7)

A. I _____ speak it pretty well when I was in school, but I've forgotten a
        (8)
lot.

B. Didn't you study French in college?

A. I _____n't go to college in my country because a war broke out and
        (9)
we had to leave.

B. Did you come to the U.S. after the war broke out?

A. Yes. We were lucky. My father _____ get us out of the country
                                        (10)
immediately. Unfortunately, many of our friends and relatives weren't

_____ leave.
     (11)

4.6 Permission

PRESENT		
Subject	Permission Words (Not)	Verb Phrase
You	can	buy aspirin without a prescription.
The pharmacist	may not	sell medicine without a prescription.
You	are permitted to	use a dictionary to write a composition.
The students	are not allowed to	talk during a test.

PAST		
Women	couldn't weren't allowed to weren't permitted to	vote before 1920.

Language Notes

1. *Can, may, be permitted to,* and *be allowed to*[3] are used for permission. These words can refer to permission from a legal authority or from a person in a superior position. (teacher to student, parent to child, police officer to citizen)

2. Do not use a contraction for *may not.*

3. *May* is not used for past permission.

EXERCISE 6   Fill in each blank with an appropriate permission word to talk about what is or isn't permitted in your country.

EXAMPLES: A man *isn't permitted to* have more than one wife.

Teachers *can* hit children.

1. People _____ own a gun.

2. Minors _____ buy alcohol.

3. Children _____ work.

4. A man _____ have more than one wife.

5. A married women _____ get a passport without her husband's permission.

6. Public schools _____ teach about religion.

7. People _____ travel freely.

8. People _____ live anywhere they want.

9. Teachers _____ hit children.

---

[3]*Permitted* and *allowed* are past participles used as adjectives.

EXERCISE 7   Work with a partner. Write a list of three questions to ask the teacher about what is permitted in this class, in this school, or during a test. Your teacher will answer.

EXAMPLES: **A. May we use our textbooks during a test?**
B. No, you may not.
A. Why can't we use our books during a test?
B. Because I want to see if you have learned the material.

4.7 Necessity

Study these affirmative sentences:

Subject	*Must*	Verb Phrase
The pharmacist	must	give you exactly what the doctor ordered.
I	must	see a doctor immediately. It's urgent.

Subject	*Have to* *Have Got to*	Verb Phrase
The pharmacist	has to	give you what the doctor ordered.
You	have got to	ask your doctor for a refill.

1. In affirmative statements, *have to, have got to,* and *must* show necessity. *Must* is stronger and more formal than *have to* and *have got to*. *Must* is usually reserved for moral and legal obligations and urgent situations. *Have to/have got to* can be used for legal or personal obligations.

2. *Have got to* is used mostly in affirmative statements. It is not generally used for questions and negatives.

3. In affirmative statements, *must* and *have to* have about the same meaning. In negative statements, *must* and *have to* are very different. *Must not* shows prohibition; *don't have to* means not necessary. COMPARE:

The pharmacist *must not* sell drugs without a prescription from the doctor. (This is prohibited.)
You *don't have to* visit your doctor for a prescription refill. (It is not required.) You can simply call the doctor.

4. *Must not* and *cannot* have about the same meaning.

You *must not* smoke on an airplane. (It is prohibited.)
You *can't smoke* on an airplane. (It is not permitted.)

5. *Must,* meaning "necessity," has no past form. The past of both *must* and *have to* is *had to.*

I *had to* go to the doctor last week.
The pharmacist *had to* give me the name-brand drug.

6. *Have to* is usually pronounced "hafta." *Got to* is often pronounced "gotta." *I've got to* is often pronounced "I gotta."

EXERCISE 8   Tell if you have to or don't have to do the following. For affirmative statements, you can also use *have got to*.

EXAMPLES: **work on Saturdays**
I have to work on Saturdays. OR **I've got to work on Saturdays.**

wear a suit to work
I don't have to wear a suit to work.

1. return to my country (meaning: you have only a temporary visa)
2. study English
3. get up early on Sundays
4. cook every day
5. wear formal clothes (a suit, a dress) to work/school
6. _____

EXERCISE 9   Work with a partner. Name some things you must not do while driving a car. (Use *you* in the impersonal sense.)

EXAMPLE: **You must not pass a car while going up a hill.**

EXERCISE 10   Fill in each blank with *don't have to* or *must not* to describe situations in a public library.

EXAMPLES: **You _must not_ write in a library book.**

**You _don't have to_ know the name of the author to find a book.
You can find the book by the title.**

1. You _____ wait until the due date to return a book. You can return it early.

2. You _____ eat or smoke in the library.

3. You _____ study in the library. You can study at home.

4. You _____ return your books to the circulation desk.
You can leave them in the book drop.

5. You _____ tear a page out of a book.

6. You _____ make noise in the library.

book drop

EXERCISE 11   Make a list of five things you have to do at your job or in your house. Find a partner. Ask your partner if he or she has the same obligations.

> EXAMPLE: A. **I've got to work on Saturdays. Do you have to work on Saturdays?**
> B. **No, I don't.**

EXERCISE 12   Write three sentences telling what you had to do when you were a child or a teenager. Share your sentences with a small group or with the entire class.

> EXAMPLE: **I had to wear a uniform to school.**

1. _____

2. _____

3. _____

EXERCISE 13   Fill in each blank to make **true** statements. Share your answers with a small group or with the entire class.

> EXAMPLE: **I've got to** _drive my son to the doctor_ **after class.**

1. I have to _____ every day.

2. I don't have to _____ every day.

3. I've got to _____ right now.

4. Before I came to the U.S., I had to _____.

5. Passengers on an airplane must _____ before the plane takes off.

6. Passengers on an airplane must not _____.

7. A driver must not _____.

8. The students must not _____ during a test.

9. The students don't have to _____.

Before you read

Have you ever been invited to a party at an American's house? Did you notice any differences between social customs at this party and social customs in your country?

Read the following article. Pay special attention to modals and related words.

SOCIAL CUSTOMS

If an American invites you to a party at his or her home, you **should** know about certain customs:

1. You**'re supposed to** respond to an invitation that says "R.S.V.P."[4] Let the host or hostess know if you plan to attend or not.
2. Children are not usually welcome at a party unless they are specifically invited. If you must take your children to the party, you**'d better** inform the host or hostess.
3. You **aren't supposed to** take an uninvited guest. However, you **can** take your spouse with you.
4. Sometimes the person who invites you may say "BYOB." This means "Bring your own booze." Booze is a slang word for alcoholic drink. You **could** bring a bottle of wine or a six-pack of beer.
5. If you are invited to a formal dinner party, you **ought to** arrive on time. At a cocktail party, a formal dinner is not served, and you **can** arrive whenever it is convenient for you.
6. If you are invited to a "potluck" party, you**'re supposed to** bring a dish of food. If you don't know what to bring, you **can** ask the host or hostess for a suggestion.
7. You **should** wear appropriate clothing. If you are not sure what is appropriate, ask the host or hostess if it is a formal or informal party.
8. You **can** leave whenever you want. However, you **ought to** leave when you see most of the other guests leaving.
9. You **should** always thank the host or hostess for a good time. You don't have to send a "thank-you" note, but you **can**.

---

[4]*R.S.V.P.* is the abbreviation of a French phrase, "Répondez s'il vous plaît," which means "Please respond."

4.8 Advisability

Subject	*Should (Not)* *Ought to*	Verb Phrase
You	should	thank the hostess.
You	shouldn't	wear jeans to a formal party.
You	ought to	invite them to your house.

Language Notes

1. *Should* and *ought to* have about the same meaning. They are used to advise, suggest, warn, or tell about an obligation.

2. *Ought* is the only modal followed by *to.* *Ought to* is usually pronounced /ɔtə/.

3. For questions and negatives, *should* is used, not *ought to.*

   Should I wear a suit? What *should* I wear?

EXERCISE 14   Tell if you *should (ought to)* or *shouldn't* do the following.

EXAMPLES: respond to an invitation
You ought to respond to an invitation.

take children to a party for adults
You shouldn't take children to a party for adults.

1. come late to a dinner party
2. invite friends to go with you
3. bring wine or beer to a party
4. wear jeans to a formal party
5. say thank you before you leave a party
6. respond to an invitation that says "R.S.V.P."
7. bring food to a "potluck" party

4.9 Suggestions/Options

We use *can* or *could* to offer suggestions.

> What should I take to the party?
> You *can* buy something, such as a bottle of wine.
> You *could* make something, such as a cake.

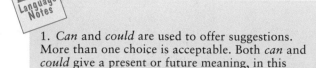

1. *Can* and *could* are used to offer suggestions. More than one choice is acceptable. Both *can* and *could* give a present or future meaning, in this case.

   You *could* bake a cake or you *can* buy one.

2. *Should* is used when there is only one good choice. *Can/Could* are used when there are several good choices.

   You *should* take food to a "potluck" party. (only one choice)
   You *can (could)* take a salad, a main dish, or a dessert. (several choices)

EXERCISE 15   Answer these questions by offering suggestions. If possible, give more than one suggestion.

> EXAMPLE: **How could I get a refill on a prescription?**
> **You can call your doctor.**
> OR
> **You could ask your pharmacist to call your doctor.**

1. How can I find out about apartments for rent?
2. How could I lose weight?
3. How could I find out the weather report?
4. How can I become more fluent in English?
5. How could I learn more about this city?

 **4.10** Warning

Had better (not) is used to give a warning.

Subject	*Had/'d Better (Not)*	Verb Phrase	Reason
You	had better	inform the hostess about your children.	She's not expecting children at the party.
You	'd better not	drink too much.	You're driving.

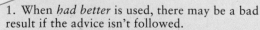

1. When *had better* is used, there may be a bad result if the advice isn't followed.

   You*'d better* be careful or you'll get hurt.

2. In fast speech, we usually say a contraction with the subject pronoun and *had*. In some fast speech, the *'d* is omitted completely:

   You*('d)* better not drink.

3. To give advice or remind someone of an obligation, we often use *had better* in a question.

   It's raining. *Hadn't you better* take an umbrella?
   Hadn't you better do your homework before you watch TV?

EXERCISE 16   Give a warning using *you'd better (not)* in the following office situations.

> **EXAMPLE:** You've been late three times this week. *You'd better come on time* , or the boss will fire you.

1. You usually take five extra minutes for lunch. _____, or the boss will dock[5] you.

2. You work too slowly. _____, or the boss will find someone else.

3. You just typed up a report. _____ an extra copy in case you lose it.

4. You are the only person who wears jeans to the office.

   _____ if you want to look appropriate.

5. You've been using the phone for your personal calls.

   _____, or clients won't be able to call.

6. One of the men in the office is a big gossip. He tells whatever you say to the

   boss. _____, or you'll be sorry later.

4.11 Expectations

Be supposed to is used to show that a certain behavior is expected because of a rule, a duty, or a custom.

Subject	Be (Not)	Supposed to	Verb Phrase
You	're	supposed to	take food to a "potluck" party.
You	aren't	supposed to	take an uninvited guest.
I	was	supposed to	call the hostess, but I forgot.

---

[5]When a company *docks* a worker, it deducts money from the worker's salary.

1. *Be supposed to* is often used for rules and laws. It is softer than *must*.

> *You're supposed to* slow down at a flashing yellow light. = You *must* slow down.
> You*'re not supposed to* park there. It's a no parking zone. = You *must not* park there.

2. The past form, *was/were supposed to,* shows that a person was expected to do something but didn't.

> We *were supposed to* have the party outdoors, but it rained.

3. Use *was/were supposed to* instead of *had to* when a rule is broken.

> I *was supposed to* stop at the stop sign, but I didn't and got a ticket.

EXERCISE 17   Use *be supposed to* to tell what people expect you to do or say in the following social situations in your country. Share your answers with the class.

> EXAMPLE: **If you are invited to someone's house for dinner,**
>
> *you're supposed to bring some food to share with the other guests.*

1. If you invite a friend to eat in a restaurant, _____

    _____

2. If you bump into someone, _____

3. If you don't hear or understand what someone says, _____

    _____

4. If you want to smoke in front of other people, _____

    _____

5. If you want to leave the dinner table, _____

    _____

6. If a woman with a small child gets on a crowded bus, _____

    _____

7. If you're invited to someone's house for dinner, _____

    _____

8. If you meet someone for the first time, _____

    _____

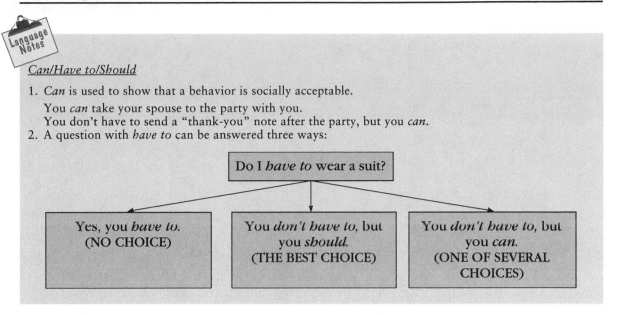

Language Notes

<u>*Can/Have to/Should*</u>

1. *Can* is used to show that a behavior is socially acceptable.

   You *can* take your spouse to the party with you.
   You don't have to send a "thank-you" note after the party, but you *can*.
2. A question with *have to* can be answered three ways:

Do I *have to* wear a suit?

| Yes, you *have to*. (NO CHOICE) | You *don't have to*, but you *should*. (THE BEST CHOICE) | You *don't have to*, but you *can*. (ONE OF SEVERAL CHOICES) |

EXERCISE 18   Answer the questions to tell if these behaviors are acceptable in your country. Discuss your answers in a small group or with the entire class.

> EXAMPLE: A. Can you eat some foods with your fingers?
> B. Yes, you can eat tacos with your fingers in Mexico.

1. Can you take children to a party?
2. Can you invite your friends to someone else's party?
3. Can you eat some foods with your fingers? Which foods?
4. Can women wear shorts on the street?
5. Can women smoke in public?
6. Can a man and woman live together if they're not married?

EXERCISE 19   Ask your teacher if he or she has to do these things. Your teacher can answer with "Yes, I do," "No, I don't have to, but I can," or "No, I don't have to, but I should."

> EXAMPLES: correct the homework
> A. Do you have to correct the homework?
> B. Yes, I do.
>
> work in the summer
> A. Do you have to work in the summer?
> B. No, I don't have to, but I can.

help students after class
A. **Do you have to help students after class?**
B. **I don't have to, but I should.**

1. work during the summer
2. give a final exam
3. teach reading
4. take more courses in the teaching of English
5. call the school when you're going to be absent
6. work in the evenings
7. have office hours
8. write lesson plans
9. take attendance
10. call the students by their last names
11. know another language in order to teach English
12. attend teachers' meetings
13. _____

EXERCISE 20   Fill in each blank. Discuss your answers in a small group or with the entire class.

    Example: **I don't have to** _clean my house_ , **but I should.**

1. I ought to _____ more, but I don't have the time.

2. Most people don't _____, but they should.

3. Many people _____, but they shouldn't.

4. Teenagers often _____, but they shouldn't.

5. The teacher doesn't have to _____, but she or he does it anyway.

6. In this class, we don't have to _____, but we can.

7. Drivers are supposed to _____, but many don't.

EXERCISE 21   Fill in each blank with the negative form of a modal or a related word. In some cases, more than one answer is possible.

    EXAMPLES: **We** _can't_ **smoke in the classroom.** (OR _are not supposed to_)

             We _shouldn't_ **talk loudly in the library.** (OR _aren't supposed to_)

             We _don't have to_ **bring our dictionaries to class.**

             One of the Ten Commandments says "You _must not_ **kill."**

1. The teacher says we _____ use our books during a test. It's not permitted.

2. The teacher says we _____ sit in a specific seat in class. We can sit in any seat we want.

3. We _____ talk to each other during a test. It's not permitted.

4. We _____ type the homework. We can write it.

5. We _____ speak our native language in class. We'll never learn English if we do.

6. We _____ come back after the final exam, but we can in order to pick up our tests.

7. Children _____ talk to strangers.

8. Children _____ enter an adult movie (an R-rated movie) without an adult. It is not permitted.

9. Children _____ attend public school. They can attend private school.

10. Teachers _____ teach summer school if they don't want to.

11. English teachers _____ talk fast to foreign students.

12. Teachers in American public schools _____ teach religion. It's not permitted.

13. In court, you _____ lie.

EXPANSION ACTIVITIES

PROVERBS   The following proverbs contain *can*. Discuss the meaning of each proverb. Do you have a similar proverb in your language?

> You can't teach an old dog new tricks.
> You can't judge a book by its cover.

DISCUSSIONS   1. In a small group or with the entire class, discuss home remedies for the following medical problems:

A. a headache	G. dizziness
B. a fever	H. a sore throat
C. a stomachache	I. a hangover
D. a cut	J. a cold
E. insomnia	K. a toothache
F. nervousness	

2. Complete these sentences in any way you want. Discuss your answers in a small group or with the entire class.

a. _____ years ago I couldn't _____, but I can now.

b. When I was younger, I could _____, but I can't now.

c. When I didn't speak English well, I wasn't able to _____.

d. I hope I will be able to _____ soon.

e. I've never been able to _____ as well as I'd like to.

3. Discuss proper behavior at a social event in your country. Tell about the guests' social obligations and the host's social obligations. Tell about what is and isn't acceptable behavior.

4. Describe your responsibilities with your family or at your job. Tell what you *can, should, are supposed to,* or *have to* do.

WRITING   1. Choose one of the following statements and tell if you agree or disagree. Write a paragraph explaining your point of view.

A. Parents should select the television programs that their children watch.
B. People under eighteen years old shouldn't get married.
C. Parents should never hit their kids.

2. Write an essay comparing medical care in the U.S. with medical care in your country. You can write about doctors, hospitals, clinics, dentists, nurses, pharmacists, medicines, and insurance.

OUTSIDE ACTIVITIES

1. Show Exercise 17 to an American. Ask him or her to fill in each blank about American customs. Share your findings with the class.

2. Most pharmacies give you information about your prescription medication—how to use it, and what side effects it has. The next time you have a prescription filled, read this information. Bring it to class if you have questions.

EDITING ADVICE

1. Don't use *to* after a modal. (Exception: *ought to*)

   You should ~~to~~ buy a new car.

2. Use a base form after a modal.

   She couldn't ~~saw~~ *see* the movie.

3. After *mind*, use a gerund.

   Would you mind ~~to close~~ *closing* the door?

4. Use *have/has* before *got to* in writing.

   We *have* got to leave.

5. Don't put two modals together.

   She should ~~can~~ *be able to* drive well in a few months.

6. Don't forget *be* or *to* in these expressions: *be supposed to, be able to, be permitted to, be allowed to.*

   They *are* supposed to leave at 6 o'clock.

   I'm able *to* work on Saturday.

7. Use correct word order in a question.

   What ~~I should~~ *should I* do?

SUMMARY OF LESSON FOUR

Ability

Pharmacists *know how to/are able to/can* read Latin.	They have this ability.

Polite Expressions

Would you mind opening the window? *Could/Would* you open the window? *Can/Will* you open the window?	These expressions are more polite than the imperative, "Open the window."
Would you *mind* if I used your pen? *Do* you *mind* if I use your pen? *May/Could/Can* I use your pen?	These expressions are more polite than the imperative, "Give me your pen."
Would you *like* a glass of water?	Do you want a glass of water?
Would you *rather* go out or stay home? *Would* you *prefer* to go out or stay home?	Which one do you prefer?

Permission

You *can/may* use your dictionary during the test. You *are permitted to/allowed to* use your dictionary during the test.	You have permission to use your dictionary. (Permission comes from an authority, the teacher.)

Advice and Necessity

You *must* take a test to get a driver's license.	It's absolutely necessary. It is the law. It is urgent.
I feel chest pains. I *must* see a doctor immediately.	
I *have to* study tonight. I have a test tomorrow.	I believe that it's necessary to study.
You*'re supposed to* say "Excuse me" when you interrupt a conversation.	You are expected to do this. It is a social custom.
You*'d better* be careful on that ladder. You might fall.	This is a warning. There may be a bad result if you don't follow this advice.
You *ought to/should* practice English as much as possible.	It's a good idea to practice English. It's a recommendation.
Do I have to bring a gift to the party? You don't have to, but you *can*.	It is not necessary, but it is acceptable.

How *can* you improve your English?
  You *can* practice with Americans.
  You *could* read American novels.
	These are some suggestions.

LESSON FOUR TEST/REVIEW

Part 1   In the following sentences, find the mistakes with modals and related words, and correct them. Not every sentence has a mistake. If the sentence is correct, write *C*.

EXAMPLES: He 's got to talk to you.

You ought to come to class earlier.   *C*

1. He must to talk to you.

2. He knows how use a word processor.

3. Would you mind open the window?

4. We not allowed to use our books during a test.

5. Before I go back to my country, I will have to apply for a passport.

6. To become a citizen, you must can speak simple English.

7. Before 1920, American women can't vote.

8. She can't find a job.

9. You'd better don't talk during the test. The teacher will get angry.

10. She knows how to type. She cans type very fast.

11. Where I can find information about garage sales?

12. You not suppose to take your friends to a party.

13. She'd like to be a doctor.

14. I'd rather not go out today. I prefer to stay at home.

Part 2   In the following sentences, choose the word or phrase that means (almost) the same as the underlined words.

EXAMPLE: You <u>should</u> study.

a. must   b. can   (c. ought to)   d. would   e. are able to

1. I <u>wasn't able to</u> find a job when I came to the U.S.

a. couldn't   b. can't   c. wouldn't   d. wasn't supposed to
e. wasn't allowed to

2. We're not permitted to talk during a test.

   a. may not   b. aren't able to   c. don't know how to   d. wouldn't
   e. would rather not

3. Do you prefer to have coffee or tea?

   a. Had you better   b. Would you rather   c. Would you mind
   d. Are you supposed to   e. Should you

4. How can I find out tomorrow's weather?

   a. should   b. will   c. could   d. must   e. ought

5. She can't swim. She never learned.

   a. may not   b. should not   c. doesn't know how to   d. must not
   e. is not supposed to

6. A tree can't live without sunlight and water.

   a. shouldn't   b. must not   c. is not permitted to   d. doesn't have to
   e. isn't able to

7. You can't park at a bus stop.

   a. shouldn't   b. would rather not   c. had better not
   d. aren't allowed to   e. wouldn't like to

8. You don't have to call the teacher by her last name. You can call her "Barbara."

   a. You must not   b. You shouldn't   c. It is not necessary to
   d. You can't   e. You aren't supposed to

9. May I use your pen?

   a. Should   b. Must   c. Could   d. Would   e. Will

10. Could you open the window, please?

   a. Should you   b. Would you   c. Would you rather   d. May you
   e. Do you mind

11. I've got to leave now.

   a. I have to   b. I'd like to   c. I'm supposed to   d. I ought to
   e. I would rather

12. You must not steal.

   a. You shouldn't steal.   b. You don't have to steal.
   c. Stealing is prohibited.   d. You are not able to steal.
   e. It is not a good idea to steal.

13. You shouldn't take your children to a party for adults.

   a. must not   b. don't have to   c. aren't supposed to
   d. aren't allowed to   e. don't need to

Part 3   Look at the job application. Then fill in each blank in the exercise that follows.

Fill out the following form. Print in black ink or type. Bring it to the personnel office or mail it to:

Ms. Judy Lipton
P.O. Box 324
Tucson, Arizona 85744

Applications must be submitted by November 15.

Name _____ _____ _____
                    (last)   (first)   (middle initial)

Address _____

Telephone (   ) _____

Marital status (optional) _____ Sex _____

Date of birth _____ _____ _____ (You must be at least 18.)
                      (month)   (day)   (year)

Social Security number ____-____-____

Educational background

                          Date graduated   Degree or major

High School   _____   _____

College   _____   _____

Graduate School   _____   _____

Employment History (Please start with your present or last job.)

Company	Position	Dates	Supervisor	Reason for leaving
_____	_____	_____	_____	_____
_____	_____	_____	_____	_____
_____	_____	_____	_____	_____
_____	_____	_____	_____	_____

Do not write in the shaded box. For office use only.

Rec'd. by _____
Amer. cit. _____
Doc. checked _____
Transcripts received _____

The Immigration Act of 1986 requires all successful applicants to present documents to prove U.S. citizenship or permanent residence with permission to work in the U.S.

This company is an Equal Opportunity Employer. Race, religion, nationality, marital status, and physical disability will not influence our decision to hire.
I certify that these answers are true.

Signature: _____   Date: _____

Fill in each blank with an appropriate modal or related expression. In some cases, more than one answer is possible.

EXAMPLES: You _should_ check over all the information carefully before handing in this application.

You (not) _shouldn't_ use a red pen to fill out this application.

(OR _aren't supposed to_)

1. You _____ read the instructions before filling out the application.

2. You (not) _____ type this form. You _____ use a black pen.

3. You (not) _____ give your marital status.

4. You (not) _____ write in the shaded box.

5. An Equal Opportunity Employer (not) _____ make its decision based on race or religion.

6. Foreigners _____ present their documents to prove that they have permission to work in this country.

7. You (not) _____ be born in the U.S. to apply for this job. You _____ be a resident alien.

8. You _____ have a Social Security number.

9. You _____ bring this application to the personnel office, or you _____ mail it.

10. In most European countries, you write the day before the month. In the U.S., however, you _____ write the month before the day.

11. The deadline for this application is November 15. Today is November 14. You (not) _____ mail it by regular mail. It probably won't get there by tomorrow. You _____ take the application to the personnel department or send it by overnight mail.

12. You _____ sign your name on the bottom line. You _____ swear that your answers are true.

13. If you don't like your present job, you _____ look for a better job.

LESSON FIVE

Lesson Focus **Modals—Additional Meanings; Continuous Modals; Modals in the Past**

- There are additional meanings for some of the modals we saw in Lesson Four:
    - *may/might* for possibility
        It *may/might* rain tomorrow.
    - *must* for present probability
        You didn't eat at all today. You *must* be hungry.
    - *be supposed to/should* for expectation about the future
        The concert *is supposed to/should* begin at 8 P.M.

- We can give a continuous meaning to modals:
    You *should be studying* now. You *shouldn't be watching* TV.

- For some modals, we use the perfect form to give a past meaning:
    His mother moved the sofa by herself. He *should have helped* his mother.
    I can't find my keys. I *might have left* them in my jacket pocket.

• •

R
E
A
D
I
N
G

Before you read:

In your country, do most people try to control the size of their families? Is the population growing quickly?

Read the following article. Pay special attention to *may, might, can,* and *could.*

THE POPULATION EXPLOSION

The world population has been growing at an alarming[1] rate. It took a million years before the earth reached its first billion people. However, the amount of time that it takes to add another billion is decreasing rapidly. Even though the birthrate has been going down in recent years, experts believe that the population will be at least eight billion by the middle of the twenty-first century. If countries do not try to limit their populations, the total **may** be as high as 11 billion, twice the population at the end of the twentieth century.

Year	Population
1800	1 billion
1930	2 billion
1960	3 billion
1975	4 billion
1990	5 billion

If the population continues to rise rapidly, many serious problems **could** occur. There **may** not be enough food for everyone in the world. There **might** not be enough petroleum or other natural resources. Species of animals **could** disappear, crowded out by

---

[1]When something is *alarming,* it makes us worry or become afraid.

humans. Pollutants **could** destroy the environment. Countries **might** even go to war to fight over diminishing[2] resources.

Some of these problems are already occurring. Many people in Third World countries[3] are already starving or going to other countries as refugees in search of food.

The United Nations, a world organization, is trying to develop a plan to prevent the population from growing so fast and destroying the environment. If this plan is not successful, the results **could** be terrible for future generations.

5.1   Possibilities for the Future

May, might, and *could* are used for possibility or uncertainty about the future.

Subject	Modal *(Not)*	Verb Phrase
Some animals	may	disappear.
Countries	might	go to war.
Serious problems	could	occur.
People	may/might not	have enough to eat.

Language Notes

1. *Will* (or *be going to*) are used for certainty about the future.

> The population *will* increase.

May/Might/Could are used for an uncertain result.

> The population *may/might/could* reach 11 million.

2. For negative possibility, we use *may not* or *might not* only. We don't usually make a contraction with these words. (Do not use *could not* for negative possibility; it means *was not able to* in negatives.)

> We *may not* finish this lesson today.
> We *might not* have enough time.

3. For questions about future possibility, we usually say "Do you think . . . *will/may/might/could* . . .?"

> Do you think it *will* rain tomorrow?
> Do you think we *might* need more practice with modals?
> Do you think he *may* call you?
> Do you think the situation *could* get worse?

NOTE: The clause after *Do you think* is in statement word order.

4. *Maybe,* written as one word, is an adverb. It is usually put before the subject. *May be,* written as two words, is a modal + verb. It follows the subject. Compare:

> The future *may be* terrible.
> *Maybe* the future will be terrible.
> We *may have* very little food in the future.
> *Maybe* we will have very little food in the future.

---

[2]*Diminishing* means becoming less.

[3]*Third World countries* are poor, underdeveloped countries.

EXERCISE 1   Change these *maybe* statements to statements with *may, might,* or *could.*
Use the word in parentheses ( ).

> EXAMPLE: **Maybe there won't be enough food. (might)**
>   **There might not be enough food.**

1. Maybe we won't have enough petroleum. (may)
2. Maybe we will use a different kind of energy. (might)
3. Maybe there will be a war. (could)
4. Maybe countries will try to control their populations. (might)
5. Maybe I won't live long enough to see these problems. (may)

EXERCISE 2   Tell about the possible results of the following situations. Use *may, might,*
or *could* for affirmative statements. (Don't use *could* for negative statements.)

> EXAMPLE: **If you buy a lottery ticket,** *you might get lucky and win a lot of money.*

1. If you don't pay your rent, _____

2. If you save a lot of money, _____

3. If you drink a lot of coffee, _____

4. If you eat a lot of sugar, _____

5. If you drive without a license, _____

6. If _____

• •

R
E
A
D
I
N
G

Before you read:

1. In your country, how long does it usually take a letter to travel from one city to
   another?
2. How long does it usually take a letter from the U.S. to arrive in your country?

Read the following article. Pay special attention to *should* and *be supposed to.*

EXPRESS MAIL

Letters and packages mailed within the United States **should** arrive at their destination within a few days. Sometimes it is very important that a letter or package arrive
quickly. In this case, it is best to use some kind of express mail service.

The U.S. Postal Service offers several types of fast mail. One kind is priority mail.
Priority mail **is supposed to** arrive within the next day or two, but it is not guaranteed.

Another service, express mail, is guaranteed to arrive the next day if mailed by a certain time. These services are more expensive than regular mail.

The Postal Service is not the only place that offers these services. There are also several private companies that guarantee next-day service.

• •

5.2 **Future Probability and Expectations**

Be supposed to and *should* are used for future probability and expectations.[4]

Subject	*Be Supposed To*	Verb Phrase	Explanation
My letter	is supposed to	arrive tomorrow.	I was told this would happen.
It	is supposed to	rain tomorrow.	The weather forecaster said that we can expect this.
The concert	is supposed to	begin at 8.	It is scheduled to begin at this time.
That restaurant	is supposed to	be very good.	I've heard this from other people.

Subject	*Should*	Verb Phrase		Explanation
You	should	receive my package in a couple of days.		You probably will receive it in a couple of days.

Language Notes

1. *Be supposed to* is used when we expect something to happen because we were told that it would happen or because it is scheduled to happen.

    Priority mail *is supposed to* arrive within a day or two.

2. *Should* is used when there is a strong probability that something will happen. *Should* = probably will.

    Student: I didn't receive my midterm grade.
    Teacher: It was mailed out a few days ago. You *should* receive it any day now. (You probably will receive it soon.)

    Customer: I'm calling about my car. Is it ready now?
    Mechanic: I'm finishing up now. The car *should* be ready in about a half hour. (It is probable.)

———————

[4]In Lesson Four, we saw that *be supposed to* is used for rules and social customs, and that *should* is used for advice. This section presents a completely different meaning of *be supposed to* and *should*.

EXERCISE 3 Fill in each blank with *should* (for strong probability) or *be supposed to* (for something that is expected or scheduled). In some cases, more than one answer is possible.

EXAMPLES: Student: When will we finish this lesson?

Teacher: We _should_ finish this lesson by Friday.

A: Do you know anything about tomorrow's weather?

B: It _is supposed to_ rain tomorrow.

1. Student: When will I be fluent in English?

   Teacher: After a few years, you _____ speak English much better.

2. Teacher to students: I don't know the results of your test today. I

   _____ know by Friday.

3. I can't go out with you tonight. My cousin _____ call me from Peru.

4. Patient: When will the doctor see me?

   Receptionist: The doctor hasn't arrived yet. He _____ be here any minute now.

5. A: When is the plane going to arrive?

   B: It _____ arrive at 6:45.

6. A: When do you expect to find out if you got the job?

   B: I _____ know by Friday.

7. A: When will we finish this lesson?

   B: We _____ be finished by Friday.

8. A: What time will you be home?

   B: There isn't much traffic at this hour. I _____ be home in about 20 minutes.

EXERCISE 4   The students have arrived, but the teacher hasn't arrived yet. Fill in each blank with *will* if the result is certain, *should* if it is probable, *be supposed to* if it is expected, and *may, might,* or *could* if it is possible.

A: Where's the teacher today?

B: No one knows. She __*might*__ be absent.

A: I'll go to the English office. They _____ know if she's absent or not.
                                                                 (1)

(A few minutes later.)

A: I asked the secretary in the English office. He said that the teacher called and

said she had a flat tire, but she _____ be here for sure tonight. She's
                                                       (2)

not far, so she _____ be here by 7:30.
                              (3)

B: We _____ have a test today. Why don't we practice modals while
            (4)

we're waiting? That _____ make her happy.
                                     (5)

· ·

R
E
A   **Before you read:**
D
I   1. What are your observations about Americans or American customs?
N   2. What questions do you have about Americans or American customs?
G

Read the following conversation. Pay special attention to the use of *must* for deductions.

DEDUCTIONS ABOUT AMERICANS

When foreigners come to the U.S. and observe American behaviors and customs, they often come to some conclusions. In the following conversation, an American (A) is interviewing a foreigner (F) about her deductions about Americans.

A: What do you think about food in America?
F: There are a lot of fast-food restaurants. Americans **must** not like to cook. And a lot of people have microwave ovens. They **must** not like to waste time.
A: What do you think about family life?
F: Americans generally have small families, and they often don't live close to their relatives. They **must** be lonely. And there is a lot of divorce. I don't understand it. People **must** not think that marriage is very important.
A: Do Americans like to talk about themselves?

F: They **must!** I watch talk shows on TV where people speak publicly about their
   problems. I can't believe some of the things people say about their personal
   lives.
A: Do you think Americans are generally happy people?
F: They **must** be happy. They're always smiling.

• •

5.3 **Present Deductions and Conclusions**
• • • • • • • • • •

Must is used when we come to a conclusion or make a deduction based on information we have or observations we make.[5]

> Many Americans live far from their relatives. They *must* feel lonely.
> She smiles all the time. She *must* be happy.

> When *must not* is used for a negative deduction, we don't make a contraction.[6]
> Americans eat a lot of fast food. They *must not* like to waste time cooking.

EXERCISE 5   You can tell[7] a lot about Americans by looking through their garbage. What
we throw out often indicates what kind of lifestyle we lead. What conclusions can you
make about a family that has the following items in their garbage can?

> EXAMPLE: **Spanish-language newspapers**
>   **They must speak Spanish.**

1. dog-food cans
2. packages from frozen foods
3. cigarette butts
4. homework papers
5. sports magazines
6. food containers from fast-food restaurants
7. disposable diapers
8. last week's cable TV guide

cigarette butts

---

[5]In Lesson Four, we studied *must* for necessity. This is a completely different meaning of *must*.

[6]When *must* means necessity, a negative contraction can be formed: "You *mustn't* drink and drive."

[7]*Can tell* is an idiom. It means to know something because there is evidence. Example: "I *can tell*
you're nervous. Your hands are shaking."

EXERCISE 6   In each of the conversations below, fill in the blank with an appropriate verb to make a logical conclusion.

> EXAMPLE: **A. Have you ever visited Japan?**
>
> **B. I lived there when I was a child.**
>
> **A. Then you must** *know how to speak*   **Japanese.**
>
> **B. I used to, but I've forgotten it.**

1. This is a conversation between two women students.
   A. Would you introduce me to Lee?
   B. Who's Lee?
   A. You must _____ who I'm talking about. He's in your speech class. He sits next to you.
   B. You mean Mr. Song?
   A. Yes, Lee Song. The tall fellow[8] with glasses.
   B. Now I know who you mean. The muscular guy. He must _____ weights.
   A. Yes. He's tall, strong, and good-looking. I'd like you to introduce me to him. He doesn't wear a wedding ring. He must _____ single.
   B. I'm not so sure about that. Not all married men wear a wedding ring.

2. This is a conversation between a married woman (M) and a single woman (S).
   M. My husband spends all his free time with our children.
   S. He must _____ kids very much.
   M. He does.
   S. How many kids do you have?
   M. We have four.
   S. Raising kids must _____ the hardest job in the world.
   M. It is, but it's also the most rewarding.

3. This is a conversation between a teacher (T) and a student (S).
   T. Take out the paper I gave you last Monday.
   S. I don't have it. Could you give me one, please?
   T. Were you in class last Monday?
   S. Yes, I was.
   T. Then you must _____ it.
   S. Oh, yes. You're right. Here it is.

4. This is a conversation between an American (A) and an immigrant (I).
   A. It must _____ hard to start your life in a new country.
   I. Yes, it is.
   A. You must _____ lonely at times.
   I. Yes. You must _____ how it feels. You went to live in Japan for a few years.
   A. It took me a long time to get used to it.

---

[8]*Fellow* means *man.*

EXERCISE 7   Find a partner. Take something from your purse or pocket that represents something about you. Show it to your partner. Your partner will make a deduction about you.

> EXAMPLE: car keys
> **You must have a car.**

Probability vs. Possibility in the Present

1. When we are sure about our information, no modal is used.

> My brother is sick. (I know this is true.)

2. *Must* is used when we think something is probably true. We make a deduction based on information we have.

> Mary is coughing. She *must* be sick.

3. We use *may, might,* or *could* when we are not sure if our conclusion is true. We are examining the possibilities.

> I don't know why Martha isn't here today. She *might* be sick.
> Her daughter *could* be sick. She *might* have to work overtime today.

4. For negative possibility, use *may* or *might.* Don't use *could* for negative possibility.

> I don't know why Paul always sits in the back row. He *might not* want the teacher to notice him.

5. Compare a statement with *maybe* to a statement using the modal *may, might,* or *could.*

> Maybe she's sick. = She may be sick.
> Maybe she has a cold. = She could have a cold.
> Maybe she wants to leave. = She might want to leave.

EXERCISE 8   A student isn't answering any questions in class today. What could be the possible reasons? Change these *maybe* statements to statements with *may, might,* or *could* to give some possibilities.

> EXAMPLES: **Maybe he's bored. (could)**
> **He could be bored.**
>
> **Maybe the question isn't clear. (might)**
> **The question might not be clear.**

1. Maybe the class is too hard for him. (could)
2. Maybe he's tired today. (might)
3. Maybe he's sick. (may)
4. Maybe he's shy. (could)
5. Maybe he has a question about the lesson. (may)
6. Maybe he needs help. (might)
7. Maybe he doesn't want to answer. (may)
8. Maybe he doesn't know the answer. (might)

EXERCISE 9   Decide if the situation is probable or possible. Fill in each blank with *must* for probability or *may/might/could* for possibility.

      EXAMPLES: A. **Where is Linda Ramirez from?**

               B. **Ramirez is a Spanish name. She _might_ be from Mexico.**

                  She _may_ be from Colombia. There are so many coun-

                  tries where Spanish is spoken that it's hard to know for

                  sure.

               A. **She _could_ be from the Philippines. Filipinos have**

                  Spanish names, too.

               B. **Where is Tran Nguyen from?**

               A. **That's a Vietnamese name. He _must_ be from Vietnam.**

   1. A. What time is it?

      B. I don't have a watch. The sun is directly overhead, so it _____ ____ be about noon.

   2. A. Where's the teacher today?

      B. No one knows. She _____ be sick.

   3. A. Does Yoko speak Japanese?

      B. She _____ speak Japanese. She's from Japan.

   4. A. Where's Washington Avenue?

      B. I don't know. We're lost. There's a woman over there. Let's ask her. She _____ know.

   5. A. Why is that student sneezing so much?

      B. I don't know. She _____ have a cold, or it _____ be an allergy.

   6. A. Is Susan married?

      B. She _____ be married. She's wearing a wedding ring.

   7. A. Why didn't Joe come to the party?

      B. Who knows? He _____ not like parties.

5.4 Modals and Related Expressions with Continuous Verbs

Certain modals and related expressions can be used with a continuous verb to talk about things that are happening now (except with nonaction verbs). We use the pattern: modal + *be* + verb-*ing*.

The following modals and related expressions can be used with a continuous verb:

may, might, could = possibility	The teacher might be planning a test now.
should, be supposed to = advisability or probability	You're supposed to be listening to the teacher. You should be paying attention. The airplane is supposed to be landing now.
must = deduction	Don't call them now. It's after midnight. They must be sleeping.
would rather = preference	I'm working now. I'd rather be watching TV.

EXERCISE 10   A student is home sick today. She looks at her watch and knows that her English class is going on right now. She knows what usually happens in class. Read the following statements and tell what *may, must,* or *should* be happening now.

> EXAMPLE: **The teacher usually asks questions. (must)**
> **He must be asking questions now.**

1. The teacher sometimes sits at the desk. (may)
2. The teacher always does the exercises. (must)
3. The teacher explains the grammar. (should)
4. The teacher always helps the students. (must)
5. The teacher sometimes reviews. (might)
6. Sometimes the students don't pay attention. (be supposed to)
7. The students are probably wondering where I am. (must)
8. I don't like to be sick in bed. I prefer to study. (would rather)

R
E
A
D
I
N
G

Before you read:

1. What do you know about the assassination of President Kennedy in 1963?
2. Has a political leader of your country ever been assassinated?

Read the following article. Pay special attention to perfect modals (modal + *have* + past participle).

THE ASSASSINATION OF PRESIDENT KENNEDY

On November 22, 1963, President John F. Kennedy, the thirty-fifth President of the United States, was assassinated in Dallas, Texas, while he was riding in an open car. Many people think it was foolish of him to be in an open car. He **should have had** a covered bulletproof car, as most world leaders do today. His death **could have been prevented.**

Immediately after the assassination, a suspect, Lee Oswald, was arrested. Two days later, as Oswald was being transferred to a jail, he himself was killed by a gunman in the crowd. An investigation took place to find out the truth behind the assassination. After examining a lot of evidence and questioning many people, the investigating committee determined that Lee Oswald **must have been** the person who shot Kennedy. However, many theories have been made about why he did it. Some people think Oswald **might have been** a crazy person who thought he could get attention by killing a famous man. Another theory states that he **might have been** the agent of another government, possibly Russia or Cuba. According to another theory, organized crime (the Mafia) **may have been** behind the assassination.

Some witnesses report gunshots coming from two different directions. If this is true, Oswald **could not have acted** alone; there **must have been** more than one gunman.

Even though the assassination occurred many years ago, people are still fascinated with this event. Books and movies have appeared through the years offering new theories about this mysterious tragedy. Because Oswald was killed before he went to trial, many questions have remained unanswered.

5.5 Modals in Past Form

Study the past of these modals. (Only *can* has a past form.)

Present/Future	Past
I *can* run a mile in 10 minutes.	When I was a teenager, I *could* run a mile in 7 minutes.
Tomorrow I *must* go to court.	Last week I *had to* go to court.
The plane *is supposed to* arrive at 8 tonight.	The plane *was supposed to* arrive at 4:30 this afternoon, but it was late.

For other modals, we use the following pattern:

Subject	Modal	*(Not)*	*Have*	Past Participle
Lee Oswald	might		have	been crazy.
He	may	not	have	acted alone.
Kennedy	should		have	used a bulletproof car.
He	should	not	have	ridden in an open car.

For a passive, use modal + *have* + *been* + past participle.

Subject	Modal	*Have Been*	Past Participle	
Kennedy	must	have been	killed	by Oswald.
He	should	have been	protected	better.
His death	could	have been	prevented.	

NOTE: In informal speech, *have* is often pronounced like *of* or /ə/. Listen to your teacher pronounce the above sentences with fast, informal pronunciation.

Language Notes

<u>Advice That Comes Too Late</u>

1. We use *should have* (less frequently, *ought to have*) to give advice too late, after someone has already done something wrong or badly.

    A. Kennedy wanted to ride in an open car.
    B. He *should have ridden* in a bulletproof car.

    A. I drove too fast, and the police officer gave me a ticket.
    B. You *shouldn't have driven* so fast.
    A. I know.

    A. You fell asleep in class.
    B. I was up late last night watching a movie.
    A. You *should have gone* to bed earlier.

2. A person who receives a gift may be a little embarrassed. This person sometimes says, "You *shouldn't have.*" This means "You shouldn't have gone to so much trouble or expense" or "You shouldn't have given me a gift. I don't deserve it."

EXERCISE 11   Jack had a party at his house, and many things went wrong. Make comments with *should have*.

> EXAMPLE: He invited a lot of people to his party, and there was no room
> to move.
> He shouldn't have invited so many people.

1. There wasn't enough food for everyone.
2. Jack forgot to fix his stereo, and there was no music at the party.
3. One man got drunk and started to act crazy.
4. The party became noisy. The neighbors called the police.
5. One woman came very late. Most of the guests were leaving when she arrived.

EXERCISE 12   A family went on vacation by car. Make comments with *should have*.

> EXAMPLE: They didn't fill up their gas tank, and they ran out of gas.
> They should have filled up their tank before they left.

1. They didn't take a map, and they got lost.
2. They didn't put air in the tires of the car.
3. They didn't check the oil.
4. They drove too fast and got a ticket.
5. They took a lot of cash, and their money was stolen.
6. They didn't take a spare tire, and they had a flat tire.
7. They didn't pack any warm clothes, and it was cold at night.

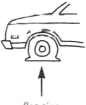

flat tire

Language Notes

<u>Past Possibility</u>

We use *might have, may have,* or *could have* to express possibility about the past. We use these words to guess about something in the past. For negative possibility, don't use *could not have* because it has a different meaning. (See "Past Possibility and Impossibility" on page 150.)

A. Why did Oswald kill Kennedy?
B. We don't know. There are several theories: He *could have been* the agent of another government. Organized crime *may have been* behind the assassination, or he *might have acted* alone.

A. Why did you get a D on your composition?
B. I don't know. The teacher *might not have liked* my topic.
A. Or you *may have had* a lot of grammar mistakes.

A. Did you receive your bank statement today?
B. I don't know. I *may have received* it. I haven't looked at my mail yet.

EXERCISE 13   A student dropped out of a course after the first few weeks. What might have been the possible reasons? Answer these questions by using *may have, might have,* or *could have* to give some possibilities. (Don't use *could* for a negative possibility.)

>   EXAMPLE: **Did he register for the wrong section?**
>   **He may have registered for the wrong section.**

1. Did he prefer an earlier class?
2. Did he want to be in his friend's class?
3. Was this class too hard for him?
4. Did he get sick?
5. Didn't he like the teacher?
6. Did he find a full-time job?
7. Did he have a lot of problems at home?

EXERCISE 14   Make statements about the possible reasons for the following.

>   EXAMPLE: **Linda was yawning during the lesson yesterday.**
>   **She could have been bored.**
>   **She might have gone to bed late the night before.**

1. She didn't answer the phone last night.
2. She didn't come to class all last week.
3. She came to class late today.
4. She looked tired this morning.
5. She didn't bring her homework to class today.

Past Deduction

We use *must have* to make a statement of deduction about the past. For negatives, use *must not have* (no contraction).

   A. Who killed Kennedy?
   B. The committee came to the conclusion that Oswald *must have killed* Kennedy.

   A. I said, "How are you?" to one of my classmates, and he answered, "I'm 34 years old."
   B. He *must have misunderstood* you.
   A. He *must have thought* I asked, "How old are you?"

   A. I was worried about you. You came home so late last night.
   B. You knew I was going to be home late.
   A. No, I didn't.
   B. You *must have known*. I left you a message on your answering machine.
   A. I *must not have looked* at my machine when I got home last night.

EXERCISE 15   Last semester, the teacher asked the students if they planned on returning the following semester. Eight students said they would return unless something happened. Read what these students said, and conclude why they aren't here this semester.

> EXAMPLE: **Linda said, "I won't return if I move to Los Angeles."**
>   **She must have moved to Los Angeles.**

1. Irma said, "I won't return if I get a high score on the TOEFL."
2. Norma said, "I won't return if I go to summer school."
3. Marlene said, "I won't return if I don't get a scholarship."
4. Ali said, "I won't return if my parents don't send me money."
5. Kim said, "I won't return if my sister comes to visit."
6. Leo said, "I won't return if I go back to my country."
7. Boris said, "I won't return if I find a job."

EXERCISE 16   Fill in each blank with an appropriate verb for past probability.

> EXAMPLE: **A. I called my friend's house. The person who answered the phone said, "Apex Car Repair."**
>
>   **B. You must _have dialed_____ the wrong number. Try again.**

1 A. I didn't see your sister yesterday.

   B. You must ___ _____ her. She was in your class yesterday.

2. A. I followed your directions to go downtown yesterday. I took the number 60 bus, but it didn't take me downtown.

   B. You must _____. I said "16," not "60."

3. A. My husband was an orphan. Both of his parents died when he was small.

   B. He must _____ a difficult childhood.

4. A. I can't find my wallet.

   B. When was the last time you saw it?

   A. When I paid for gas at the gas station.

   B. Why don't you go back there? You must _____ it there.

5. A. Didn't we meet at Sue's party last week?

   B. I wasn't there. You must _____ my brother Tom. We're twins. We look alike.

6. A. My family and I escaped from our country by boat.

B. It _____ a difficult trip.

A. Yes, it was.

Past Possibility and Impossibility

1. *Could have* is used to express a past possibility that was not taken. The opportunity presented itself, but it wasn't used.[10]

A. Did Kennedy have to ride in an open car?
B. He *could have ridden* in a closed, bullet-proof car, but he didn't want to.

A. I tried to call you last Saturday, but you weren't home.
B. I moved last month.
A. Why didn't you tell me? I *could have helped* you.
B. I didn't want to bother you.

A. My sister decided to go to City College.
B. Why didn't she go to the state university? Was it too expensive for her?
A. No. She had a scholarship. She *could have gone* to the state university, but she wanted to be closer to home.

2. Compare *could* (past ability or possibility) with *could have* (past opportunity not taken).

When I was a child, I *could* speak French. (I was able to speak French; I spoke French at that time.)
I *could have studied* German, but my parents thought it would be better for me to learn French. (I had the opportunity to study German, but I didn't.)

3. *Couldn't have* is used to show disbelief or to show that someone's statement is absolutely impossible.

A. I voted for Kennedy in 1964.
B. What? You *couldn't have voted* for him in 1964! He died in 1963.

A. I had a test on December 25.
B. You *couldn't have had* a test on December 25. That's Christmas Day. The school is closed on Christmas.

A. I think I saw your brother at the library yesterday.
B. You *couldn't have seen* him. He's in Europe now on vacation.

4. Compare *couldn't* (inability) with *couldn't have* (disbelief or impossibility).

A. Why didn't you help me last Saturday?
B. I *couldn't* help you. I had to work.

A. I moved that piano all by myself.
B. What? You *couldn't have moved* it alone! It's impossible. That piano is too heavy.

NOTE: When we want to show gratitude or appreciation for someone's help, we often say, "Thanks so much. I *couldn't have done* it without you."

EXERCISE 17 A husband and wife are talking about a different direction their lives could have taken. They are discussing what they did and what they could have done instead. Finish each statement with *could have* + past participle.

EXAMPLE: We got married at home, but we *could have gotten married* in church.

1. We had a small wedding, but we _____ a big one.

2. We spent our honeymoon in San Francisco, but we _____ it in Florida.

[10]As we saw in "Past Possibility" on page 147, *could have* also means *might have*.

3. We bought a house, but we _____ a condo.

4. We got married when we were 28, but we _____ right after we graduated from college.

5. We (have) _____ children, but we decided not to have any.

6. We decided to live in the city, but we _____ in a suburb.

7. Wife: I _____ a full-time housewife, but I decided to have a career.

EXERCISE 18   Fill in the blanks to tell about an opportunity that you did not take. Find a partner and explain your sentence to him or her.

> I could have _____ _____ instead of (gerund = verb + -*ing*)
>
> _____, but
>
> _____.

> EXAMPLE: I could have gone to Israel instead of coming to the U.S., but it's easier to find a job in my profession in the U.S.

EXERCISE 19   Fill in each blank to make statements of disbelief.

> EXAMPLE: A. When I was a child, I saw President Kennedy.
>
> B. You _couldn't have seen him!_____ He died before you were born.

1. A. U.S. athletes won ten gold medals at the 1980 Olympics.

   B. They _____. The U.S. didn't participate in the 1980 Olympics.

2. A. We had an English test on December 25.

   B. You _____. The school was closed for Christmas Day.

3. A. I got a letter from my mother last Sunday.

   B. You _____. The post office doesn't deliver the mail on Sundays.

4. A. President Kennedy ran for reelection in 1964.

   B. He _____. He died in 1963.

5. A. Oswald went to prison for many years for killing Kennedy.

   B. He _____. He was killed before he went to trial.

6. A. Hi. Don't you remember me?

   B. No, I'm sorry.

   A. We met in a math class last year.

   B. We _____ last year. I just came to this country two weeks ago.

7. A. Thanks for driving me to my cousin's house.

   B. It was nothing.

   A. I _____ there without you. I don't have a car.

8. A. I got an A on my math test.

   B. That's impossible. The teacher said that the highest grade was a B+. You

   _____ an A.

EXERCISE 20   A student will read one of the following problems out loud to the class. The student will pretend that this is his or her problem. Other students will ask for more information and give advice about the problem. Try to use modals, past and present.

Problem 1   My mother-in-law came to the U.S. last May. She stayed with us for three months. I told my husband that he had to find another apartment for her. He didn't want to. I finally said to my husband, "Tell her to leave, or I'm leaving." So he helped her move into her own apartment. Now my husband is mad at me. Do you think I did the right thing?

Problem 2   I had a beautiful piano. I got it from my grandmother, who bought it many years ago. When I moved into my new apartment, I couldn't take the piano because it was too big for the entrance. So I sold it. Do you think I did the right thing?

Problem 3   My wife gave me a beautiful watch last Christmas. While I was on a business trip in New York last month, I left my watch in my hotel room. A few days later, I called the hotel, but they said that no one reported finding a watch. So far, I haven't told my wife that I lost the watch. What should I do?

Problem 4   My friend gave me $1.00 to buy her a lottery ticket. I bought one for her and one for me, put both tickets in my pocket, and forgot about them for a few days. One of the tickets had the winning number. So far I haven't told my friend. I want to keep all the money. Do you think this is alright?

Problem 5   *Write your own problem, real or imaginary.*

EXPANSION ACTIVITIES

POEM

The following short poem contains a past modal. Discuss the meaning of this poem.

> Of all sad words of tongue or pen,
> The saddest of these: "It might have been." (John Greenleaf Whittier)

WRITING

1. Write about a big mistake you once made. Tell about what you should have done to avoid the problem.

2. Use Exercise 18 to write a short composition about another direction your life could have taken. What made you decide not to go in that direction?

OUTSIDE ACTIVITY

1. The next time you are in the post office, ask how much it costs to send a letter or package by Priority Mail and by Express Mail.

2. Look in the Yellow Pages under "Delivery Service" for the names of companies that offer express mail service. Call two of these companies to compare prices.

SUMMARY OF LESSON FIVE

Example	Explanation
Americans spend a lot of money on pets and pet care. They *must love* their animals.	A present deduction.
When Kennedy was killed, Americans *must have felt* sad.	A past deduction.
Susan isn't here today. She *may/might be* sick.	A present possibility.
I *may/might* work on Saturday.	A future possibility.
Overpopulation *may/might/could* cause starvation.	A future result.
Susan wasn't here last night. She *might have had* to work overtime.	A past possibility.
This package *is supposed to/should arrive* tomorrow.	A future probability or expectation.
My package *should have arrived* yesterday./My package *was supposed to arrive* yesterday.	A past expectation that was not met.
Kennedy *should have used* a bullet-proof car.	Advice that comes too late.
I *could have gone* to the University of California, but I chose Stanford University instead.	An opportunity not taken.
A. I was in Dallas when Kennedy was assassinated. B. You *couldn't have been* in Dallas at that time. You weren't born yet!	An absolute impossibility.

Review Lesson Four before going on to the Test/Review.
For a complete listing of Modals and Related Words, see Appendix I.

Part 1　　Fill in each blank with a modal (or related word) that refers to the present or future. In some cases, more than one answer is possible. The words in brackets [ ] give you a clue.

SITUATION: A foreigner (F) is asking an American (A) about American customs.

F: Excuse me. _May/can/could_ I talk to you for a minute?

A: Of course. What _____ you like to talk to me about?
　　　　　　　　　　　　　　(1)

F: A co-worker of mine invited me to a party, and I don't know much about

　　American customs. _____ you mind giving me some advice? You're an
　　　　　　　　　　　　　　　　(2)

　　American. You ___ _____ know the right thing to do. [You probably
　　　　　　　　　　　　　(3)

　　know.]

A: I'll try to help.

F: _____ I bring something to the party? [Do you advise me to bring
　　　　　　(4)

　　something?]

A: You _____ bring anything [it's not necessary], but it's always nice to
　　　　　　(5 not)

　　come with a small gift.

F: What _____ I bring? [What's your advice?]
　　　　　　　　(6)

A: You _____ bring a bottle of wine or some beer.
　　　　　　(7)

F: You know, I'm a Moslem, and my religion says we _____ drink.
　　　　　　　　　　　　　　　　　　　　　　　　　　　　(8 not)

　　[It is prohibited.] So I don't feel good about bringing wine.

A: Oh. You _____ bring a box of candy or some flowers. [This is a
　　　　　　　　(9)

　　suggestion.]

F: I see. _____ I invite my friends to the party? [Is this acceptable?]
　　　　　　　(10)

A: It's not a good idea. You _____ take your wife with you, of course.
　　　　　　　　　　　　　　　　　(11)

　　[This is acceptable.]

F: In my country, guests _____ come with as many people as they want
    (12)

to someone's party. [This is permitted or acceptable.] In fact, the more people,
the better the party.

A: Well, Americans usually prepare enough food for a certain amount of people. If

everyone brings extra guests, there _____ be enough food for
                                          (13 not)

everyone. [Possibly there won't be enough.]

F: What about my children? _____ I take them to the party? [Is this
                                    (14)

acceptable?]

A: No. You _____ take your children. [People expect no children.]
              (15 not)

F: What _____ I wear? [What's your advice?]
              (16)

A: I really don't know. It _____ be a formal party, or it _____
                                  (17)   (18)

be a casual party. [There are two possibilities.] You _____ ask the
                                                              (19)

hostess. [This is my advice.]

F: You _____ think I'm stupid for asking all these questions. [You
          (20)

probably think I'm stupid.]

A: I don't think you're stupid. You're a foreigner, and you _____ know
                                                                    (21 not)

everything about American customs. [You aren't expected to know.]

F: Well, I hope I don't make any silly mistakes.

A: Don't worry so much. Just enjoy yourself. Everything _____ be fine.
                                                                  (22)

[Everything will probably be fine.]

Part 2   Fill in each blank with the past of the modal or expression in parentheses ( ).

After Alan (A) has waited for two hours for his friend Bill (B) to arrive for dinner,
Bill finally arrives.

A: Why are you so late? You _*were supposed to be*_ here two hours ago.

B: I'm sorry. I got lost on my way to your house.

A: You _____ a road map.
            (1 should/take)

B: I did, but I _____ it while I was driving. I
                (2 can/not/read)

_____ a wrong turn.
   (3 must/make)

A: Where did you get off the highway?

B: At Madison Street.

A: You _____ off at Madison Street. There's no exit there.
        (4 can/not/get)

B: Oh. It _____ Adams Street, then.
        (5 must/be)

A: But Adams Street is not so far from here.

B: I know. But I had a flat tire after I got off the highway.

A: Did you fix it yourself?

B: Yes. I'm a member of a motor club, and I _____ for a tow
                (6 can/call)

truck, but I thought it would take too long. So I changed the tire myself.

A: But you're over two hours late. How long did it take you to change the tire?

B: It _____ about 15 minutes, but then I _____
    (7 may/take)   (8 must/go)

home, take a shower, and change clothes. I was so dirty.

A: You _____ me.
       (9 should/call)

B: I wanted to, but I _____ the paper where I had your phone
          (10 can/not/find)

number. I _____ it while I was changing the tire.
     (11 must/lose)

A: Well, thank goodness you're here now. But you'll have to eat dinner alone. I

got hungry and _____ for you.
          (12 can/not/wait)

Part 3   Look at the completed job application below. Then fill in each blank in the sentences that follow.

Fill out the following form. Print in black ink or type. Bring it to the personnel office or mail it to:

Ms. Judy Lipton
P.O. Box 324
Tucson, Arizona 85744

Applications must be submitted by November 15.

Name _Wilson_____ _Jock_____ _N_____
          (last)   (first)   (middle initial)

Address _5040 N. Albany Ave._____

Telephone (   ) _539 - 2756_____

Marital status (optional) _Divorced_ Sex _yes_

Date of birth _18_____ _2_____ _64_____ (You must be at least 18.)
               (month)   (day)   (year)

Social Security number _549 - 62 - 7149_

Educational background

		Date graduated	Degree or major
High School	Roosevelt	1892	
College			
Graduate School			

Employment History (Please start with your present or last job.)

Company	Position	Dates	Supervisor	Reason for leaving
Apex	Stock boy	3/84 – 3/88	R. Wilmot	personal
Smith, Inc.		5/88 – 12/92	M. Smith	pay
Olson Co.	loading dock	1/93 – present	B. Adams	

Do not write in the shaded box. For office use only.

Rec'd. by _J.W._
Amer. cit. _yes_
Doc. checked _?_
Transcripts received _yes_

The Immigration Act of 1986 requires all successful applicants to present documents to prove U.S. citizenship or permanent residence with permission to work in the U.S.

This company is an Equal Opportunity Employer. Race, religion, nationality, marital status, and physical disability will not influence our decision to hire.
I certify that these answers are true.   _Catholic_

Signature: _Jack N. Wilson_____   Date: _13/11/93_____

Write a past modal or related words plus a verb to describe the problems in the job application. (In some cases, more than one answer is possible.)

EXAMPLES: He didn't write his zip code. He _should have written_ his zip code.

He included his religion. He _wasn't supposed to include_ it.

1. He wrote his application with a pencil. He _____ a pen.

2. He put the day before the month. He _____ the month before the day.

3. He didn't fill in any college attended. He (not) _____ any college.

4. He didn't fill in his reason for leaving his last job. He _____.

5. His printing is hard to read. He _____ his application.

6. He wrote in the shaded box. He (not) _____ the directions carefully. [He probably didn't read them carefully.]

7. He wrote that he graduated from high school in 1892. He (not) _____ in 1892. That's more than 100 years ago! He _____ 1982.

8. He forgot to include his area code. He _____.

9. He said that he left his first job for personal reasons. He _____ because he couldn't get along with his boss. Or _____ because he had problems at home.

10. He mailed the application on November 13. It (not) _____ on time.

11. He printed his name on the bottom line. He _____.

12. In the blank next to "sex," he wrote "yes." He (not) _____ the meaning of this question.

13. He included his marital status. He (not) _____ to include it. This information is optional.

LESSON SIX

GRAMMAR

Adjective Clauses

CONTEXT

Halloween
Selling Information
Income Tax
Puerto Rico
Alaska

**Lesson Focus Adjective Clauses**[1]

- An adjective clause is a clause that describes a noun.

              Noun   Adjective Clause
                ↓   ↓
  I saw the man *who stole the bike.*

        Noun Adjective Clause
          ↓   ↓
  The bike *that he stole* is worth $300.

  Relative pronouns introduce adjective clauses. *Who(m)* is for people, *which* is for things, and *that* is for people or things.

- Some adjective clauses are essential to the meaning of the sentence. Other adjective clauses add extra, but nonessential information. Commas are used with nonessential adjective clauses only.   *extra commas*

    Cars *that are made in Japan* are popular in the U.S.
    Toyota, *which is a Japanese company,* sells many cars in the U.S.

· ·

R
E
A
D
I
N
G Before you read:

1. In your country, is there a special holiday for children? How is it celebrated?
2. Is there a special day in your country when people wear costumes?

Read the following article. Pay special attention to adjective clauses.

HALLOWEEN

Halloween is a special day **that American children love.** On this day, October 31, children wear costumes. Some children wear costumes **that represent spooky**[2] **characters** such as ghosts, monsters, witches, and skeletons. In the past, people believed that these spooky characters would scare away the evil spirits. Nowadays, however, Halloween is just for fun, and any kind of costumes can be worn. Children often like to dress up like characters **that they see on TV or in current popular movies.**

Children in costumes go from house to house. They carry a big bag and say "trick or treat" to the person **who answers the door.** "Treat" refers to the candy **that they expect to be given.** "Trick" refers to the activities **that they plan to do** if they don't get a treat. Some children throw eggs or spray shaving cream on windows.

---

[1]An *adjective clause* is sometimes called a relative clause.

[2]*Spooky* means *scary*.

If you have small children, it is best to take them to the houses of people **whom you know and trust.** In recent years, some of the fun has been taken out of Halloween by people **who put harmful things in children's bags.**

The colors **you see** on Halloween are orange and black. Orange represents the color of harvest;[3] black represents death. People often decorate their homes with these colors and with figures of spooky characters. Many people put a "jack o'lantern" in their windows. This is a pumpkin **that has been emptied out** and **on which a scary face has been carved.** A lit candle is placed inside the pumpkin to provide a spooky effect.

6.1 Defining an Adjective Clause

- An adjective is a word that describes a noun.

    I live in a *big* house.

- A clause is a group of words that contains a subject and a verb. A sentence is one kind of clause.

            S   V
    The house has five bedrooms.

    A sentence is an independent clause.

- An adjective clause is a clause that describes a noun.

    I live in a house *that has five bedrooms.*

---

[3]*Harvest* is the time in the fall when farmers pick their crops.

1. An adjective clause is a dependent clause. It is never a sentence.

> NOT: I live in a house. That has five bedrooms.

2. An adjective comes before a noun. An adjective clause comes after a noun.

> a *big* house
> a house *that has five bedrooms*

3. Relative pronouns introduce adjective clauses. *Who(m)* is for people, *which* is for things, and *that* is for people or things.

> I saw the man *who* stole the bike.
> I saw the man *that* stole the bike. (less formal)
> The bike *which*[4] he stole is worth $200.
> The bike *that* he stole is worth $200.

6.2   Relative Pronoun as Subject

A relative pronoun can be the subject of an adjective clause.

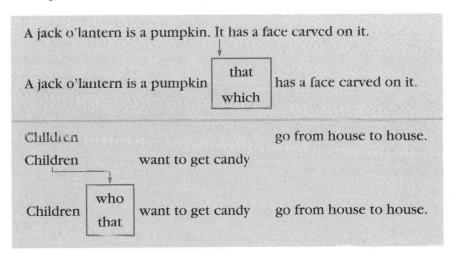

1. A present tense verb in the adjective clause must agree in number with its subject.

> Children who *eat* a lot of candy can get sick.
> A child who *eats* a lot of candy can get sick.

2. Avoid using an adjective clause when a simple adjective is enough.

> WEAK: Children who are young like Halloween.
> BETTER: Young children like Halloween.

'Most writers prefer *that* over *which* in this situation.

EXERCISE 1   In each sentence below, underline the adjective clause.

> EXAMPLES: A jack o'lantern is a pumpkin <u>that has a face carved on it</u>.

1. Some schools have a contest for the best costume. The child who has the best costume can win a prize.
2. Costumes that represent spooky characters are traditional.
3. People who put bad things in children's bags should be sent to jail.

EXERCISE 2   Complete each statement with an adjective clause. Make sure that the verb in the adjective clause agrees with its subject.

> EXAMPLE: I know a woman . . .
>   I know a woman who doesn't want to have children.

1. I like movies . . .
2. I don't like movies . . .
3. I have never met a person . . .
4. I can't understand people . . .
5. I like a teacher . . .

EXERCISE 3   Complete each statement with an adjective clause. Make sure that the verb in the adjective clause agrees with its subject. The subject of the adjective clause is general.

> EXAMPLE: Classes _that meet in the evening_ aren't convenient for me.

1. A student _____ gets good grades.

2. Teachers _____ are usually popular.

3. Teachers _____ are bad for foreign students.

4. A grammar book _____ is useful for foreign students.

5. A college _____ is popular with foreign students.

6. Classes _____ are convenient for me.

EXERCISE 4   Each subject contains an adjective clause. Complete the statement with a verb phrase.

> EXAMPLE: Colleges that have ESL classes . . .
>   Colleges that have ESL classes attract students from all over the world.

1. People who have children . . .
2. Foreigners who come to the U.S. . . .
3. Americans who go to my country . . .
4. People who use drugs . . .
5. Apartments that don't have air conditioning . . .

EXERCISE 5   Complete this sentence. Discuss your answers in a small group or with the entire class.

> **EXAMPLE:** **I don't like people who . . .**
> **I don't like people who don't keep their promises.**

6.3   **Relative Pronoun as Object**
• • • • • • • • • • •

A relative pronoun can be the object of an adjective clause.

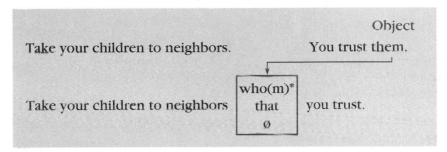

*NOTE: The correct relative pronoun for people is *whom*. However, in conversation, *who* is heard more often.

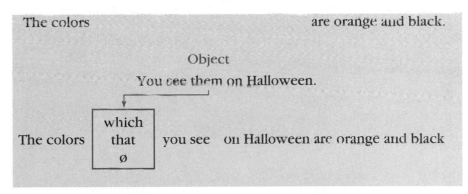

[Language Notes]

1. The relative pronoun can be omitted completely. In fact, in conversation, it usually is.

   Take your children to neighbors *(who, that)* you trust.
   The child *(who, that)* I saw was wearing a ghost costume.

2. In an adjective clause, don't use the relative pronoun with an object pronoun.

   The colors that you see ~~them~~ on Halloween are orange and black.

EXERCISE 6   In the sentences below, underline the adjective clause.

> **EXAMPLE: Halloween is a holiday <u>American children love</u>.**

1. The costumes children wear represent spooky characters.
2. Parents should inspect the candy their children bring home.
3. The candle you put inside a jack o'lantern gives it a spooky look.
4. Children shouldn't go to the houses of people they don't know.
5. The tricks children play sometimes annoy adults.

EXERCISE 7   Fill in each blank to make an appropriate adjective clause.

> **EXAMPLE: My friend just bought a new dog. The last dog _(that) he had_ died a few weeks ago.**

1. I have a hard teacher this semester. The teacher _____ last semester was much easier.

2. I studied British English in my country. The English _____ now is American English.

3. The teacher gave a test last week. Almost everyone failed the test _____.

4. When I read English, there are many new words for me. I use my dictionary to look up the words I _____.

5. I had a big apartment in my country. The apartment _____ now is very small.

6. Did you return the wallet _____ on the street?

7. I write poetry. One of the poems _____ won a prize.

8. The last book _____ was very sad. It made me cry.

6.4   Relative Pronoun as Object of Preposition

The relative pronoun of an adjective clause can be the object of a preposition.

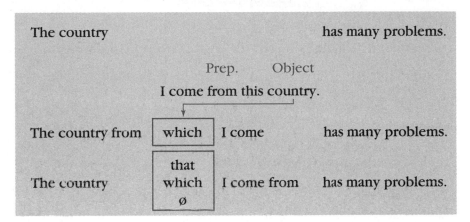

The country   has many problems.

                                     Prep.   Object
                          I come from this country.

The country from | which | I come   has many problems.

                  | that |
The country | which | I come from   has many problems.
                  | ø |

1. In very formal English, the preposition comes before the relative pronoun.

   The person *about whom* I am speaking was a great hero.
   This is the pen *with which* I signed the document.

   Which must be used for things; *whom* must be used for people. *That* cannot be used after the preposition. The relative pronoun cannot be omitted if the preposition comes first.

2. In informal speech, the preposition comes at the end of the adjective clause. *Who(m), that,* or *which* may be used or omitted.

   The person (who) I'm speaking *about* was a great hero.
   This is the pen (that) I signed the document *with*.

EXERCISE 8   Complete each statement. Then change your statement to more formal English by putting the preposition before the relative pronoun.

> EXAMPLE: The country I come from . . .
> The country I come from is now involved in a civil war.
> The country from which I come is now involved in a civil war.

1. The country I come from . . .
2. The city I come from . . .
3. The house/apartment I lived in . . .
4. The high school I graduated from . . .
5. The teacher I studied beginning grammar with . . .
6. Most of the people that I went to school with . . .

EXERCISE 9   This is a conversation between two friends. One just came back from an island vacation where he had a terrible time. Fill in each blank with an adjective clause.

A. How was your trip?

B. Terrible.

A. What happened? Didn't your travel agent choose a good hotel for you?

B. The hotel *(that) he chose for me* didn't have air conditioning. It was too hot.

A. What kind of food did they serve?

B. The food _____ made me sick.
                        (1)

A. Did you meet any interesting travelers?

B. I didn't like the other travelers _____. They were unfriendly.
                                                    (2)

A. Did you travel with an interesting companion?

B. The person _____ was boring.
                        (3)

A. Did you take pictures?

B. The pictures _____ didn't come out.
                            (4)

A. Did you find any interesting souvenirs?

B. The souvenirs _____ were cheaply made. I didn't buy any.
                            (5)

A. Could you communicate with the people on the island? Do they speak English?

B. No. I don't understand the language _____.
                                                        (6)

A. Did you spend a lot of money?

B. Yes, but the money _____ was wasted.
                                (7)

A. Why didn't you change your ticket and come home early?

B. The ticket _____ couldn't be changed.
                        (8)

A. Are you going to have another vacation soon?

B. The next vacation _____ will be in December. I think I'll just
                                (9)
   stay home.

• •

Before you read:

1. Do you receive phone calls from companies that are trying to sell you something? How do you respond to these calls?
2. Do you receive mail that you haven't asked for? What do you do with this mail?

Read the following article. Pay special attention to adjective clauses that begin with *whose*.

SELLING INFORMATION

You probably receive phone calls from companies that have your name. Or you may get catalogs in the mail that you have not asked for. Most Americans do. How do these companies get your name?

The information industry is a growing business in the U.S. When a person opens a bank account, applies for a credit card, or selects a phone company, information about that person is compiled. There are companies **whose primary business it is** to collect and sell this personal information to other companies. A person **whose name is on a list** starts to receive unsolicited[5] calls, letters, and catalogs, trying to sell him new products and services.

What kind of information do these companies have? They may know a person's age, hobbies, income, marital status, number of children, Social Security number, whether he rents or owns, what kind of car he drives, and what types of products he buys. In some ways, a person may benefit from what this information can bring. A person who shops for baby products may appreciate receiving coupons for these products. However, sometimes a company may have information that a person would like to keep private. For example, a person **whose medical record shows that he has AIDS or other serious health problems** might lose medical benefits or even his job.

Because of computer technology, private information can be bought and sold easily.

• •

---

[5]When you receive something *unsolicited,* it means that you didn't ask for it.

6.5 *Whose* + Noun as the Subject or Object of an Adjective Clause

Whose is the possessive form of *who.*
Whose + noun can be the subject of the adjective clause:

A person		may start to receive catalogs.
	Her name is on a list.	
A person	*whose* name is on a list	may start to receive catalogs.

Whose + noun can be the object of the adjective clause:

There are companies.   It is their business to collect personal
                                        information about you.
There are companies *whose* business it is to collect personal information about you.

Language Notes

1. *Whose* substitutes for *his, her, its, their,* or the possessive form of the noun.
2. *Whose* cannot be omitted from the sentence.

3. Do not confuse *whose* with *who's. Whose* is a possessive form.

   People *whose* names are sold may receive catalogs. *(whose = their)*
   A woman *who's* in my math class received five catalogs today. *(who's = who is)*

EXERCISE 10   Underline each adjective clause.

> EXAMPLE: A person <u>whose name is on a list</u> will receive catalogs.

1. The TOEFL is a test for students whose native language isn't English.
2. A student whose homework has a lot of mistakes should do it over.
3. Teachers get angry at students whose homework is always late.
4. The woman whose wallet I found and returned gave me a reward.
5. She doesn't know the person whose car she bought.

EXERCISE 11   Use the sentence in parentheses ( ) to form an adjective clause.

> EXAMPLES: **There are many American children** *whose parents are divorced.*
> **(Their parents are divorced.)**
>
> **There is one student** *whose handwriting the teacher can't read.* **(The teacher can't read her handwriting.)**

1. There are many American children _____ (Their mothers work.)

2. Working parents _____ need to find day-care centers. (Their children are small.)

3. People _____ can get food stamps. (Their incomes are below a certain level.)

4. A widow is a woman _____ (Her husband has died.)

5. There is one student _____ (The teacher loves to read her compositions.)

6. The student _____ is absent today. (I borrowed his book.)

7. There are a few students _____ (I can't remember their names.)

8. The teacher _____ can advise you on what course to take next semester. (You are taking her class.)

- -

R
E
A
D
I
N
G

Before you read

1. In your country, do people pay income tax?
2. Besides income, what else is taxed in your country?

Read the following article. Pay special attention to clauses that begin with *where* and *when*.

INCOME TAX

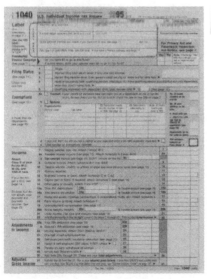

Everyone who earns money in the U.S. must file[6] an income tax return with the federal government. Your tax rate depends on your income. People with higher incomes pay at a higher tax rate.

In addition to federal income tax, most people must also pay income tax in the state **where they live.** Some states have no state income tax. Alaska is one state **where residents pay no income tax.** Other states have a very high tax. In California, the rate can be as high as 11% (for people with high incomes).

April 15 is the date **when income taxes are due.**[7] If we do not pay our taxes on or before this date, we

---

[6]*File* a return means to fill out and send in the tax form.

[7]When something is *due* on a certain date, this means it must be submitted on or before this date: "My library books are due on March 8."

have to pay a penalty. Some people submit their tax forms well in advance of that date. But many people put off doing their taxes until the last day. In some locations, the post office stays open until midnight on April 15. The Internal Revenue Service (the federal tax collection agency) accepts as on time any envelope that is post-marked before midnight of April 15.

Benjamin Franklin, a famous American, once said, "In this world, nothing is certain but death and taxes."

6.6 Adjective Clauses with *Where* and *When*

Where and *when* can introduce adjective clauses of place and time.

> April 15 is the day.
>
> The post office is open late on this day.
>
> April 15 is the date when the post office is open late.

> You must pay income tax in the state.
>
> You live in the state.
>
> You must pay income tax in the state where you live

1. *When* may be omitted.

   April 15 is the date (*when*) taxes are due.

2. Study the difference between *where, that,* and *which* in the following sentences.

   The state *where* I live has high taxes.
   The state *in which* I live has high taxes.
   The state *that/which* I live *in* has high taxes.
   The state I live *in* has high taxes.

   If *where* is used, a preposition is not used in the adjective clause. If *which* or *that* is used, the preposition is included.

EXERCISE 12   Change the sentences so that they include an adjective clause. Begin with the words given.

EXAMPLES: **People pay no state income tax in Alaska.**
Alaska *is a state where people pay no state income tax.*

Income tax is due on April 15.
April 15 *is the date (when) income tax is due.*

1. The President lives in the White House.

   The White House _____

2. A presidential election is held in November.

   November _____

3. President Kennedy was killed in 1963.

   1963 _____

4. President Kennedy was killed in Dallas, Texas.

   Dallas _____

5. The original capital of the U.S. was located in Philadelphia.

   Philadelphia _____

6. Americans celebrate Labor Day in September.

   September _____

EXERCISE 13   Use the sentence in parentheses ( ) to add an adjective clause to the first sentence.

EXAMPLES: **I buy my groceries at a store** *where I can buy food from my country.*
(I can buy food from my country at that store.)

1. The teacher didn't give a test on the day _____

   _____. (Some students celebrated a religious holiday on that day.)

2. You should study at a time _____

   _____. (The house is quiet at that time.)

3. Saturday is the day _____.
   (I am busiest on this day.)

4. The bookstore _____
   is having a sale this week. (I bought my books at the bookstore.)

5. The bank _____
   is open late on Fridays. (I cash my checks at the bank.)

6.7 Adjective Clauses After Indefinite Compounds

An adjective clause can follow an indefinite compound *(someone, something, everyone, nothing, anything, everywhere,* etc.).

Compound	Adjective Clause	Verb Phrase
Everyone	who earns money	must pay taxes.
Something	(that) I said	made him angry.

Subject	Verb Phrase	Compound	Adjective Clause
I	didn't understand	anything	(that) he said.
She	said	something	that made me angry.

Language Notes

1. When the relative pronoun is the object of the clause, it is usually omitted.

   Something *(that) I said* made him angry.

2. An adjective clause does not usually follow a personal pronoun. However, there are some proverbs that use a personal pronoun before an adjective clause.

   He *who hesitates* is lost.
   He *who laughs last* laughs best.

3. An adjective clause always needs a noun before it.

   WRONG: Who fails the test can take it again.
   RIGHT: *Anyone* who fails the test can take it again.
   RIGHT: *A student* who fails the test can take it again.

4. An indefinite pronoun takes a singular verb.

   Everyone who *drives* a car *needs* insurance.
   I don't know anyone who *speaks* Armenian.

EXERCISE 14   Fill in each blank with an adjective clause. Use information from nearby sentences to help you.

A woman (W) is trying to break up with a man (M).

M. I heard you want to talk to me.

W. Yes. There's something *I want to tell you.*

M. What do you want to tell me?

W. I want to break up.

M. Are you angry at me? What did I say?

W. Nothing _____ made me angry.
                           (1)

M. Did I do something wrong?

W. Nothing _____ made me mad.
                           (2)

M. Then what's the problem?

W. I just don't love you anymore.

M. But I can buy you anything _____.
                                (3)

W. I don't want anything from you. In fact, I'm going to return everything

   _____.
                 (4)

M. But I can take you anywhere _____.
                                (5)

W. I don't want to go anywhere with you. You haven't heard anything

   _____. I said that I just don't love you any more. Good-bye.
              (6)

EXERCISE 15   Fill in each blank with an adjective clause.

EXAMPLE: I know someone *who can help you with your car problem.*

1. I don't know anyone _____.

2. I know someone _____.

3. Everyone _____ can go to the next level.

4. Anyone _____ should ask the teacher.

5. Everything _____ is useful.

Before you read

In your country, is there any group of people that wants independence from the rest of the nation?

Read the following article. Pay special attention to the adjective clauses. Notice that these adjective clauses are separated from the rest of the sentence with commas.

PUERTO RICO

Puerto Rico, **which is a small Caribbean island,** is an American territory. This territory, **which is sometimes called a commonwealth or associated free state,** is not counted as one of the fifty American states. However, Puerto Ricans are considered U.S. citizens and can travel freely from their island to any of the fifty states. Puerto Ricans, **whose native language is Spanish,** have the same rights and privileges as any U.S. citizen. However, they cannot vote in a national election, and they do not pay taxes to the federal government. If a Puerto Rican moves to one of the fifty states and takes up residence there, he or she has all the rights and duties of an American citizen.

Some Puerto Ricans would like Puerto Rico to become the fifty-first state of the U.S. A small group of Puerto Ricans, **who call themselves "independentistas,"** would like Puerto Rico to become an independent nation.

6.8 Nonessential Adjective Clauses

Subject	Comma	Nonessential Clause	Comma	Verb Phrase
Puerto Rico	,	which lies between the Atlantic Ocean and the Caribbean Sea	,	has a tropical climate.

Subject	Verb Phrase	Comma	Nonessential Clause
My cousin	lives in Puerto Rico	,	which is an American territory.

1. A nonessential adjective clause adds extra information to the main clause. However, the main idea of the sentence is complete without it.

> Main Idea: Puerto Rico has a tropical climate.
> Extra Information: Puerto Rico lies between the Atlantic Ocean and the Caribbean Sea.
> Main Idea: My cousin lives in Puerto Rico.
> Extra Information: Puerto Rico is an American territory.

A nonessential adjective clause and a main clause are two complete, independent ideas.

2. A nonessential adjective clause is separated from the main clause by commas.

3. An adjective clause that describes a unique person or place *(Puerto Rico, France, my father, her husband)* is always nonessential.

> My father, *who lives in Puerto Rico,* works as a carpenter.
> Ms. Henderson, *who teaches English 101 in the morning,* is a very popular teacher.

4. In a nonessential adjective clause, use *who(m)* for people, *which* for things, and *whose* for possession. Do not use *that*.

> Puerto Rico, ~~that~~ *which* *is an island,* has a tropical climate.
> My father, ~~that~~ *who* *comes from Puerto Rico,* lives in New York.

5. An essential adjective clause gives information that is necessary to identify or limit the noun it describes. Commas are not used.

> Puerto Ricans *who live in New York* can vote in a national election. (Not all Puerto Ricans live in New York.)
> Puerto Ricans *who speak English* have an easier time adapting to life in New York. (Not all Puerto Ricans speak English.)

EXERCISE 16 Decide which of the following sentences contain a nonessential adjective clause. Put commas in those sentences.

> EXAMPLES: Puerto Rico which is an island is an American territory.
> Nonessential: Puerto Rico, which is an island, is an American territory.
>
> A piece of land which is surrounded by water is called an island.
> Essential: No commas.

1. Puerto Ricans who take up residence in the U.S. can vote in a national election.
2. Puerto Ricans who live on the island can't vote in a national election.
3. Puerto Rico which was once a colony of Spain has a tropical climate.
4. Puerto Ricans who live in the U.S. usually learn to speak English.
5. The Spanish which is spoken in Puerto Rico is different from Mexican Spanish.
6. Spanish which is a Romance language is the principal language of Puerto Rico.
7. Puerto Ricans who want Puerto Rico to become an independent nation are in the minority.
8. San Juan which is the capital of Puerto Rico attracts many tourists.
9. Hawaii which is a group of Pacific islands has been an American state since 1959.
10. Puerto Rico which is sometimes called a commonwealth is not one of the fifty states.

EXERCISE 17   Combine the two sentences into one. The sentence in parentheses ( ) is not essential to the main idea of the sentence. It is extra information.

>   EXAMPLE: **Puerto Ricans can travel to any of the fifty states. (Puerto Ricans are American citizens.)**
>
>   *Puerto Ricans, who are American citizens, can travel to any of the fifty states.*

1. Puerto Rico is a very small island. (It has a population of about three million.)

    _____

2. Colombians can communicate with Puerto Ricans. (Their native language is Spanish.)

    _____

3. New York City is the biggest city in the U.S. (Many Puerto Ricans live there.)

    _____

4. John Kennedy was assassinated in 1963. (Kennedy was one of the youngest American Presidents.)

    _____

5. Kennedy was the 35th President of the U.S. (We saw his picture on page 145.)

    _____

. . . .

R
E
A
D
I
N
G

Before you read

Is there a region of your country where very few people live? Why is this region underpopulated?

Read the following article. Pay special attention to the descriptive phrases.

ALASKA

Alaska, **the largest state in the United States,** is the northernmost region of the U.S. and is separate from the mainland. In spite of its size, it has the smallest population of any state, with about a half million people.

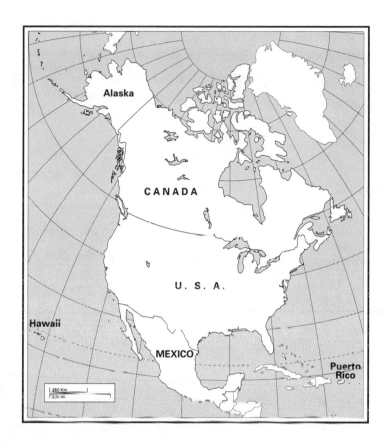

Alaska, **purchased from Russia in 1867 for only $7 million (about two cents an acre),** proved to be a good investment for the United States. Gold, oil, and other valuable minerals **discovered there** attracted people from other parts of the U.S.

The Eskimos, Indians, and Aleuts, **the natives of Alaska,** make up 16% of the population today.

In 1959, Alaska became the forty-ninth state of the U.S.

6.9 Shortening an Adjective Clause

Adjective clauses that have a subject pronoun followed by the verb *be* may be shortened to phrases. The following kinds of phrases result.

• Prepositional Phrase

California, which is on the West Coast, has a large population.
California,   *on the West Coast,* has a large population.

• Participial Phrase

Alaska, which was purchased from Russia, was a good investment.
Alaska,   *purchased from Russia,* was a good investment.
              (past participle)

Puerto Ricans who are living in a state of the U.S. can vote.
Puerto Ricans   *living in a state of the U.S.* can vote.
              (present participle)

• Appositive (a noun or noun phrase that explains or defines the noun before it)

Aleuts, who are natives of Alaska, have their own language.
Aleuts,   *natives of Alaska,* have their own language.

Language Notes

1. An adjective clause with *whose* cannot be shortened.

The man *whose wife you met* is from Alaska.

2. If the phrase is nonessential, it is separated from the main clause with commas. If it is essential, commas are not used.

Puerto Rico, *in the Caribbean,* is an American territory.
Puerto Ricans *in New York* usually speak English.

EXERCISE 18   Shorten the adjective clause to a phrase by crossing out the unnecessary words.

EXAMPLE: Alaska, ~~which is~~ the largest state, has the smallest population.

1. English, which is the official language of Alaska, is not the only language.

2. There are many languages that are spoken in Alaska.

3. Eskimos, who are natives of Alaska, have their own language.

4. Alaska, which was purchased from Russia, proved to be a good investment.

5. Gold, which was discovered in Alaska in 1896, attracted people from all over the U.S.

6. Many non-Alaskans who were searching for jobs in the oil fields went to Alaska in the 1960s.

7. Puerto Ricans who are residing in one of the fifty states can vote in a national election.

8. Puerto Rico, which was once a colony of Spain, uses Spanish as its official language.

9. Puerto Ricans speak Spanish, which is a Romance language.

10. The languages that are used in Puerto Rico are Spanish and English.

11. San Juan, which is the capital of Puerto Rico, is on the northern coast.

EXERCISE 19   Combine the two sentences. Use a phrase for the sentence in parentheses ( ).

> EXAMPLE: **Los Angeles is one of the largest American cities. (It is in California.)**
>
> *Los Angeles, in California, is one of the largest American cities.*

1. Alaska is separate from the other American states. (It is the largest state.)

_____

2. Rhode Island is the smallest American state. (It is on the East Coast.)

_____

3. Arizona has a dry climate. (It is in the Southwest.)

_____

4. The White House is in Washington, D.C. (It is the home of the President.)

_____

5. Puerto Rico is an American territory. (It's a Caribbean island.)

_____

6. Hawaii is a group of islands. (It is located in the Pacific Ocean.)

_____

EXPANSION ACTIVITIES

DISCUSSION   Fill in each blank to tell about people in your country. Discuss your answers in a small group or with the entire class.

1. People _____ have an easy life.

2. No one likes or respects people _____

3. People _____ want to go to the U.S.

4. People who have very little education _____

5. There are a lot of people _____

PROVERBS   1. The following proverbs use prepositional phrases. Discuss the meaning of each proverb. Do you have a similar proverb in your language?

A bird in the hand is worth two
   in the bush.
A stitch in time saves nine.

— stitch

2. The following proverb contains an adjective clause. Discuss the meaning of this proverb. Do you have a similar proverb in your language?

People who live in glass houses shouldn't throw stones.

ACTIVITIES   1. Bring to class something typical from your country. Demonstrate how to use it.

EXAMPLE: a samovar
This is a pot that we use in Russia to make tea.

2. We often give a definition with an adjective clause. Work with a partner to give a definition of the following words by using an adjective clause. Try to be precise. Share your definitions with the class.

EXAMPLES: **a currency exchange**

A currency exchange is a place where you can cash checks, buy money orders,

and pay bills.

a fire fighter

A fire fighter is a person whose job it is to put out fires.

A. a dictionary _____

B. an island _____

C. the TOEFL _____

D. directory assistance _____

E. a zoo _____

F. a mechanic _____

G. _____

WRITING

1. You read about Alaska and Puerto Rico. Write about a specific region, territory, or ethnic group in your country.

2. Write a paragraph about an unforgettable teacher you had. Begin:

    I once had a teacher whom I liked very much.
    OR
    I once had a teacher whom I didn't like at all.

    Give reasons why you feel this way. Give examples of the teacher's behavior.

3. Write about the day you left your country. What happened that day? Write about what you did that day, who you were with, and how you felt.

EDITING ADVICE

1. Never use *what* as a relative pronoun.
                          who
   She married a man ~~what~~ has a lot of money.
                     (that)
   Everything ~~what~~ you did was unnecessary.

2. You can't omit a relative pronoun that is the subject of the adjective clause.
                    who
   I know a man ∧ speaks five languages.

3. If the relative pronoun is the object of the adjective clause, don't put an object after the verb.

   The car that I bought ~~it~~ has a stick shift.

4. Make sure you use subject-verb agreement.

   I know several English teachers who speak~~s~~ Spanish.
                     has
   A car which ~~have~~ a big engine is not economical.

5. Only nonessential adjective clauses need commas.
                   x   x
   People~~,~~who commit crimes~~,~~should be put in jail.

6. Always put a noun before an adjective clause.
   The student   *w*
   ∧ ~~W~~ho wants to leave early should sit in the back.

7. Put the adjective clause near the noun it describes.

   The teacher (speaks Spanish) ⟨whose class I am taking.⟩

8. Don't confuse *whose* with *who's*.
                  whose
   A student ~~who's~~ grades are good may get a scholarship.

9. Put the subject before the verb in an adjective clause.
                      my cousin bought
   The house which ~~bought my cousin~~ is very beautiful.

10. An adjective clause is a dependent clause. It is never a sentence.
                              w
    She'd like to marry a man ~~W~~ho knows how to cook.

SUMMARY OF LESSON SIX

Adjective Clauses and Phrases

1. Pronoun as Subject—Essential
   I saw the man *who (or that) stole your wallet.*
   A car *that (or which) has a large engine* uses a lot of gas.
2. Pronoun as Subject—Nonessential
   George Washington, *who was from Virginia,* was the first American President.
   My brother lives in Alaska, *which is the biggest state in the U.S.*
3. Pronoun as Object—Essential
   The costumes *(that/which) children wear on Halloween* are often spooky.
   The child *(that/whom/who) I saw* was wearing a ghost costume.
4. Pronoun as Object—Nonessential
   Jerry Smith, *whom you met at the party,* is Mary Smith's husband.
   Puerto Rico, *which I visited in 1989,* is a beautiful island.
5. Pronoun as Object of a Preposition—Essential
   The teacher *to whom I was speaking* couldn't understand me. (FORMAL)
   The teacher *(whom/who/that) I was speaking to* couldn't understand me. (INFORMAL)
6. Pronoun as Object of a Preposition—Nonessential
   Alaska, *about which we read,* is an interesting place. (FORMAL)
   Alaska, *which we read about,* is an interesting place. (INFORMAL)
7. *Whose* + Noun as Subject of Adjective Clause—Essential
   The teacher *whose class meets in room 103* is absent today.
8. *Whose* + Noun as Subject of Adjective Clause—Nonessential
   Mr. Jackson, *whose class meets in room 206,* is absent today.
9. *Whose* + Noun as Object—Essential
   The student *whose dictionary I borrowed* didn't come to class today.
10. *Whose* + Noun as Object—Nonessential
    Ms. Kaplan, *whose class I took last semester,* does not teach at this college anymore.
11. Clause with *Where*—Essential
    The restaurant *where she met her husband* is out of business now.
12. Clause with *Where*—Nonessential
    Last year she went to Alaska, *where she met her husband.*
13. Clause with *When*—Essential
    I'll never forget the day *(when) I met you.*
14. Clause with *When*—Nonessential
    December 12, *when I met you,* was a cold day.
15. Adjective Clause After an Indefinite Compound—Pronoun as Subject (Always Essential)
    Do you know anyone *who speaks Irish*?
16. Adjective Clause After an Indefinite Compound—Pronoun as Object (Always Essential)
    You can say anything *(that) you want.*
17. Phrase—Essential
    Japan has a special holiday *for children.*
18. Phrase—Nonessential
    Halloween, *a day for children,* is on October 31.

LESSON SIX TEST/REVIEW

Part 1   Find the mistakes with adjective clauses, and correct them. Not every sentence has a mistake. If the sentence is correct, write *C*.

EXAMPLES: The students should correct the mistakes that they make ~~them~~.

The students about whom we were speaking entered the room.   *C*

1. The teacher what we have is from Canada.

2. Five students were absent on the day when was given the TOEFL test.

3. The room where we took the test was not air-conditioned.

4. Who missed the test can take it next Friday.

5. Students who knows a lot of English grammar can take a composition course.

6. The teacher whose class I'm taking speaks English clearly.

7. A tutor is a person whom helps students individually.

8. Everyone wants to have a teacher whose pronunciation is clear.

9. The student whose sitting next to me is trying to copy my answers.

10. A teacher helped me at registration who speaks my language.

11. The teacher gave a test had 25 questions.

12. The student which sits near the door always leaves early.

13. Do you know anyone, who has a German car?

14. The textbook we are using has a lot of exercises.

15. The people, who live upstairs of me, make a lot of noise in the morning.

Part 2   Fill in each blank to complete the adjective clause.

EXAMPLES: A. Do you like your new roommate?

B. Not really. The roommate *I had last year*   was much nicer.

A. Do you remember the names of all the students?

B. No. There are some students *whose names I can't remember.*

1. A. I heard you had a car accident. You hit another car.

    B. Yes. The woman whose _____ wants me to pay her $700.

2. A. My office uses IBM computers.

    B. Not mine. The computers _____ are Macintosh.

3. A. Did you buy your textbooks at Berk's Bookstore?

    B. No. The store _____ is about ten blocks from school. Books are cheaper there.

4. A. My husband's mother always interferes in our married life.

    B. That's terrible. I wouldn't want to be married to a man whose

    _____

5. A. Do you have a black-and-white TV?

    B. Of course not. I don't even know anyone _____ anymore.

6. A. What did the teacher say about registration?

    B. I don't know. She spoke very fast. I didn't understand everything

    _____

7. A. Did you buy that coat in the U.S.?

    B. No. I bought it during the time _____

8. A. The teacher is talking about a very famous American, but I didn't hear his name.

    B. The man _____ is Martin Luther King, Jr.

9. A. Did you buy the dictionary I recommended to you?

    B. No. The dictionary _____ is just as good as the one you recommended.

10. A. Are there any teachers at this school _____?

    B. Yes. Ms. Lopez speaks Spanish.

Part 3   Complete each statement. Every sentence should have an adjective clause.

✓   EXAMPLE: **The library is a place** _where you can read._____

1. The teacher _____ doesn't teach here anymore.

2. Everything _____ is important to me.

3. Teachers _____ aren't good for foreign students.

4. The teacher will not pass a student whose _____

5. I would like to live in a house _____

6. The classroom _____ is clean and pleasant.

7. Saturday is usually the day _____

Part 4   Combine each pair of sentences into one sentence. Use the words in parentheses ( ) to add a nonessential adjective clause to the first sentence.

EXAMPLE: **Puerto Ricans are American citizens. (Their native language is Spanish.)**

_Puerto Ricans, whose native language is Spanish, are American citizens._____

1. Alaska was purchased from Russia. (Gold was discovered there in 1896.)

_____

2. My friend lives in Alaska. (It is the largest state in the U.S.)

_____

3. Mr. Smith lives in Alaska. (You met his wife.)

_____

4. Mr. Jones comes from Alaska. (You saw him at the party.)

_____

Part 5   Shorten each adjective clause by crossing out unnecessary words.

EXAMPLE: **Thanksgiving, ~~which is~~ an American holiday, is in November.**

1. The English that is spoken in the U.S. is different from British English.

2. A lot of Americans like to eat at McDonald's, which is a fast-food restaurant.

3. Do not disturb the students who are studying in the library.

4. In the U.S. there are many immigrants who are from Mexico.

Extra Credit

Part 6   Write *E* if the adjective clause is essential. Write *NE* if the adjective clause is nonessential. Put in commas for the nonessential adjective clauses.

EXAMPLES: **The last article we read was about Alaska.** *E*

Alaska, which is the largest state, has the smallest

population. *NE*

1. Puerto Ricans who live in Puerto Rico cannot vote in a national election. _____

2. Puerto Rico which is a very small island has a tropical climate. _____

3. A piece of land which is surrounded by water is called an island. _____

4. I don't like teachers who give a lot of homework. _____

5. Ms. Kessell who is studying Spanish understands how hard it is to learn

   another language. _____

Part 7   Complete each statement with an adjective clause. You may use *who, whom, that, which, whose, when,* or *where* to introduce the adjective clause. (In some cases, no word is necessary to introduce the adjective clause.)

EXAMPLES: I have a friend *I can trust with my secrets.*

I like magazines *that have pictures of the latest fashions.*

New Year's Eve is a time *when I get together with my friends and drink*

champagne.

There are some students *whose names I can't remember.*

1. Most women want to marry a man _____

2. I don't like teachers _____

3. The President is a person _____

4. English is a language _____

5. The U.S. is a country _____

6. A day-care center is a place _____

7. Alaska is a state _____

8. I don't know anyone _____

9. (Fill in the name of a special day or holiday in your country.)

_____ is a time _____

LESSON SEVEN

GRAMMAR

Infinitives
Causative Verbs

CONTEXT

Drunk Driving
Great Expectations
A College Education
Advertising

Lesson Focus Infinitives; Causative Verbs

- An infinitive is *to* + the base form of the verb. An infinitive can be used in these patterns:

    He decided *to leave* his country. (after a verb)
    His parents wanted him *to get* an American education. (after an object)
    To get a visa took four months. (as a subject)
    It was difficult *to say* goodbye. (after a phrase beginning with *it*)
    He's happy *to be* in the U.S. (after an adjective)

- After some causative verbs, the *to* of the infinitive is deleted.

    She *made* her daughter *clean* her room.
    She *had* the mechanic *fix* her car.

• •

R
E
A
D
I
N
G

Before you read

In your country, is the law strict about drunk driving?

Read the following article. Pay special attention to infinitives.

DRUNK DRIVING

Drunk driving is a factor in about 50% of all fatal[1] traffic accidents. Television ads have tried **to influence** drivers not **to drive** if they are going to drink. If a group of people is going to be drinking, one person should be the "designated driver." This means that one of the people in the group agrees not **to drink** so that he or she can drive the others to their destination. The others in the group are free **to drink.** Having a designated driver is especially important on a holiday, such as New Year's Eve, when people often drink a lot.

Of course, it is against the law for a person **to drive** while drunk. However, whether a person is considered drunk differs from state to state. Each local government decides what is an acceptable level of alcohol in the blood. In most states, if a person has a blood/alcohol concentration (BAC) of .10% or higher, he or she is considered too drunk **to drive.** When police suspect a driver of driving under the influence of alcohol, the driver may be asked **to get** out of the car and walk a straight line. Or the driver may be asked **to blow** into a machine that tests blood/alcohol concentration. A drunk driver may lose his or her license.

Mothers Against Drunk Drivers (MADD) is a citizens' organization that was started by a group of mothers whose children had been killed by drunk drivers. MADD tries **to get**

---

[1]A *fatal* accident results in a death.

lawmakers **to make** stricter laws against drunk driving. MADD also wants them **to crack down**[2] on advertising aimed at young people that makes drinking look attractive. They want local police departments **to declare** a driver drunk with a BAC of .08% or lower. In addition, this organization believes it is important **to educate** people about the consequences of drunk driving.

7.1 Verb Plus Infinitive

We use an infinitive in this pattern:

Subject	Verb	(Not)	Infinitive Phrase
He	appears		to be drunk.
I	decided		to drive.
They	agreed	not	to drink.

1. The verbs below can be followed by an infinitive:

agree	expect	need	refuse
appear	forget	offer	seem
be able	hope	plan	start*
begin*	know how	prefer*	tend
can('t) afford*	learn	prepare	try
choose	like*	pretend	want
decide	manage	promise	would like

*These verbs can also be followed by a gerund. See Lesson Eight.

2. In a sentence with two infinitives connected by *and*, the second *to* is usually omitted.

   I want *to read and write* English well.

---

[2]To *crack down* means to be strict with people who break a rule.

EXERCISE 1   Fill in each blank with an infinitive. Share your answers with the class.

    EXAMPLE: I like _to eat Chinese food._

    1. I don't like _____, but I have to do it anyway.

    2. I can't afford _____

    3. I've decided _____

    4. I want _____

    5. I sometimes forget _____

    6. I love _____

    7. I need _____ every day.

    8. I don't know how _____, but I'd like to learn.

EXERCISE 2   Find a partner. Ask each other these questions.

    EXAMPLE: Why did you want to leave your country?
               I wanted to leave my country because there is little opportunity
               for me to go to college there.

    1. Why did you want to leave your country?
    2. Why did you decide to come to the U.S.? To this city?
    3. What did you need to do before you left your country?
    4. Did you learn to speak English before you came to the U.S.?
    5. What did you expect to find or see in the U.S.?
    6. What do you hope to accomplish in the U.S.?
    7. Do you plan to go back to your country?
    8. Do you want to become an American citizen?

7.2 Object Before Infinitive

Some verbs can be followed by an object + infinitive.

Subject	Verb	Object	Infinitive Phrase
MADD	wants	lawmakers	to crack down on drunk drivers.
It	urges	them	to change the laws.
I	don't want	him	to drive.
They	expect	me	to be the designated driver.
I	expect	her	to be responsible.
Our parents	allowed	us	to use their car.

Language Notes

1. The verbs below can be followed by noun/pronoun + infinitive:

advise	encourage	persuade
allow	expect	select
appoint	forbid	teach*
ask	force	tell
beg	invite	urge
choose	need	want
convince	permit	would like

*After *teach, how* is often used: "He taught me (how) to ski."

2. *Let* and *permit*:

   Let is always followed by the base form.
   She let him *drive* her home.

   Permit or *allow* is followed by the infinitive.
   She permitted him *to drive* her home.
   She allowed him *to drive* her home.

3. *Help* can be followed by either the base form or the infinitive. The infinitive is more formal.

   The teacher helped me *write* a composition.
   OR
   The teacher helped me *to write* a composition.

EXERCISE 3   Tell if you want or don't want the teacher to do the following.

EXAMPLES: speak fast
I don't want the teacher to speak fast.

answer my questions
I want him to answer my questions.

1. explain the grammar
2. review modals
3. give us a lot of homework
4. give us a test on gerunds and infinitives
5. explain American customs
6. speak slowly
7. _____

EXERCISE 4   Tell if the teacher expects or doesn't expect you to do the following.

EXAMPLES: come on time
The teacher expects us to come on time.

wear a suit to class
The teacher doesn't expect us to wear a suit to class.

1. write perfect compositions
2. learn English in six months
3. do the homework
4. stand up to answer a question
5. raise our hands to answer a question

6. ask questions
7. study on Saturdays
8. practice English every day
9. speak English without an accent
10. _____

EXERCISE 5   Use the words given to tell what your family wanted from you when you were growing up.

EXAMPLES: want/come to the U.S.
My parents didn't want me to come to the U.S.

expect/get married
My mother expected me to get married as soon as I graduated from high school.

let/play a lot
My parents let me play a lot when I was young.

1. expect/respect older people
2. let/stay out late at night
3. want/come to the U.S.
4. expect/get good grades in school
5. encourage/have a lot of friends
6. want/be obedient
7. want/be independent

8. let/choose my own friends
9. expect/get married
10. encourage/be religious
11. advise/be honest
12. encourage/go to college
13. _____

· ·

R
E
A
D
I
N
G

Before you read

When you came to the U.S., what surprised you? What disappointed you?

Read the following article. Pay special attention to infinitives.

GREAT EXPECTATIONS

Before coming to the U.S., people usually have ideas about what they will see when they get there. Some people find that the U.S. is better than they expected. Others find that it is worse. Most people find that it is different from what they thought.

Many people say that they are **surprised to learn** that the streets are not made of gold. Others are **amazed to see** so many poor and homeless people in such a rich country. Some are **disappointed to find** that health care is so expensive. Other people are **surprised to find** out that there is so much crime and that people in some places are **afraid to walk** on the street at night.

On the other hand, some people are **delighted to learn** that things are not as bad as they thought. People who expected to see gangsters in Chicago are **happy to learn** that Al Capone[3] and his men have been gone for many years.

How did your expectations of life in the U.S. compare to the reality?

- -

7.3 Adjective Plus Infinitive

Some adjectives can be followed by an infinitive in this pattern.

Subject	*Be*	Adjective	Infinitive (Phrase)
I	am	afraid	to walk alone at night.
He	is	amazed	to see so many poor people.
They	are	happy	to be in the U.S.

Language Notes

1. The adjectives below can be followed by an infinitive.

afraid	happy	sad
ashamed	lucky	sorry
delighted	pleased	surprised
disappointed	prepared	willing
eager	proud	
glad	ready	

NOTE: Many of these adjectives describe an emotion or a mental state.

2. Notice how we respond when we are introduced to someone.

A. I'd like you to meet my brother.
B. (I'm) *pleased to meet* you.
A. (I'm) *glad to meet* you.

3. Notice how we respond to news of a death.

A. My father died last week.
B. I'm (so) *sorry to hear* about it.

---

[3]Al Capone was a famous Chicago gangster in the 1920s.

EXERCISE 6   Fill in each blank with an infinitive (phrase). Share your answers with the class.

       EXAMPLE: **Before I came to the U.S., I was afraid** *to speak English.*

1. When I left my country, I was eager _____

   _____

2. When I came to the U.S., I was surprised (to see, learn, find out) _____

   _____

3. When I lived in my country, I was afraid _____

   _____

4. In the U.S., I'm happy _____

5. In the U.S., I'm afraid _____

· ·

R
E
A   **Before you read**
D
I   1. Is a college education in your country expensive?
N   2. Can everyone go to college? Why or why not?
G

   Read the following article. Pay special attention to gerunds and infinitives as subjects.

A COLLEGE EDUCATION

   Nowadays it is very expensive **to go to college** in the U.S. During the past decade, college tuition rose much faster than the rate of inflation. At one time, it was inexpensive **to study** at a state university or a community college. However, tuition even at these schools has gone up considerably in the past few years. **To save for a child's education** takes many years. Often parents start to save for their child's college education as soon as the child is born.

   About 60% of American high school graduates attend college at some point in their lives. More than one-third of college students are over 25 years old. This indicates that many students can no longer rely on their parents to pay for their education; it is necessary for many people **to work and pay** for their own education or **to apply** for grants and loans. Over 50% of college students get financial aid. Two-fifths of all students are part-timers.

   Colleges get less money from the government than they used to. **Raising tuition** every year seems to be the primary way that colleges meet the cost of educating students.

· ·

7.4   Infinitive as Subject

An infinitive (phrase) can be the subject of a sentence.

Subject (Infinitive Phrase)	Verb	Complement
To attend college	is	expensive.
To save for college	takes	many years.

For + an object can be used to give the infinitive a specific subject.

It	*Be*	Adjective	*For* + Noun/Pronoun	Infinitive Phrase
It	is	hard	for a student	to work and go to school at the same time.
It	was	important	for me	to come to the U.S.

Beginning a sentence with an infinitive phrase is very formal. It is more common to use an infinitive phrase at the end of a clause and put *It* at the beginning of the sentence.

To save for college takes many years. (formal)
It takes many years *to save for college.* (informal)

To have a satisfying career is important. (formal)
It is important *to have a satisfying career.* (informal)

EXERCISE 7   Complete each statement with an infinitive (phrase).

EXAMPLES: It isn't polite . . .
             It isn't polite to interrupt a conversation.

             It's impossible . . .
             It's impossible for me to return to my country.

1. It's dangerous . . .
2. It isn't healthy . . .
3. It isn't polite . . .
4. It's illegal . . .
5. It's important for me . . .
6. It's boring for me . . .
7. It's fun for me . . .
8. It's easy for Americans . . .

EXERCISE 8   Make a sentence with the words given. Share your sentences with a small group or with the entire class.

     EXAMPLE: **dangerous/children**

         It's dangerous for children to play with matches.

     1. fun/children

     2. necessary/children

     3. important/a family

     4. difficult/a large family

     5. necessary/working parents

     6. difficult/women in my country

     7. hard/single parents

     8. difficult/the teacher

EXERCISE 9   Complete each statement.

     EXAMPLE: . . . to be perfect.
              It's impossible to be perfect.

     1. . . . to work hard.   4. . . . to make mistakes.
     2. . . . to fall in love.   5. . . . to be lonely.
     3. . . . to get married.   6. . . . to help other people.

EXERCISE 10   Complete each statement. Remember, statements that begin with an infinitive are very formal.

> **EXAMPLE: To succeed at one's job** _requires hard work._ _____
>
> 1. To find a job _____
>
> 2. To lose one's job _____
>
> 3. To raise children _____
>
> 4. To have a lot of friends _____
>
> 5. To travel _____
>
> 6. To meet new people _____
>
> 7. To do the same things every day _____

Language Notes

1. We can use *cost* + an infinitive in the following pattern.

It	Cost	(Object)	Price	Infinitive Phrase
It	costs		$150	to take this course.
It	cost	me	$500	to fix my car.

2. We can use *take* + an infinitive in the following pattern.

It	Take	(Object)	Time	Infinitive Phrase
It	takes		four hours	to fly from New York to Los Angeles.
It	took	him	five years	to finish college.

EXERCISE 11   Complete each statement by using *cost* (any tense). (NOTE: present = *it costs*; past = *it cost.*)

> **EXAMPLE: It** _cost me $75.00_ _____ **to buy my books.**
>
> 1. It _____ to come to the U.S.
>
> 2. It usually _____ to eat lunch in the cafeteria.
>
> 3. It _____ to take a taxi from downtown to my house.
>
> 4. It _____ to send a letter to my country.
>
> 5. It _____ to make a ten-minute long-distance call to my country.

EXERCISE 12 Complete each statement by using *take* (any tense).

EXAMPLES: It _will take me two years_ to get my bachelor's degree.

It _took me a half hour_ to do my homework.

1. It _____ to get to class.

2. It _____ to get ready to leave the house in the morning.

3. It _____ to come to the U.S.

4. It _____ to do my homework.

5. It _____ to learn English.

Language Notes

Too and Enough

1. *Too* can precede an adjective or adverb. *Too* shows that the adjective or adverb is excessive for a specific purpose. A *too* phrase is often followed by an infinitive.

> He's only fifteen years old. He's *too young to go* to college.
> She's from a poor family. She's *too poor to pay* for a college education.

2. With quantities, we use *too much* + noncount noun and *too many* + count noun.

> I can't help you today. I have *too many things to do.*
> She earns *too much money to get* financial aid.

3. *Enough* follows an adjective or adverb. It shows that the adjective or adverb is sufficient for a specific purpose. An *enough* phrase is often followed by an infinitive.

> She's *old enough to drive.*
> She speaks English *well enough to attend* an American university.

4. The infinitive phrase can be preceded by *for* + an object noun or pronoun.

> His grades are not good enough *for him to get* a scholarship.
> The exercise is short enough *for us to do* in five minutes.

5. *Enough* can be used with nouns. It usually precedes a noun, but it sometimes follows the noun.

> He has *enough money* to buy a car. (more common)
> He has *money enough* to buy a car. (less common)

6. The infinitive can sometimes be omitted.

> A. Can you help me this afternoon?
> B. I'm sorry. I can't. I'm *too busy.*

EXERCISE 13 Fill in each blank with an adjective or adverb and *too* or *enough*.

EXAMPLES: It's <u>*too late*</u> for a student to register for this semester.

I don't speak English <u>*well enough*</u> to be a translator.

1. I arrived _____ to hear the teacher's explanation.

2. This lesson is _____ to finish in fifteen minutes.

3. This exercise is _____ to finish in a few minutes.

4. The cafeteria is _____ for me to study there.

5. Some Americans speak English _____ for me to understand.

6. The bus is sometimes _____ for me to get a seat.

7. I (don't) type _____ to get a secretarial job.

8. It's _____ to go swimming today.

9. It's _____ to predict next week's weather.

10. She earns _____ to get a scholarship.

11. I can't go out with you. I have _____ things to do this afternoon.

• •

R
E
A
D
I
N
G

Before you read

1. What do you think of commercials on American TV? How are they different from commercials in your country?
2. Are you influenced by commercials or other kinds of ads?

Read the following article. Pay special attention to the verbs *get, persuade, make,* and *have.*

ADVERTISING

A company uses advertising to **get** consumers **to buy** its products. Ads (advertisements) are everywhere—on television, on the radio, in newspapers, in magazines, and on billboards. Advertising agencies believe that if they show you the same ad enough times, they can **make** you **prefer** a certain product. Ads

billboard

want to **persuade** you **to believe** that a product washes cleaner, lasts longer, protects you better, makes you more attractive, or impresses your friends.

Ads are not only for products; they are also for services. An ad may try to tell you where to **have** a muffler **installed,** where to get good legal advice, or where to **have** your eyes **examined.**

You have to use your own judgment and not let ads **persuade** you **to spend** money on something you do not need or want.

7.5 Causative Verbs

A *causative* verb shows that the subject causes another person to do something.

Subject	*Get/Persuade*	Object	Infinitive Phrase
Ads	persuade	you	to spend money.
Companies	get	you	to believe that their product is the best.

Subject	*Make/Have*	Object	Base Form + Complement
The robber	made	me	give him my wallet. (I had no choice.)
I	had	the mechanic	fix my car. (I paid him to do it.)
He	had	the optician	examine his eyes.

Subject	*Have/Got*	Object	Past Participle
I	had	my car	fixed.
He	got	his eyes	examined.

1. *Get* and *persuade* have the same meaning. These verbs are followed by an infinitive.

2. *Make* and *have* are followed by a base form. *Make* shows a much stronger influence of one person over another than *have* does.

3. *Have* or *get* can be used with a past participle for a passive meaning. The agent is usually omitted.

EXERCISE 14   Fill in each blank with an appropriate infinitive or base form.

EXAMPLE: **When I was a child, my parents made me** _wash the dishes after every_

meal.

1. The teacher had us _____ a composition.

2. We would like to persuade the teacher _____

3. When I was a child, my parents made me _____

4. It is hard to get children _____

EXERCISE 15   Answer the questions. Follow the pattern.

EXAMPLE: **Are you going to defend yourself in court? (a lawyer)**
I'm going to have a lawyer defend me.

1. Are you going to take your blood pressure yourself? (a nurse)
2. Are you going to prepare your tax form yourself? (an accountant)
3. Are you going to wash your windows yourself? (a window washer)
4. Are you going to watch your kids yourself? (a baby-sitter)
5. Are you going to install your phone yourself? (the phone company)

EXERCISE 16   Complete the sentences with a past participle.

EXAMPLE: **I went to a mechanic and had my car . . .**
I went to a mechanic and had my car fixed.

1. I went to a barber to get my hair . . .
2. I hired a painter and had the walls of my house . . .
3. I went to the bank and got my check . . .
4. I went to a photographer and had my picture . . .
5. I took my suit to the cleaner's to get it . . .
6. I went to the dentist to have my teeth . . .
7. I went to a mechanic to have the oil in my car . . .

An infinitive can be made passive as follows:

    Verb + *to be* + past participle

Compare:

ACTIVE: Someone needs to answer the question.
PASSIVE: The question needs *to be answered.*

ACTIVE: You have to sign the check.
PASSIVE: The check has *to be signed.*

EXERCISE 17   Fill in each blank with the passive infinitive of the verb in parentheses ( ).

EXAMPLE: I prefer ___*to be called*___ by my first name.
                              (call)

1. I don't like _____ what to do.
                        (tell)

2. She has _____ to the doctor immediately.
                   (take)

3. Children need _____ love.
                          (give)

4. The students want _____ if there will be a test.
                               (inform)

5. She doesn't want _____ in that awful dress.
                             (see)

EXPANSION ACTIVITIES

PROVERBS   1. The following proverb contains a causative verb. Discuss the meaning
                          of this proverb. Do you have a similar proverb in your language?

                          You can lead a horse to water, but you can't make it drink.

                    2. The following proverbs contain *too*. Discuss the meaning of each
                          proverb. Do you have a similar proverb in your language?

                          Too many cooks spoil the broth.
                          You're never too old to learn.

ACTIVITY   Find a partner. Talk about teachers and students in your countries. What
                       do students expect from teachers? What do teachers expect from stu-
                       dents? Compare your country to your partner's country and to the U.S.
                       Share some of your information with the class.

                       EXAMPLE: **Teachers expect students to call them by their title:**
                                         Professor.

FAMOUS   Discuss the meaning of the following sentences.
QUOTATIONS
                       "To err is human, to forgive divine." (Alexander Pope)
                       "To be or not to be, that is the question." (William Shakespeare)
                       "It's better to have loved and lost than never to have loved at all." (Alfred
                         Tennyson)

**OUTSIDE
ACTIVITIES**

1. Look through magazines and newspapers for ads. Find an interesting ad. Bring it to class and explain why you think the ad is clever or interesting.

2. Go to the reference desk at the library and ask to see the latest edition of one of the following books:

   Lovejoy's College Guide
   Cass and Birnbaum's Guide to American Colleges
   Peterson's Four-Year College Directory
   Peterson's Two-Year College Directory

   Look for the names of a few colleges or universities that interest you. Compare tuition costs and any other information you want to know about these colleges. Share this information with the class.

WRITING

1. Write about an expectation your parents had for you that you did not meet. Explain why you did not do what they expected.

2. Write about an expectation you have for your children (or future children).

3. Use the questions from Exercise 2 to write a short composition about yourself or about your partner. Read your composition to the class.

EDITING ADVICE

1. Don't forget *to* when introducing an infinitive.

   He needs ∧ leave.
   to

   It's necessary ∧ have a job.
   to

2. After the causative verbs *make, let,* and *have,* use the base form.

   He let me ⨉ borrow his car.

   She made her daughter ⨉ do her homework.

   I had the nurse ⨉ check my blood pressure.

3. Don't omit *it* when introducing an infinitive phrase.

   ∧ ⨉s important to know a second language.
   It i

4. After *want, need, expect,* and similar verbs, use the object pronoun followed by the infinitive.

   She wants ~~that I~~ speak English.
   me to

5. Use the correct word order after the causative verb *have.*

   He had ~~fix his car the mechanic.~~
   the mechanic fix his car.

   He needs to have ~~fixed his car.~~
   his car fixed.

6. With a compound infinitive, use the base form after *and.*

   He needed to finish the letter and ~~went~~ to the post office.
   go

SUMMARY OF LESSON SEVEN

1. An infinitive follows certain verbs.
   > I want *to go.*
   > I need *to leave.*
2. An object sometimes comes before an infinitive.
   > They wanted *me to help* them.
   > I expect *you to teach* me grammar.
3. *Let* and *help* are followed by a base form. (*Help* is sometimes followed by an infinitive.)
   > She let me *talk.*
   > I helped her *(to) move* the piano.
4. An infinitive can follow an adjective.
   > He's happy *to be* here.
   > I'm sorry *to see* you go.
5. An infinitive can be used with *too* and *enough.*
   > He's too young *to drink.*
   > He's old enough *to vote.*
6. An infinitive can be used as a subject.
   > It is expensive *to go* to college.
   > *To go* to college is expensive.
7. Use *for* + an object to give an infinitive a specific focus.
   > It's hard *for me* to read English.
8. An infinitive is used after *cost* + price and *take* + time.
   > It cost me $400 *to fly* to Miami.
   > It takes me ten minutes *to walk* to school.
9. After causative verbs *get* and *persuade,* an infinitive is used.
   > She got him *to marry* her.
   > He persuaded her *to give* him some money.
10. After causative verbs *make* and *have,* a base form is used.
    > The movie made her *cry.*
    > I had the mechanic *fix* my car.
11. After *have* and *get,* a past participle can be used.
    > I had my car *fixed.*
    > I'm going to get my hair *cut.*
12. An infinitive can be used in the passive voice.
    > The car needs *to be repaired.*

For a list of verbs that are followed by gerunds and infinitives, see Appendix D.

LESSON SEVEN TEST/REVIEW

Part 1   Find the mistakes with infinitives, and correct them. Not every sentence has a mistake. If the sentence is correct, write *C*.

EXAMPLES: He was surprised ∧ get the job.
                                    to

                    To make mistakes in English is natural.   *C*

1. She let me to use her phone.

2. I want that you call me.

3. Do you like to watch TV?

4. She's enough old to get married.

5. She wanted me to come early.

6. He decided to rent a car and drove to San Francisco.

7. It took me five minutes finish the job.

8. Is she old enough drive?

9. He helped me move the piano.

10. Live in a foreign country is difficult.

11. He had his car fix last week.

12. He had the mechanic fix his car.

13. It cost to me a lot of money to take this course.

14. She needs speak with you.

15. He learned how to speak English well.

16. I got her to tell me the secret.

17. The teacher made the student take the test a second time.

18. It was hard to me to find a job.

19. She persuaded her son to wash the dishes.

20. She got him to wash the dishes.

21. She made him to wash the dishes.

22. Costs a lot of money to buy a house.

Part 2   Fill in each blank to complete these sentences.

EXAMPLE: **I don't know how** *to speak Chinese.* _____

   1. When I was a child, my parents didn't let me _____

   2. When I was a child, my parents made me _____

   3. I'm too young _____

   4. The teacher wants _____ study before a test.

   5. Are you glad _____ in the U.S.?

   6. It's difficult _____ _____

   7. To _____ requires hard work.

   8. It's easy for _____ speak English.

   9. To be or (negative infinitive) ___ _____ ___, that is the question.

  10. It _____ ten minutes to wash the floor this morning.

  11. I went to a photographer and had my picture _____

  12. This check needs to _____ before you can cash it.

  13. She decided to stay home and _____ a book.

  14. _____ to work full time and go to school.

  15. He went to the barber and got his hair _____

LESSON EIGHT

GRAMMAR

Gerunds

CONTEXT

Illegal Aliens
Driving to California
Changes
Seasons

Lesson Focus Gerunds

A gerund is formed by putting an *-ing* ending on a verb. A gerund is used as a noun (as a subject, object of a verb, or object of a preposition).

Subject	Verb Phrase		Gerund Subject	Verb Phrase	
Tennis	is fun.		Swimming	is fun.	

S	Verb	Object		S	Verb	Gerund Object	
I	enjoy	conversation.		I	enjoy	talking.	

S	Verb	Prep.	Object		S	Verb	Prep.	Gerund Object
I	dreamed	about	a mountain.		I	dreamed	about	falling.

• •

R
E
A
D
I
N
G

Before you read:

Are there groups of foreigners who want to enter your country? From what country? Why do they want to go to your country?

Read the following article. Pay special attention to gerunds.

ILLEGAL ALIENS

Illegal aliens are foreigners who do not have permission to live in the U.S. Some foreigners come to the U.S. with a visa but do not leave when their visa has expired. Others simply cross the border **without obtaining** any permission at all. Undocumented workers are foreigners who work in the U.S. without permission.

The government estimates that as many as 400,000 illegal aliens enter the U.S. each year and that the population of "illegals" in the U.S. is between 2 million and 4 million. It is impossible to know the exact number of illegals because of the difficulty **in counting them.**

It is believed that about 85–90% of illegals come from Mexico. Most plan **on finding** jobs in the U.S. because wages in Mexico are 60% lower than in the U.S. They usually enter the U.S. **by crossing** the border on foot at night. The U.S. government tries to prevent these people **from crossing** the border. However, it is almost impossible to do an effective job. The border between the U.S. and Mexico is about 2,000 miles long, but there are only 300 border patrol guards responsible **for patrolling** this area. About 3,000 Mexicans cross the border every day into the U.S., and only one-third of these are caught and returned to their country. The rest succeed **in entering** the U.S. At best, the U.S. government only limits the number.

The U.S. has even more trouble **finding** people who come with short-term visas and stay. It is believed that about 50% of people who enter with limited visas stay permanently.

Some Americans complain that undocumented workers take jobs away from American citizens and legal residents. However, most American citizens would not consider **working** at such difficult or low-paying jobs.

In general, most people who break the immigration laws do so because they are looking for a better life for themselves and their families. While the U.S. often accepts political refugees, it often turns away "economic" refugees, people who face serious economic hardships in their countries. **Coming** to the U.S. seems like the only choice they have.

8.1 Gerund as Subject

A gerund (phrase) can be the subject of the sentence.

Subject (Gerund Phrase)	Verb	Complement
Entering the U.S. without a visa	is	illegal.
Patrolling the border between the U.S. and Mexico	is	difficult.

1. A gerund subject takes a singular verb.
   Counting illegal aliens *is* difficult.
2. To make a gerund negative, *not* is put before the gerund.
   Not knowing English makes me feel bad.

3. Remember, an infinitive can also be used as a subject. COMPARE:
   Counting illegal aliens is difficult.
   It is difficult *to count illegal aliens.*
   To count illegal aliens is difficult.

It is very formal to begin a sentence with an infinitive. It is more common to use a gerund or *it* + infinitive phrase.

from: Grammar in Context 2nd ed. #3
Sandra N. ELBaum   pp. 226-139

EXERCISE 1   Complete each statement. Share your answers.

>   EXAMPLE: Leaving my country . . .
>   Leaving my country was the most difficult decision I have ever
>   made.

1. Living in the U.S _____

2. Making new friends _____

3. Not understanding American customs _____

4. Learning a new language _____

5. Finding an apartment _____

6. Thinking about my country ___ _____

7. Getting a college education _____

8. _____

EXERCISE 2   Complete each statement with a gerund (phrase) as the subject. Share your
answers.

>   EXAMPLE: . . . relaxes me at the end of the day.
>   Taking a warm bath relaxes me at the end of the day.

1. _____ is important for everyone.

2. _____ is difficult for foreigners.

3. _____ is an important decision in a person's life.

4. _____ is against the law.

5. _____ is a healthy activity.

6. _____ is not polite.

7. _____ isn't good for you. (is an unhealthy activity)

8. _____ takes a long time.

8.2 Gerund After Verb

In Lesson Seven, we saw that some verbs are usually followed by an infinitive (phrase).

Subject	Verb	Infinitive Phrase
They	want	to come to the U.S.
She	expects	to get her visa soon.

Some verbs are commonly followed by a gerund (phrase).

Subject	Verb	Gerund Phrase
I	enjoy	living in the U.S.
She	considered	going to Canada.

Some verbs can be followed by either a gerund or an infinitive with almost no difference in meaning.

Subject	Verb	Gerund or Infinitive
He	likes	living in the U.S.
He	likes	to live in the U.S.

Language Notes

1. The verbs below are followed by a gerund.

admit	can't help*	discuss	imagine	permit	quit	suggest
advise	consider	dislike	keep	postpone	recommend	
appreciate	delay	enjoy	mind*	practice	regret	
avoid	deny	finish	miss	put off	risk	

2. *Go* + gerund is used in many idiomatic expressions.

go boating	go dancing	go hunting	go shopping	go skiing
go bowling	go fishing	go jogging	go sightseeing	go swimming
go camping	go hiking	go sailing	go skating	

She *went fishing* last Saturday.
She *goes shopping* every Thursday.

3. The verbs below can be followed by either a gerund or an infinitive.

attempt	can't stand*	deserve	like	prefer
begin	continue	hate	love	start

He likes *driving*.
He likes *to drive*.

4. Study the definitions of starred verbs.

- *Can't help* means to have no control: "When I see a sad movie, I can't help crying."
- *Mind* is a verb. *I mind* means that something bothers me. *I don't mind* means that something is OK with me; it doesn't bother me: "Do you mind living with your parents?" "No, I don't mind."

EXERCISE 3   Complete the sentences with a gerund (phrase). Share your answers.

> EXAMPLE: I avoid . . .
>   I avoid walking alone at night.

1. The teacher doesn't permit . . .
2. I don't mind . . .
3. It's difficult to quit . . .
4. I enjoy . . .
5. I don't enjoy . . .

6. I need to start . . .
7. I don't like to go . . .
8. I can't stand . . .
9. Everyone appreciates . . .

Review verbs followed by an infinitive in the last lesson before doing Exercise 4.

EXERCISE 4   Fill in each blank with the gerund or infinitive of the verb in parentheses ( ).
In some cases, either a gerund or an infinitive may be used.

A. When did you begin __*studying/to study*__ English?
                       (study)

B. When I was in high school. I continued _____ it in college, but I
                                             (1 study)

   didn't start _____ it until I came to the U.S.
                  (2 speak)

A. Do you like _____ English now?
                 (3 study)

B. Yes. But I'm shy, and I avoid _____ with Americans.
                                  (4 talk)

A. You'll never learn _____ English if you don't practice.
                        (5 speak)

B. But I'm afraid of making mistakes.

A. A foreigner can't help _____ some mistakes. It's only natural. You
                            (6 make)

   can't expect _____ perfect.
                  (7 be)

B. You're right, of course. How about you? Do you enjoy _____ English?
                                                          (8 speak)

A. Yes. My English is not perfect, but I manage _____ with Americans.
                                                  (9 communicate)

   But I dislike _____ homework. I don't mind _____ in the
                   (10 do)   (11 fill)

   blanks in a grammar exercise, but I hate _____ a composition.
                                              (12 write)

B. Me too. I always put off _____ it until the night before.
                             (13 do)

8.3 Gerund After Preposition

A gerund can be used as the object of a preposition in several patterns.

PATTERN A:

Subject	Verb	Prep.	Gerund Phrase
I	thought	about	coming to the U.S.
I	plan	on	going back to my country some day.

PATTERN B:

Subject	Verb	Adjective	Prep.	Gerund Phrase
He	was	successful	in	getting his visa.
Guards	are	responsible	for	patrolling the border.

PATTERN C:

Subject	Verb	Object	Prep.	Gerund Phrase
They	prevented	him	from	entering the U.S.
They	suspected	him	of	not having a work permit.

Language Notes

1. These are some common verb + preposition combinations:

care about	talk about	look forward to*	plan on*
complain about	think about	object to	believe in
dream about	worry about	depend on (or upon)	succeed in
forget about	adjust to	insist on (or upon)	

2. These are some common adjective + preposition combinations:

afraid of*	concerned about	accustomed (or used) to	good at
fond of*	excited about	responsible for	(un)successful at
proud of*	upset about	famous for	interested in
tired of	worried about	grateful to . . . for	

3. These are some common verb + preposition combinations that take an object:

accuse . . . of	blame . . . for	stop . . . from
suspect . . . of	thank . . . for	warn . . . about
apologize to . . . for	prevent . . . from	

4. Study the starred verbs.

- *Look forward to* means to wait for a future event, usually with pleasure: "I look forward to seeing my sister next month." (In this expression, *to* is not the beginning of an infinitive but a preposition.)
- *Plan* can also be followed by an infinitive: "I plan *to go*," "I plan *on going*."
- *Afraid* can also be followed by an infinitive: "I'm afraid *to go* out," "I'm afraid *of going* out."
- *Fond of* means to like very much: "I'm fond *of gardening*."
- *Proud* can also be followed by an infinitive: "I'm proud *to be* an American. I'm proud *of passing* my citizenship test."

EXERCISE 5   Complete the sentences with a gerund (phrase). Share your answers.

EXAMPLE: **I plan on . . .**
I plan on getting a degree in electrical engineering.

1. I (don't) believe in . . .
2. I'm sometimes afraid of . . .
3. I'm grateful to my parents for . . .
4. I hope I will succeed in . . .
5. I'm not accustomed to . . .
6. I'm (not) very good at . . .
7. When I finish this course, I plan on . . .

Language Notes

1. We use a gerund after the preposition in the following expressions.

in danger of	reason for
in favor of	technique for
need for	

What was your *reason for coming* to the U.S.?
Many factory workers are *in danger of losing* their jobs.

2. We use a gerund after the noun in the following expressions.

have a difficult time	have a hard time
have difficulty	have a problem
have experience	have trouble
have fun	spend time
have a good time	there's no use

I had *trouble getting* a visa.
I had a *hard time getting* to the U.S.

EXERCISE 6   Complete the questions with a gerund (phrase). Find a partner. Ask your partner these questions.

> EXAMPLE: **Are you lazy about . . .?**
>   **A. Are you lazy about writing compositions?**
>   **B. Yes, I am.**

1. Are you tired of . . .
2. Are you worried about . . .
3. Do you ever complain about . . .
4. Are you interested in . . .
5. Do you have a hard time . . .
6. What is (was) your reason for . . .
7. After class, do you ever spend time . . .

EXERCISE 7   Fill in each blank with a preposition (if necessary) and the gerund of the verb in parentheses ( ). In some cases, no preposition is necessary.

A. I'm worried __*about*__ __*losing*__ my job. A lot of workers in my factory are in
                    (lose)

   danger _____ _____ laid off.
               (1 get)

B. I don't blame you _____ _____ worried. These are hard times. Have
                   (2 be)

   you thought _____ _____ a new career?
               (3 start)

A. I'd have to go back to school to retrain. I'd have a hard time

   _____ now that I'm married and have children.
         (4 study)

B. Maybe you could take a short course. It doesn't take long to study to be a
   licensed practical nurse.

A. I'm not interested _____ _____ a nurse.
              (5 become)

B. What about medical records?

A. I'm not good _____ _____ with records. Besides, I can't spend time
            (6 work)

   _____ to school, even for six months. I need a job right away.
   (7 go)

B. Well, I don't know what to tell you. I hope you succeed _____ _____ a
                         (8 find)

   job soon.

EXERCISE 8   Ask a question with the words given. Use the correct preposition (if necessary) and a gerund. Another student will answer.

> EXAMPLES: fond/read
> > A. **Are you fond of reading?**
> > B. **Yes, I am.**
>
> > care/get a good grade
> > A. **Do you care about getting a good grade?**
> > B. **Of course I do.**

1. accustomed/eat American food
2. in favor/prohibit smoking at this school
3. have trouble/understand Americans
4. lazy/do the homework
5. have a technique/learn new words
6. afraid/fail this course
7. good/spell English words
8. interested/study computer programming
9. have experience/translate
10. think/buy a house some day

Language Notes

1. Some adverbial phrases contain a preposition followed by a gerund.

   He came to the U.S. *by crossing* the border
   He came to the U.S. *without obtaining* permission.

2. Adverbial phrases can begin with these words:

after	in addition to
before	instead of
by	without

EXERCISE 9   Answer each question with *by* + a gerund phrase.

> EXAMPLE: **How can you get a good grade?**
> > **By studying hard, coming to class, and doing the homework.**

1. How can you learn a foreign language?
2. How can you get rich?
3. How can you lose weight?
4. How can you find out today's temperature?
5. How can you improve your accent?
6. How can you find out the meaning of a new word?

EXERCISE 10   Fill in each blank with a gerund (phrase).

EXAMPLE: After *jogging in the park*_____, I always feel good.

1. After _____, I always need a rest.

2. Before _____, I need to study.

3. I can't read an English novel without _____

4. You can type your homework instead of _____

5. In addition to _____ English, I would also like to learn

   _____ (*fill in a subject*)

6. It's hard to find a good job without _____

7. You can increase your vocabulary by _____.

R
E
A
D
I
N
G

Before you read:

Do you think parents should give advice to their grown children? Why or why not?

Read the following conversation between a son (S) and his mother (M). Notice that **stop** and **remember** are sometimes followed by an infinitive and sometimes followed by a gerund.

DRIVING TO CALIFORNIA

S. Hi, Mom. I'm calling to say good-bye. I'm leaving tomorrow.
M. Where are you going?
S. To California.
M. You didn't tell me.
S. Of course I did. I **remember telling** you about it when I was at your house for dinner last week.
M. Oh, yes. Now I **remember hearing** you say something about it. Are you flying?
S. No, I'm driving with a friend.
M. Are you driving straight through?[1]
S. Yes.
M. If you get tired, you can **stop to rest** at a rest area. You should **stop to get** a cup of coffee every few hours.

---

[1]*Straight through* means *directly,* without a stop.

S. I will.

M. Don't **stop to pick up** hitchhikers. It could be dangerous.

S. I won't.

M. Did you **remember to check** the oil and tire pressure?

S. Yes, I did.

M. **Remember to call** me when you get there. Otherwise I'll worry.

S. **Stop worrying** so much. And **stop giving** me so much advice. I'm 24 years old!

M. I can't help it. I'm your mother.

• •

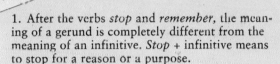

1. After the verbs *stop* and *remember*, the meaning of a gerund is completely different from the meaning of an infinitive. *Stop* + infinitive means to stop for a reason or a purpose.

> You should *stop to get* a cup of coffee if you're sleepy.
> We're going to *stop to rest*.

Stop + gerund means to quit or discontinue doing something.

> *Stop worrying* so much, Mother.
> *Stop giving* me advice.

2. *Remember* + infinitive means to remember to do something later. First you remember; then you do something.

> *Remember to check* your oil.
> *Remember to call* me.

Remember + gerund means to remember that something happened earlier. First you do something; then you remember that you did it.

> I *remember telling* you about my trip last week. (I remember that I told you.)
> Oh, yes. Now I *remember hearing* something about it.

EXERCISE 11   Fill in each blank with an appropriate infinitive.

EXAMPLE: Remember _to put air in_ your tires before you leave on a car trip.

1. Remember _____ your oil.

2. Remember _____ your gas tank.

3. Remember _____ a map.

4. Remember _____ me a postcard.

5. Don't stop _____ hitchhikers.

6. Stop _____ a cup of coffee if you're tired.

7. Stop _____ at a motel if you are very tired.

8. Don't stop _____ a drink (alcohol) while you're traveling by car.

EXERCISE 12   Fill in each blank with an appropriate gerund.

> **EXAMPLE:** Stop _giving me_____ advice. I'm 24 years old!

1. Stop _____ me what to do.

2. You worry too much. Stop _____.

3. She doesn't remember _____ about her son's trip.

4. He remembers _____ his mother about the trip.

5. She won't stop _____ her son questions.

6. She won't stop _____ about her son until he calls her from California.

7. Do you remember _____ advice from your parents when you were young?

EXERCISE 13   Fill in each blank with the gerund or infinitive of the verb in parentheses ( ).

> **EXAMPLES:** Stop _bothering_ me. I'm trying to study.
> (bother)
>
> The teacher always says, "Remember _to do_ your homework."
> (do)

1. When the teacher came in, the students stopped _____.
(talk)

2. The teacher usually remembers _____ the homework papers.
(return)

3. When you learn more English, you will stop _____ your dictionary so much.
(use)

4. You should remember _____ an infinitive after certain verbs.
(use)

5. When you're tired of studying, stop _____ a break.
(take)

6. Will you remember _____ the homework during Christmas vacation?
(do)

7. Do you remember _____ the passive voice last month?
(learn)

8. Remember _____ the passive voice when the subject does not
(use)

perform the action of the verb.

9. I remember not _____ much English when I arrived in the U.S.
(understand)

10. I remember _____ the present perfect tense even though I don't
       (study)
    always use it correctly.

11. I saw my friend in the hall, and I stopped _____ to her.
                                                  (speak)

12. My sister and I had a fight, and we stopped _____ to each other. We
                                                   (speak)
    haven't spoken to each other for two weeks.

• •

R
E
A   **Before you read:**
D
I   What are some experiences you have had in the U.S. that you never had before?
N
G   Read the following conversation between an American (A) and a foreign student
    (F). Notice that *used* is sometimes followed by an infinitive and sometimes fol-
    lowed by a gerund or noun.

CHANGES

A. I know you're from Russia. What city are you from?
F. I'm from Leningrad.
A. Why do you say Leningrad? Isn't the name of your city St. Petersburg?
F. The name was changed in 1991. But I can't **get used to saying** St. Petersburg
   after saying Leningrad for so many years.
A. How do you like living in the U.S.?
F. I can't **get used to** the hot summers here.
A. Don't you have a summer season in St. Petersburg?
F. Yes, but the summers there are mild. It's never as humid as it is here.
A. I heard your winters are very dark. There's very little sunlight. I don't think I'd
   like that.
F. Yes. Our winters are very dark, but it doesn't bother me. I'**m used to it.**
A. How was your life different there?
F. I **used to live** with my wife, my daughter, and my wife's parents—three gener-
   ations lived in one apartment. Now her parents live separate from us. And our
   daughter went away to college. There **used to be** five of us in two rooms. Now
   there are two of us in five rooms!
A. How else was your life different?
F. We **used to spend** a lot of time waiting in line. There was very little to buy in
   the market. Here I'm in and out of a supermarket in a short time.
A. So you think the food situation here is better?

F. Of course. You have lots of food. But I'**m not used to eating** some kinds of American food. You Americans like everything fast. You buy frozen food, put it in the microwave, and have a meal ready in five minutes. In my opinion, this is not food.

A. Are there any other differences?

F. Yes. In Russia, we didn't have a car. We **used to go** everywhere by bus or metro (subway). Here we have a car. I never use public transportation here. I've **gotten used to driving** everywhere.

A. So your life here is better, isn't it?

F. Well, in spite of all the conveniences here, it's still hard to **get used to living** in a new country.

8.4 *Used to/Be Used to/Get Used to*

Compare:

Subject	*Used to*	+	Base Form	Rest of Sentence
I	used to		live	with my whole family, but now I live alone.
I	used to		take	public transportation. Now I have a car.

Subject	*Be Used to*	+	Gerund/Noun	Rest of Sentence
He	isn't used to		eating	American food. He's never eaten frozen food before.
He	is used to		dark winters	because he has experienced them all his life.

Language Notes

1. *Used to* + a base form shows that an activity was repeated or habitual in the past. This activity has usually been discontinued.

> He *used to live* in Russia. Now he lives in the U.S.
> He *didn't use to own* a car.

NOTE: Omit the *d* in the negative form.

2. *Be used to* + a gerund or noun means "be accustomed to."

> American are *used to eating* fast food.
> Alaskans are *used to a cold climate.*

3. *Get used to* + gerund or noun means "become accustomed to."

> It's hard to *get used to the customs* of another country.
> The Russian man has been saying Leningrad all his life. He can't *get used to saying* St. Petersburg.

4. The *d* in *used to* is not pronounced.

EXERCISE 14   Write sentences comparing the way you used to live in your country with the way you live now.

EXAMPLES: *I used to live with my whole family. Now I live alone.*

I used to work in a restaurant. Now I am a full-time student.

I didn't use to speak English at all. Now I speak English pretty well.

Ideas for sentences:

school	job	hobbies
apartment/house	family life	friends

1. _____

2. _____

3. _____

4. _____

5. _____

EXERCISE 15   Fill in the blanks with four different answers.

Examples: When I came to the U.S., it was hard for me to get used to:

living in a small apartment.

American pronunciation

When I came to the U.S., it was hard for me to get used to:

1. _____

2. _____

3. _____

4. _____

• •

Before you read:

1. What is your favorite season? Why?
2. Are the seasons in this city different from the seasons in your hometown?

Read the following article. Pay special attention to sense-perception verbs and the words that follow them.

SEASONS

Fall is a beautiful season in many parts of the U.S. The New England states[2] have an especially beautiful fall season. Many people go there to see the fall colors. If you spend a few weeks there, you can observe the leaves **changing** colors. Then you will see the leaves **falling** from the trees. It is such a pretty time of year that you will see many tourists **taking** pictures of the trees.

Another beautiful seasonal change occurs in Washington, D.C., in the spring. There are many cherry trees, and people like to see the flowers **blooming** on the trees.

Skiers like the winter season. When they see the snow **falling,** they look forward to taking their ski equipment and going to the nearest hilly or mountainous area. Others prefer cross-country skiing, which is done on flat land.

Summer is the season when families take vacations together. You will often see recreational vehicles (RVs) and cars **pulling** campers on the highways as people leave the cities to look for the beauty of nature.

• •

8.5 Sense-Perception Verbs

Sense-perception verbs are: *hear, listen to, feel, smell, see, watch, observe, notice.* After sense-perception verbs, two patterns are used.

Subject	Sense Verb	Object	Base Form
I	saw	the child	fall.

Subject	Sense Verb	Object	*-ing* Form[3]
I	saw	the leaves	falling.

---

[2]The New England states are in the northeast section of the U.S.

[3]The *-ing* form in this case is not a gerund. It is a present participle. I saw her *stealing* the money means "I saw her while she *was stealing* the money."

1. The base form shows that one sensed (saw, heard, etc.) a completed action.

   I *heard* her *sing* at the concert.
   (I heard the whole thing.)

2. The *-ing* form shows that something is sensed while it is in progress.

   I *smell* something *burning*.
   (I smell it now. It's burning now.)

EXERCISE 16 Fill in each blank with an *-ing* form.

(Two teachers are talking.)

A. I'm upset with one of my students.

B. What happened?

A. I was giving a test, and I saw two students _cheating_.

B. Are you sure?

A. Yes. I noticed one student _____ a note to another student.
   (1)

B. Are you sure it was an answer on the test?

A. Yes. And I heard them _____ to each other.
   (2)

B. Did you tell them to stop?

A. As soon as they saw me _____ at them, they stopped talking.
   (3)

Sometimes the gerund has a subject that is different from the subject of the sentence.

1. In formal English, we give the gerund a subject by adding a possessive form.

  I thought about *my son's* going to California.
  I don't remember *his* telling me about the trip.
  He's upset about *my* asking so many
    questions.

2. In informal, conversational English, people often put the object form before a gerund.

  I thought about *my son* going to California.
  I don't remember *him* telling me about the trip.
  He's upset about *me* asking so many questions.

EXERCISE 17   Fill in each blank with a possessive form + gerund to complete the statements.

> **EXAMPLE:** **My neighbors make a lot of noise. I'm upset about** _their making_
>
> **so much noise. I'm tired of** _their playing_ **their music so loud.**

1. A. I found a job.

   B. I'm happy about _____ a job.

2. A. My mother-in-law is coming to visit.

   B. I bet your husband is upset about _____.

3. My parents are finally coming to the U.S. I always dreamed about

   _____ some day.

4. My son likes to go out with his friends every night. I'm worried about

   _____ every night.

5. My brother's going to visit next month. I'm really looking forward to

   _____ time with my family.

6. Our teacher gives so much homework. Some of the students complained about

   _____ us to write three compositions in one week.

7. You complain too much. I'm tired of _____ about everything I do.

8. I told you that your boyfriend likes to drink a lot. Don't tell me that I didn't

   warn you about _____.

9. My neighbor's children broke my vase. Do you think the parents should be

   responsible for _____ the vase?

A gerund can be made passive as follows:
Being (or *Getting*) + Past Participle
An illegal alien risks *getting caught*.
He's in danger of *being sent* back to his country.

EXERCISE 18 Fill in each blank with the passive gerund of the verb in parentheses ( ).

EXAMPLE: I'm afraid of ___*being told*___ that my composition is no good.

(tell)

1. I dislike _____

(criticize)

2. I enjoy _____ a compliment.

(give)

3. I'm tired of _____ what to do.

(tell)

4. She's afraid of _____ from her job.

(fire)

5. I don't mind _____ when I make a mistake.

(correct)

6. I dislike _____ at.

(laugh)

7. He's in danger of _____ by the police.

(catch)

EXPANSION ACTIVITIES

PROVERB   The following proverb contains a gerund. Discuss the meaning of this proverb. Do you have a similar proverb in your language?

There's no use crying over spilled milk.

DISCUSSIONS   1. Fill in the blank. Discuss your answer in a small group or with the entire class.

Before I came to the U.S., I used to believe that _____, but it's not true.

2. Fill in each blank. Discuss your answers with your classmates.

A. People in my country are not used to _____

B. Americans are not used to _____

C. I'm used to _____ because I've done it all my life.

D. I'm not used to _____ because _____.

3. Describe an interesting event that you experienced (a sporting event you attended, a crime you witnessed, a performance you saw, an earthquake you experienced). Write four sentences to describe this event. Share your sentences with the class.

EXAMPLES: There was an earthquake in my hometown in 1989. I felt the building shake. I saw my wife run to pick up the baby. I heard the baby crying.

In my country, there is a changing of the guard every hour in front of the palace. You can hear the clock strike the hour. You can see the soldiers marching. You see tourists taking pictures.

4. Fill in each blank. Discuss your answers in a small group or with the entire class.

EXAMPLE: In my country, I was worried about _giving my political_ _opinion_, but I'm not worried about it in the U.S.

A. In the U.S., I worry about _____, but I never worried about it before.

B. In my country, I had difficulty _____, but I don't anymore.

C. In the U.S., I have difficulty _____, but I never had this problem in my country.

WRITING

1. Write a paragraph or short essay telling how your life in the U.S. is different from your life in your country.

2. Write a paragraph or short essay telling how life in your country in general has changed over the last twenty to fifty years.

3. Write about a belief you used to have that you no longer have. What made you change your belief?

EDITING ADVICE

1. Use a gerund or an infinitive, not a base form, as a subject.

   Finding
   ~~Find~~ a good job takes time.

2. Be careful with *used to* and *be used to*.

   I ~~X~~ used to live in New York. Now I live in Boston.

   I've lived alone all my life. I ᵢₘ₎used to liv*ing* alone.

3. Be careful after *stop*.

   His doctor told him to stop ~~X~~ smok*ing*.

4. Don't use an infinitive after a sense-perception verb.

   I saw the child ~~X~~ leave the school.

5. Use a gerund after a preposition.

   He got a ticket for driv*ing* without a seat belt.

SUMMARY OF LESSON EIGHT

Using Gerunds

1. A gerund follows certain verbs.
   I enjoy *swimming*.
   I dislike *taking* tests.
2. A gerund is used in many idiomatic expressions with *go*.
   I went *shopping*.
   He goes *fishing* every Sunday.
3. A gerund is used after prepositions.
   I'm tired *of living* in the city.
   She complains *about driving* to work.
4. A gerund is used after certain nouns.
   He had difficulty *finding* an apartment.
   She has experience *working* with computers.
5. A possessive form or an object form can be used with a gerund.
   I don't mind *his leaving* early. (FORMAL)
   I don't mind *him leaving* early. (INFORMAL)
6. A gerund can be used in the passive voice.
   I dislike *being told* a lie.

Using a Gerund or an Infinitive

1. Some verbs can be followed by either a gerund or an infinitive with little or no difference in meaning.
   I like *to cook*.
   I like *cooking*.
2. A gerund or an infinitive can be used as a subject.
   It is expensive *to go* to college.
   To go to college is expensive.
   Going to college is expensive.
3. After sense-perception verbs, a base form indicates a completed action. An *-ing* form (present participle) indicates that the action was in progress as it was sensed.
   I saw the robber *enter* the bank. (= I saw the completed action.)
   I saw the robber *entering* the bank. (= I saw the robber as he was entering the bank.)
4. After *be used to* and *used to,* the meaning of the sentence with a gerund is completely different from the meaning of a sentence with an infinitive.
   I *used to live* with my family. Now I live alone.
   My American friend has lived alone all his adult life. He*'s used to living* alone.
5. After *stop* and *remember,* the meaning of the sentence with a gerund is completely different from the meaning of a sentence with an infinitive.
   I met my friend at the supermarket, and I stopped *to talk* to her.
   I had a fight with my neighbor, and I stopped *talking* to her.

Review infinitives in Lesson Seven. Also, for a list of words followed by gerunds and infinitives, see Appendix D.

LESSON EIGHT TEST/REVIEW

Part 1   Find the mistakes with gerunds, infinitives, and base forms, and correct them. Not every sentence has a mistake. If the sentence is correct, write *C*.

watching
EXAMPLES: **Do you enjoy ~~to watch~~ TV?**

Finding a good apartment is not easy.   *C*

1. After smoking for many years, he quit to smoke all of a sudden.

2. The teacher wants us to stop to talk when the test begins.

3. I like to cook, but I dislike to wash the dishes.

4. I had a good time talking with my friends.

5. We went swim yesterday.

6. Does my smoking bother you?

7. I used to living with my parents, but now I live alone.

8. My sister couldn't get used to live in the U.S., so she went back to our country.

9. Did you see the man jump off the bridge?

10. I can hear my neighbors to fight.

11. I can smell the dinner cooking.

12. Get a good job takes time.

13. He improved his English by talk with Americans.

14. Look at this old picture of you. Do you remember wearing that silly hat?

15. She thanked me for take care of her dog while she was on vacation.

16. Did you have trouble to find my apartment?

17. Please remember to turn off the lights before you go to bed.

18. Do you like to go shopping?

19. She read the book without to use a dictionary.

20. I started learning English when I was a child.

Part 2   Fill in each blank with the gerund, infinitive, or base form of the verb in parentheses ( ). In some cases, either a gerund or an infinitive may be used. If you see a pronoun, change it to its correct form.

A. I had a technician (fix) _____*fix*_____ my typewriter last year, but it broke
                            (fix)

   down again. I plan on _____*buying*_____ a new one. Do you have any suggestions?
                              (buy)

B. Instead of _____ a typewriter, you should consider _____ a
              (1 buy)   (2 buy)
   computer or word processor.

A. I don't think I can afford _____ a word processor.
                          (3 buy)

B. They're not much more expensive than a typewriter.

A. Why is a word processor better?

B. It's so easy _____ changes with a word processor. _____ out
               (4 make)   (5 take)

   or _____ some words or sentences just takes a few seconds. If you use
        (6 add)

   a typewriter, it's impossible _____ these changes without
                          (7 make)

   _____ the paper. A year ago I bought a word processor, and now I
   (8 retype)

   can't imagine _____ it to write a composition.
              (9 not/use)

A. But I don't know how _____ a word processor. I'm used to
                 (10 use)

   _____ a typewriter. I'll have _____ a lot of new things before
   (11 use)   (12 learn)
   I can use it.

B. I'll help you _____. It's not so hard. You only need _____ a
            (13 learn)   (14 learn)
   few commands, and you can start _____ it immediately.
                          (15 use)

A. I hope so. Our teacher wants _____ our compositions. He won't let
                      (16 we/type)

   _____ him a handwritten composition. Last week I gave him a
   (17 we/give)

   handwritten composition, and he made me _____ it over. I'm upset
                               (18 do)

   about _____ on typewritten homework.
      (19 he/insist)

B. If you get a word processor, you won't mind _____ a composition.
   (20 type)

You might even enjoy _____. When your teacher asks _____
   (21 write)   (22 you/rewrite)

your composition, it will only take you a few minutes _____ it.
   (23 do)

(A few days later)

A. I thought about your advice. I decided _____ a typewriter after all.
   (24 not/buy)

I'm going to buy a word processor.

B. That's great. I forgot _____ you that there's going to be a big sale next
   (25 tell)

week. Can you put off _____ it for another week? If you want, I'll go
   (26 buy)

_____ with you and help you _____ one out.
   (27 shop)   (28 pick)

A. I hate _____ you.
   (29 bother)

B. It's no bother. I'm happy _____ you. Besides, I'm interested in
   (30 help)

_____ a new printer, so I was planning on _____ to that store
   (31 buy)   (32 go)

anyway.

Part 3   Fill in each blank with the correct preposition.

EXAMPLE: **We must concentrate** *on* ____ **learning English.**

1. What is the reason ____ doing this exercise?

2. Your grade in this course depends ____ passing the tests and doing the
   homework.

3. Students complain ____ writing compositions.

4. The teacher insists ____ giving tests.

5. We talked ____ having a party at the end of the semester.

6. I hope I succeed ____ passing this course.

7. Most students care ____ getting good grades.

8. The teacher objects ____ students' talking during a test.

9. Students are interested _____ improving their pronunciation.

10. Are you afraid _____ getting a bad grade?

11. Are you worried _____ getting a bad grade?

12. Instead _____ writing a composition today, let's have a discussion.

13. I'm not used _____ speaking English all the time.

Part 4   Tell if these pairs of sentences mean about the same thing or have completely different meanings. Write *same* or *different*.

EXAMPLES: **It's important to spell correctly.**

To spell correctly is important.   *Same*

I used to live in New York.

I'm used to living in New York.   *Different*

1. I can't remember to brush my teeth.

   I can't remember brushing my teeth.   _____

2. I like to cook.

   I like cooking.   _____

3. Going to college is expensive.

   It's expensive to go to college.   _____

4. I plan to buy a computer.

   I plan on buying a computer.   _____

5. I stopped smoking.

   I stopped to smoke.   _____

6. He had the mechanic fix his car.

   He had his car fixed by the mechanic.   _____

LESSON NINE

GRAMMAR

Adverbial Clauses and
  Phrases
Result Clauses

CONTEXT

Home Schooling
Inequalities in American Life
Columbus and the Discovery of
  America
Phone Services
The Ozone Layer

Lesson Focus **Adverbial Clauses and Phrases; Result Clauses**

• A clause is a group of words that contains a subject and a verb. In addition to a main clause, a sentence sometimes has another clause or phrase that gives information about reason, purpose, time, contrast, or condition.

| Main Clause | Time |
| I went to China | before I went to Japan. |

| Main Clause | Reason |
| I went to China | because I wanted to see the Great Wall. |

| Main Clause | Purpose |
| I went to China | in order to learn Chinese. |

| Main Clause | Contrast |
| I went to China | even though it was expensive. |

| Main Clause | Condition |
| I will go to China | if I win the lottery. |

The extra information can come before or after the main clause. If it comes before, it is separated from the main clause by a comma.

Because I wanted to see the Great Wall, I went to China.
I went to China because I wanted to see the Great Wall.

• A result can follow expressions with *so . . . that* or *such . . . that.*

He was *so* tired *that* he fell asleep in class.

We had *such* a good time at the party *that* we didn't want to go home.

• •

R
E
A
D
I
N
G

Before you read:

1. Do you think education is better in the U.S. or in your country? Why?
2. Do you have children in school in this city? Are you satisfied with your child's school?

The following words show reason or purpose: *because, because of, since, (in order) to,* and *so (that).* Read the following article. Pay special attention to these words.

HOME SCHOOLING

Because of dissatisfaction with American schools, some parents have decided to educate their children at home. About half a million American children are now getting their education at home, ten times as many as a decade ago.

The movement for home schooling was begun by Christian religious groups that were dissatisfied with schools **because of** the lack of values taught there. **In order to** teach their children their own religious or moral values, some parents decided to educate their children themselves.

Other parents say that schools do not allow children to be creative and free. **Since** all children must work on the same project for the same period of time, schools take away a child's natural curiosity and creativity. A child may just begin to get interested in a subject, but when the bell rings she must stop what she is doing and start a new project. Home educators usually do not set a time limit on a project **so that** the child may continue with what she is doing until she is finished.

Some parents prefer home schooling because they believe that schools offer a poor quality of education. **Because of** classroom overcrowding, children often don't get enough attention from their teachers. In addition, parents are worried that schools are not safe **because of** the presence of drugs and weapons.

To provide their children with a safe environment, to give them a lot of attention, and to teach their family's moral and/or religious values, more and more parents have decided to educate their children themselves.

• •

9.1   Reason and Purpose

Study the ways to show reason.

Main Clause	*Because/Since* + Clause
Mrs. Watson doesn't like the schools	because they are unsafe.
She decided to educate her children at home	since the schools don't teach family values.

Main Clause	*Because Of* + Noun Phrase
She decided to educate her daughter	because of her dissatisfaction with public schools.
Students don't get enough attention in class	because of overcrowding.

Study the ways to show purpose.

Main Clause	*(In Order) To* + Verb Phrase
She decided to educate her children at home	(in order) to teach them religious values.

Main Clause	*So (That)* + Subject + Modal + Verb
She decided to educate her children at home	so that she could teach them religious values.

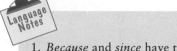

1. *Because* and *since* have the same meaning. They both introduce a clause.

> *Because* he was late, he missed the class.
> *Since* he was late, he missed the class.

2. *Because of* introduces a noun, a noun phrase, or a gerund.

> *Because of* traffic, he came late.
> *Because of* the good grades she got, she won a scholarship.
> *Because of* overcrowding, students don't get enough of the teacher's attention in the classroom.

3. *In order to* can be shortened to *to*.

> *In order to* get a good job, you need an education.
> *To* get a good job, you need an education.

4. *So that* can be shortened to *so*. *So (that)* is usually followed by a clause containing a

modal: *can, will,* and *may* for present and future, and *could, would,* and *might* for past.

> She wants to educate her children at home so they *can* learn in a safe environment.
> She wanted to educate her children at home so that they *could* get more attention.

5. Don't follow *so that* with *want*. *Want* shows a reason, not a purpose.

> She decided to educate her children at home
> *because*
> ~~so that~~ she wanted them to have a good education.

6. A question about reason or purpose begins with *why*. In informal speech, *how come* is often used for reason, and *what . . . for* is used for purpose. After *how come*, statement word order is used.

> Why did he leave school?
> What did he leave school for?
> How come he left school?

EXERCISE 1   Fill in each blank with the correct word or words: *because, because of, since, (in order) to, so (that).*

> **EXAMPLE:** Parents educate children at home <u>*in order to*</u> teach them religious values.

1. Children go to school _____ they can learn.

2. Children go to school _____ learn.

3. _____ dangerous conditions in some schools, some parents want to educate their children at home.

4. Some parents educate their children at home _____ teach them about religion.

5. Parents are unhappy _____ classrooms are overcrowded.

6. Parents are unhappy _____ unsafe conditions in the schools.

7. Parents educate children at home _____ they can control what their children learn.

8. Parents educate children at home _____ control what their children learn.

EXERCISE 2   Complete each sentence.

EXAMPLES: Because <u>*I need to learn more grammar*</u> , I'm taking this course.

To <u>*look up words I don't know*</u> , I bring a dictionary to class.

1. So that _____ ,
   the teacher gives us tests.

2. Because _____ ,
   the teacher gives us tests.

3. To _____ ,
   the teacher gives us tests.

4. Since _____ ,
   the teacher doesn't let us use our books during a test.

5. Because of _____ ,
   most parents send their children to school.

6. Since _____ ,
   most parents send their children to school.

7. In order to _____ ,
   some parents prefer to educate their children at home.

8. So that _____ ,
   most schools ring a bell at the end of a class period.

9. Because _____ ,
   I think it's better to educate children in school/at home. (choose one)

Language Notes

1. *For* + noun (phrase) can be used to show a purpose.
   A. Why do you take vitamins?
   B. For my health.
   A. Why does she watch TV?
   B. For relaxation.

2. Do not use *for* with a verb. Use *(in order) to*.
   WRONG: I take vitamins for improve my health.
   RIGHT: I take vitamins *in order to improve* my health.
   RIGHT: I take vitamins *to improve* my health.
   RIGHT: I take vitamins *for my health.*

EXERCISE 3   Complete each sentence with a noun or a verb.

EXAMPLE: People have pets for *companionship.*

1. People take vitamins for _____

2. Most people get married for _____

3. Some immigrants come to America for _____

4. Students come to this college for _____

EXERCISE 4   Fill in each blank with a reason or purpose to talk about yourself. Share your answers.

EXAMPLE: I came to the U.S. because *my country has an unstable government.*

1.   I came to the U.S. because _____

2.   I came to the U.S. so that _____

3.   I came to the U.S. for _____

4.   I (don't) want to go back to my country since _____

_____

5.   I (don't) like the U.S. because of _____

6.   I (don't) like this city since _____

7.   I (don't) like this school because _____

8.   I come to this school for _____

9.   I use my dictionary to _____

10. I'm saving money because _____

11. I'm saving money so _____

12. I'm saving my money for _____

13. I'm saving my money in order to _____

EXERCISE 5   Fill in each blank with *because, because of, since, so (that)*, or *(in order) to*.

(Two women are talking.)

A. I heard you moved.

B. Yes. We moved last month. We bought a big house _so that_____ we would

 have room for my parents. They're coming to the U.S. next month

 _____ they want to be near their children and grandchildren.
        (1)

A. Where's your new house?

B. It's in Deerfield.

A. Why did you move so far from the city?

B. We prefer the suburbs _____ the schools are much better.
              (2)

A. But isn't it expensive to live in Deerfield?

B. Yes, it is, _____ pay the mortgage, I'm working two jobs.
        (3)

A. How do you get to work? You have only one car.

B. _____ it is impossible for me to get to work by public transportation, I
    (4)

 take the car. But my husband works downtown, so he takes the train. He

 doesn't like to drive downtown _____ the expense of parking.
            (5)

A. Maybe I should start to think about buying a house.

B. You really should start saving your money now _____ you will be able
            (6)

 to buy a house soon.

R
E
A
D
I
N
G

Before you read:

Are there inequalities in your country? Is there discrimination[1] against a certain group of people? What does the government do to protect these people?

Words that connect contrasting ideas are **even though, although,** and **in spite of (the fact that).** Read the following article. Pay special attention to contrasts.

INEQUALITIES IN AMERICAN LIFE

Even though the U.S. Constitution says that all people have equal rights under the law, there have always been inequalities in American life. At the time the Constitution was written, slaves were being brought to America from Africa. Slavery continued until 1865. **In spite of the fact that** African Americans were freed at that time, they didn't achieve equality because they did not have the education or skills to find good jobs. As a result, their economic level was very low. **Even though** other minorities have suffered discrimination, nothing compares to the effects of slavery and segregation.[2] **In spite of** the constitutional guarantee of equality, the American dream was out of reach for most African Americans.

In 1964 a law was passed that prohibited discrimination because of race, color, religion, sex, or national origin. The government started a program of "affirmative action" to help minorities get more education and better jobs. **Although** this policy has helped many middle-class blacks and minorities achieve success, it has done little to help the very poor. While only 10% of white Americans live in poverty, 33% of black Americans and 26% of Hispanics do. Thirty-nine percent of white Americans attend college, but only 31% of blacks do.

Although there has been some progress toward equality for all in the U.S., the inequalities in American life still exist.

---

[1]*Discrimination* means treating one group of people as inferior to another. There can be discrimination in jobs, housing, and education.

[2]*Segregation* means that the races are separated, especially in neighborhoods and schools.

9.2 Contrast

For an unexpected result, use a clause beginning with *although, (even) though,* or *in spite of the fact that.*

Even Though/Although/ In Spite of the Fact That + Clause	Main Clause
Even though the Constitution states that all people have equal rights under the law,	Africans were brought to America as slaves.
Although "affirmative action" has helped some disadvantaged people,	it has done little to help the very poor.
In spite of the fact that the slaves were freed,	they didn't achieve equality.
In Spite of + Noun Phrase	Main Clause
In spite of his education,	he couldn't find a job.

Language Notes

1. *Anyway* or *still* can be used in the main clause to emphasize the contrast. (*Anyway* is informal.)

   Even though he has a good education, he *still* can't find a job.

   Even though he has a good education, he can't find a job *anyway*.

2. Compare *because* and *even though*.

   Many immigrants come to the U.S. *because* there are many opportunities here.

   Many immigrants come to the U.S. *even though* it is difficult to start a new life.

3. Compare *because of* and *in spite of*.

   Because of his talent, he found a wonderful job.

   In spite of his talent, he can't find a job.

EXERCISE 6 Fill in each blank with *in spite of* or *in spite of the fact that.*

EXAMPLES: The football game continued _in spite of_ the rain.

The football game continued _in spite of the fact that_ it rained.

1. A lot of people like big cities _____ the crime.

2. Some people drink and then drive _____ the combination of drinking and driving is dangerous.

3. Many immigrants come here _____ the difficulty of starting a new life.

4. I like living in the U.S. _____ I miss my friends and family back home.

5. _____ I speak with an accent, people understand me.

6. _____ my accent, people understand me.

EXERCISE 7   Complete each statement with an unexpected result.

EXAMPLE: **I like the teacher even though** *he gives a lot of homework.*

1. I like my apartment even though _____

_____

2. I like this city even though _____

_____

3. I like the U.S. even though _____

_____

4. I like this school even though _____

_____

5. I like my job in spite of (the fact that) _____

_____

6. Some student fail tests in spite of (the fact that) _____

_____

EXERCISE 8   Complete each statement by making a contrast.

EXAMPLE: **Even though Alaska is the biggest state,** *it has the smallest population.*

1. Even though the U.S. is a rich country, _____

_____

2. Even though the Constitution says that everyone is equal, _____

_____

3. Even though I don't speak English perfectly, _____

   _____

4. In spite of the fact that my teacher doesn't speak my language, _____

   _____

5. Even though I miss my friends and family, _____

   _____

● ●

R
E
A
D
I
N
G

Before you read:

In your country, is there a holiday that honors an important person? Does every-one agree that he or she was a great person?

Read the following article. Pay special attention to time words.

COLUMBUS AND THE DISCOVERY OF AMERICA

Every American school child knows that on October 12, 1492, Christopher Columbus discovered America. **While** Columbus was looking for a western sea route from Europe to Asia, he arrived in America. **During** this voyage,[3] members of his crew[4] were ready to rebel[5] **after** being at sea **for** over a month without seeing land. Finally, land was spotted, and Columbus became a hero to future generations. **Since** 1892, the 400th anniversary of Columbus's voyage, Americans **have been celebrating** Columbus Day.

Some people believe that Columbus's arrival was the first step in the creation of the United States and democracy. However, in 1992 **when** Americans were ready to celebrate the 500th anniversary of the discovery of their continent, many minority groups protest-ed that this event was not a cause for celebration but an occasion to remember the tragedy suffered by the native peoples[6] who had been living in America **before** Columbus arrived. The arrival of Columbus and other Europeans brought slavery, cruelty, disease, and the destruction of the natural environment. **Until** recently, American history text-books began the story of America with the landing of Columbus. However, newer history books include information about the native peoples that lived in America before

---

[3]A *voyage* is a trip.

[4]The *crew* consists of the people working on a ship.

[5]To *rebel* means to go against the orders of a leader.

[6]The plural form *peoples* means *nations* or *tribes*.

Columbus's arrival and the suffering they experienced as a result of the European colonization of America.

Until the day he died, Columbus did not realize that he had discovered a new continent. In spite of his mistake, he changed the course of life in America.

9.3 Time

Study the meanings and uses of the following time words.

Example	Explanation
When Columbus arrived in America, he saw native American people.	*When* means "at that time" or "after that time."
Until Columbus arrived in America, certain diseases were unknown there.	*Until* means "up to that time."
Since the fifteenth century, foreigners have been coming to America. *Ever since* Columbus discovered America, foreigners have been coming here.	*Since* or *ever since* means "from that time in the past to the present." Use the present perfect (continuous) in the main clause.
Columbus was at sea *for* thirty-three days. Americans have been celebrating Columbus Day *for* over 100 years.	Use *for* with the amount of time.
Columbus's men almost rebelled *during* the voyage.	Use *during* with an event (a trip, a vacation, a class, a meeting, a lifetime) or with a specific period of time (the month of August, the week of March 2, the evening of April 3).
While they were traveling to America, Columbus's crew wanted to rebel.	Use *while* with a continuous action.
Whenever we read a story, we learn new words.	*Whenever* means "any time" or "every time."

Language
Notes

1. In a negative sentence, either *for* or *in* can be used with the amount of time.

> I haven't seen my sister *for* three months.
> I haven't seen my sister *in* three months.

2. Use the simple past tense with *for* + amount of time if the action does not continue to the present. Use the present perfect if the action continues to the present.

> She lived in Boston from 1985 to 1992. She *lived* in Boston *for* seven years.
> She lives in Los Angeles now. She *has lived* in L.A. *for* four years.

3. Observe sentences that use the simple past and the past continuous:

> While *she was climbing* a tree, she *fell* and *broke* her arm.
> She *was climbing* a tree when she *fell* and *broke* her arm.

Use *while* with the past continuous tense. Use *when* with the simple past tense.

4. In a future sentence, use the present tense after the time word and the future tense in the main clause.

> I *will call* you when I *get* home.
> After he *finds* a job, he *will buy* a car.

EXERCISE 9   Fill in each blank with an appropriate time word. (In some cases, the tense will determine which word to use.)

EXAMPLE: ___*Until*___ Columbus died, he thought he found a short way to get to Asia.

1. Immigrants have been coming to America _____ many years.

2. _____ his lifetime, Columbus believed that he found a short way to Asia.

3. _____ Europeans started coming to America, they brought diseases to the native peoples.

4. We have been talking about Columbus _____ about ten minutes.

5. We have been talking about Columbus _____ the class began.

6. Columbus found America _____ he was looking for Asia.

7. _____ recently, American history textbooks did not include any

information about native American peoples who were living in America

_____ Columbus arrived.

8. _____ Columbus's voyage, members of his crew wanted to rebel.

9. _____ the teacher explained the grammar, he used the story about Columbus to give examples of time words.

10. _____ the teacher explains the grammar, he uses real examples.

11. We haven't had a test _____ over a week.

EXERCISE 10   Fill in each blank with an appropriate expression.

EXAMPLES: For _seven years_____, she has been working in a bank.

　　　　　　Since _1992_____, she has been working in a bank.

1. During _____, she lived in Poland.

2. For _____, she has lived in England.

3. Since _____, she has lived in England.

4. While _____, she met her future husband.

5. When _____, she was living in Poland.

6. Until _____, she lived with her parents.

7. She hasn't visited Poland in _____.

8. While _____, he broke his arm.

9. For _____, he watched TV.

10. During _____, she cried.

11. When _____, she started to laugh.

12. Until _____, she couldn't go out.

13. Whenever _____, she takes a walk in the park.

EXERCISE 11   Complete the statements that apply to you. If the time expression is at the beginning of the sentence, add a comma before the main clause.

EXAMPLES: Whenever I have a job interview, _I feel nervous._____

　　　　　　Ever since I found a job, _I haven't had much time to study._____

1. Ever since I was a child _____

2. When I was a child _____

3. _____ ever since I arrived in the U.S.

4. _____ when I arrived in the U.S.

5. _____ until I came to the U.S.

6. When the semester began _____

7. Since the semester began _____

8. _____ when I was _____ years old.

9. _____ until I was _____ years old.

10. _____ ever since I was _____ years old.

11. When I got married _____

12. Since I got married _____

13. Until I got married _____

14. _____ when I found a job.

15. _____ since I found a job.

16. _____ until I found a job.

Language Notes

If the subject of a time clause and the subject of a main clause are the same, the time clause can be changed to a participial phrase. The subject is omitted, and the present participle (-*ing* form) is used.

Subject   Same Subject

Columbus returned to Spain after he discovered America.

Columbus returned to Spain after discovering America.

EXERCISE 12   Change the time clause to a participial phrase.

EXAMPLE: Before I came to the U.S., I couldn't speak English.
          Before coming to the U.S., I couldn't speak English.

1. Before I take a test, I study.
2. Maria will go back to her country after she graduates.

3. While Jack was traveling through Europe, he learned about Italian architecture.
4. After Susan got married, she moved to London.
5. After Columbus was at sea for many days, he saw land.

R
E
A
D
I
N
G

Before you read:

1. Do you have an answering machine? Did you have one in your country?
2. In addition to basic phone service, do you use any special services offered by the phone company?

Read the following article. Pay special attention to *if, even if,* and *unless.*

PHONE SERVICES

There are many services you can add to your regular phone service. One popular service is "call waiting." **If** you are using the phone and another person calls, you hear a special tone that lets you know that someone is trying to reach you. You can put the first caller on hold and talk to the second caller. Then you can go back to the first, **if** you like. **If** you need to make an important call and you don't want to be interrupted, you can cancel the call-waiting feature by dialing a few numbers before you make your call. However, you can't cancel call waiting **unless** you make the call. **If** you receive a call, call waiting is always in effect.

Another service, "call forwarding," lets you receive your calls **even if** you're not home. **If** you know where you will be, you can enter the phone number of the place where you want your calls to go. **If** someone calls your phone number, your call will automatically go to the number you entered.

Another service is called "voice mail." Voice mail takes messages, just like an answering machine. However, this service allows you to receive messages **even if** you are talking on the phone. Because you use a special password,[7] no one else can hear your messages.

Most people today have an answering machine. Some people don't pick up the phone **even if** they're home. They want to "screen" their calls (to find out who is calling before picking up the phone).

---

[7]A telephone *password* is a personal identification number that you choose. Other people will not know this number unless you give it to them.

9.4   Conditions[8]

Study the meaning and uses of the following condition words.

Example	Explanation
If you're not home, I'll leave a message. *If* your phone is busy, I'll call back. You must pay extra money *if* you want these extra phone services.	Use *if* to show that the condition affects the result.
With call forwarding, you can receive your calls *even if* you're not home. With voice mail, you can receive a recorded message *even if* you are talking on the phone.	Use *even if* to show that the condition doesn't affect the result.
You can't cancel call waiting *unless* you make the call. If you receive the call, you can't cancel it. The phone company will put your number in the directory *unless* you ask for an unlisted number.	Use *unless* to mean *if not*. *Unless* gives an exception.
He *will call* me even if it *is* late. I *won't call* you unless you *want* me to. I *might call* you if I *need* you.	In a future sentence, use the simple present tense in the time clause.

EXERCISE 13   Complete each statement about the future.

EXAMPLES: **If you make a lot of long distance calls . . .**
If you make a lot of long-distance calls, your phone bill will be very high.

I'll get a good grade if . . .
I'll get a good grade if I study hard.

1. If you don't exercise, . . .
2. If you drink a lot of coffee, . . .
3. If you eat a lot of sugar, . . .
4. My English will improve if . . .
5. I won't get a good grade if . . .
6. I'll go back to my country if . . .

---

[8]For unreal conditions, see Lesson Eleven.

EXERCISE 14   Change the sentence from an *if* clause to an *unless* clause.

>   **EXAMPLE: You can't visit France if you don't have a passport.**
>   **You can't visit France unless you have a passport.**

1. Bars and restaurants cannot serve liquor if they don't have a license.
2. Children cannot see R-rated movies if they're not accompanied by an adult.
3. Children of immigrants will forget their language if they don't use it.
4. Illegal aliens will continue to come to the U.S. if conditions in their countries don't improve.
5. You cannot travel to most foreign countries if you don't have a passport.
6. An American citizen can't be President if he or she was not born in the U.S.
7. You shouldn't give friends advice if they don't ask for it.
8. If it's not an emergency, you shouldn't dial 911.

EXERCISE 15   Complete each statement.

>   **EXAMPLES: I don't usually drink unless . . .**
>   **I don't usually drink unless I'm at a party.**
>
>   **Unless you have a license . . .**
>   **Unless you have a license, you can't own a gun.**

1. I work/study every day unless . . .
2. I'm usually in a good mood unless . . .
3. I usually answer the phone unless . . .
4. I'm going to stay in this city unless . . .
5. I will continue to study at this college unless . . .
6. Poor students can't afford to go to college unless . . .
7. You won't be able to take the next course unless . . .
8. You can't get a refund from a store unless . . .

EXERCISE 16   Complete each statement.

>   **EXAMPLE: I have call waiting. Even if my line is busy,** _I can receive an incoming call._

1. They have call forwarding. They can receive calls even if _____

   _____

2. My phone rings very loudly. I can hear it even if _____

   _____

3. I have an answering machine. Even if _____,
   I sometimes don't pick up my phone.

4. Cold weather doesn't bother me. I go out even if _____

_____

5. Making mistakes is OK. People will understand you even if _____

_____

6. A lot of people in the U.S. have a foreign accent. People will understand you

even if _____

7. Will they call off the football game for bad weather? No. They will play football

even if _____

8. He will fail the course because he never does his homework and he's absent a

lot. Even if _____,
he will fail the course.

9. I always do my homework. I may be absent next week, but I'll do my home-

work even if _____

10. I may move to a suburb. I will continue to study in the city even if

_____

EXERCISE 19   Fill in each blank in this conversation between two middle-aged men about
health. Use *if, even if,* and *unless.*

A. I see you're still smoking. I'm sure you know that *unless* _____ you quit
smoking, you will cut years off your life.

B. I know. I've tried to quit, but I can't.

A. I quit ten years ago. And I've become a vegetarian. They say that _____
(1)
you eat less meat, you will live longer.

B. I still prefer a good steak.

A. Do you get much exercise?

B. I play golf on Sundays.

A. Golf is a nice sport, but you won't extend your life _____ you do
   (2)
   strenuous exercise like tennis or running. I get a lot of exercise. I jog every
   day. Nothing stops me. I jog _____ it rains or snows.
                              (3)

B. That's great. I've tried to jog, but I find it boring. I can't do it
   _____ someone goes with me.
     (4)

A. I usually do it alone. _____ you want, we can jog together. Why don't
                            (5)
   we start tomorrow?

B. Uh . . . thanks. I'll call you tomorrow _____ I have time.
                                            (6)

A. I think you're not really interested in good health.

B. Let's face it; we're men, so _____ we do all these healthy things, we
                                  (7)
   probably won't live as long as most women.

A. But we will die a lot sooner _____ we take better care of ourselves.
                                  (8)

• •

R
E
A   **Before you read:**
D
I   What kind of products do you use that come in spray cans?
N
G   Read the following article. Pay special attention to *so . . . that* and *such . . . that*
    followed by a result.

THE OZONE LAYER

The ozone layer above the earth protects all living things from the sun's ultraviolet light. In the 1980s, scientists discovered that a hole in the ozone had opened up above the South Pole. Ultraviolet light, which comes through this hole, is **so dangerous that** it greatly increases the risk of skin cancer and cataracts[9] and damages plant life.

This problem is caused by artificial chemicals called CFCs (chlorofluorocarbons). These chemicals are used in refrigerators, air conditioners, and spray cans. At first it was thought that CFCs were short-lived; however, now it is known that these chemicals stay in the atmosphere for **such a long time that** they will continue to cause damage decades after they enter the atmosphere.

―――――――
[9]A *cataract* is a disease of the eye.

Companies that produce these chemicals have started to use less dangerous substitutes, but **so many** CFCs are already in the atmosphere **that** they continue to deplete[10] the ozone layer.

9.5   *So . . . That/Such . . . That*

We use *so . . . that* and *such (a) . . . that* + clause to show the result of the main clause. Study the following patterns:

Subject	Verb Phrase	*So* Adj/Adv	*That* + Result Clause
Ultraviolet light	is	so dangerous	that it can cause skin cancer.

Subject	Verb Phrase	*Such (a/an)* Adjective + Noun	*That* + Result Clause
CFCs	stay in the atmosphere	such a long time	that they will continue to cause damage for many years.

Subject	Verb	*So Much/Many Little/Few*	*That* + Result Clause
There	are	so many chemicals in the atmosphere	that they have created a hole in the ozone layer.

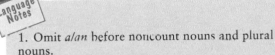

Language Notes

1. Omit *a/an* before noncount nouns and plural nouns.

   She baked *such good bread that* everyone wanted to know the recipe.
   The teacher gave the students *such interesting activities that* they didn't want to go home.

2. Use *many* and *few* for count nouns, *much* and *little* for noncount nouns.

   The teacher has *so much patience that* she never gets tired of explaining.
   The teacher gave *so little time* for the test *that* no one finished it.
   So few students passed the test the first time *that* the teacher decided to give it again.

3. *That* is often omitted in informal speech.
   She is so nice everyone loves her.

4. The result is not always mentioned.
   I like my teacher. She's *so* nice.
   In this case, *so* means "very."
   I have *so much* homework.
   In this case, *so much* means "a lot of."

---

[10]To *deplete* means to make less.

EXERCISE 18   Two students are talking about their English class. Fill in each blank with *so, so much, so many,* or *such (a/an).*

A. How do you like your new English teacher?

B. She's nice, but she gives _____*so much*_____ homework that it's impossible to

do it all. And I work _____ hours that I'm sometimes too tired
                              (1)

to do my homework. Last week the teacher gave _____ hard
                                                           (2)

test that almost everyone failed.

A. American teachers are _____ different from teachers in my
                              (3)

country that I sometimes don't know what to expect.

B. What do you mean?

A. Well, in my country they give tests only once a year. The tests are

_____ important that we get one month to study for them.
          (4)

B. There is _____ big difference between the American educational
              (5)

system and the system in my country that it's hard for me to get used to it. In

my country, students often talk to each other during a test. But here, the

teacher gets _____ mad that she tears up the student's test.
                    (6)

A. On the other hand, some teachers here are _____ friendly that
                                                       (7)

they let you call them by their first names.

EXERCISE 19   Fill in each blank with *so, so much/many/little/few,* or *such (a/an).* Then
complete each statement with a result.

EXAMPLES: **Michael is** ___*such a*___ **good student** *that he gets 100% on all his tests.*

Learning another language is ___*so*___ **hard** *it can take a lifetime to do it.*

1. My math class is _____ easy _____

_____

2. Peter is taking _____ classes this semester _____

_____

3. The teacher gives _____ homework _____

_____

4. Sometimes the teacher talks _____ fast _____

_____

5. My roommate is from India. She speaks English _____ well _____

_____

6. My biology class is _____ boring _____

_____

7. Ms. Stevens is _____ good teacher _____

_____

8. English has _____ irregular verbs _____

_____

9. We had _____ long test _____

_____

10. I had _____ mistakes on my test _____

_____

11. The teacher gave _____ confusing explanation _____

_____

EXPANSION ACTIVITIES

COMMON SAYINGS

The following sayings use *so* with a result clause. Do you have a similar saying in your language?

I'm so hungry I could eat a horse.
It's so hot today you could fry an egg on the street.

DISCUSSIONS

1. Write three sentences to complain about this city, your job, or this school. Discuss your sentences in a small group or with the entire class.

   EXAMPLES: There is so much crime in my neighborhood that I'm afraid to go out at night.

   Registration at this school is so confusing that some people leave and never come back.

   A. _____

   B. _____

   C. _____

2. Fill in each blank. Discuss your answers in a small group or with the entire class.

   A. My friends like me because _____

   B. My friends like me even though _____

3. In a small group or with the entire class, explain why people from your country immigrate to the U.S. or come to the U.S. to study.

4. What do you think about educating children at home? What does a child miss when he or she is educated at home? Do people in your country ever educate their children at home?

CHILDREN'S RHYME

There was an old woman
Who lived in a shoe
She had *so many* children
She didn't know what to do.

WRITING

1. Write about a problem in your country, in the U.S., or in the world (examples: overpopulation, crime, poverty, shortages, bad medical care). Tell what the result of this problem is or may be in the future.

2. Write about a problem in your life (examples: not enough time, too many responsibilities, homesickness, lack of friends, family worries). Tell what the result of this problem is.

3. Choose one of the following topics and defend your point of view.

   Why parents should send their children to school
   Why it is better to live in the city OR Why it is better to live in a suburb
   Why men have an easier life than women OR Why women have an easier life than men

4. Write about a famous person who is/was a hero to some people and a bad person to others.

OUTSIDE ACTIVITIES

1. Interview an American. Ask this person to tell you about his or her personal hero.

2. Ask an American these questions. Then ask *why* or *what for.* Report something interesting to the class.

   A. Do you watch a lot of TV?
   B. Do you have a microwave oven?
   C. Do you eat in fast-food restaurants?
   D. Do you like your apartment?
   E. Do you think the schools in this city are good?
   F. Do you wear your seat belt when you drive or ride in a car?
   G. _____

3. Interview an American. Ask these questions:

   A. In your opinion, what is unfair about life in the U.S.?
   B. What are your complaints about life in this city?

   Report the answers to the class.

4. Call your local phone company. Ask for a booklet that explains the different phone products and services you can buy. Share this information with the class.

EDITING ADVICE

1. Don't separate a dependent clause from a main clause with a period.

   He went home early. Because he was sick.
   (early,̶ B̶ecause — x/b correction)

2. Don't put a comma before a dependent clause that follows the main clause.

   I'll help you, if you need me.
   (you,̶ — x correction)

3. Don't use a sentence connector (*so, but, therefore, however,* etc.) and a dependent connector together.

   Even though she speaks English well, ~~but~~ she can't write.

   Because he was late, ~~so~~ he didn't hear the explanation.

4. Use *to,* not *for,* to show purpose.

   She went to the doctor ~~for~~ to get a checkup.

5. Use *because of* when a noun phrase follows.

   He came late because of bad traffic.

6. Don't use *even* without *though* or *if* to introduce a clause.

   Even though he's a poor man, he's happy.

   I won't call you even if I need your help.

7. Put a comma after a long dependent clause that comes at the beginning of the sentence.

   Because she was always fighting with her brothers and sisters at home, Mary decided to find an apartment of her own.

8. Don't put a comma before *that* when a result follows.

   He's so tall, that he can touch the ceiling.
   (tall,̶ — x correction)

SUMMARY OF LESSON NINE

1. REASON WORDS
   because/since + clause
   > It took him a long time to get home *because/since* traffic was very bad.
   because of + noun (phrase)
   > It took him a long time to get home *because of* bad traffic.
2. PURPOSE WORDS
   (in order) to + infinitive (phrase)
   > He exercises *(in order)* to lose weight.
   so (that) + clause with modal verb
   > He exercises *so (that)* he can lose weight.
   for + noun (phrase)
   > He exercises *for* his health.
3. CONTRAST WORDS
   even though/although/in spite of the fact that + clause
   > *Even though/although* he's rich, he's not happy.
   > *In spite of the fact that* he's rich, he's not happy.
   in spite of + noun (phrase)
   > *In spite of* his wealth, he's not happy.
4. CONDITION WORDS
   if = condition affects result
   > *If* it snows, we won't drive.
   even if = condition doesn't affect result
   > We'll drive *even if* it rains.
   unless = if not; an exception
   > I won't go *unless* you go with me.
5. TIME WORDS
   when = at this time, shortly after this time
   > *When* I find a job, I'll buy a car.
   whenever = every time
   > *Whenever* I work overtime, I make extra money.
   until = up to this time
   > I worked *until* 8 o'clock.
   > I worked *until* the store closed.
   while + continuous time
   > *While* I was slicing the bread, I cut my finger.
   since + starting time of an action that continues to the present
   > I have been working *since* 9 a.m.
   > I have been working *since* I got up.
   for + amount of time
   > I have been working *for* three hours.
   during + event
   > I worked *during* my summer vacation.
6. RESULT WORDS
   so + adjective or adverb + *that*
   > I was *so tired that* I fell asleep during class.
   so much/many little/few + noun + *that*
   > I worked *so many hours that* I didn't have time to study.
   such (a/an) + adjective + noun + *that*
   > I had *such* a bad week *that* I couldn't wait for it to be over.
7. Sentences with Mixed Tenses

Main Clause	Time Clause
I *have lived* in New York	since I *came* to the U.S.
Columbus *found* America	while he *was looking* for Asia.
I *will call* you	when I *get* home.

8. Using a Present Participle Instead of a Verb
   COMPARE:
   > Before he left on his vacation, he bought a map.
   > Before *leaving* on his vacation, he bought a map.

LESSON NINE TEST/REVIEW

Part 1   Find the mistakes in the following sentences, and correct them. Not every sentence has a mistake. If the sentence is correct, write *C*.

EXAMPLES: **When he met her, he fell in love with her immediately.**

Before I came to class, I stopped in the cafeteria to get a cup of coffee. *C*

1. The teacher will help you, if you go to her office.

2. She always gets good grades. Because she studies hard.

3. When I was in Mexico, I visited the pyramids.

4. Even though owning a dog has some disadvantages. There are more advantages overall.

5. Since she came to Chicago, she has been living with her sister.

6. If you need me, I'll help you.

7. Students can't go to level 6, unless they pass level 5.

8. He failed the test because, he didn't study.

9. She closed all the windows before she left the house.

10. Before he got married. His friends gave a party for him.

11. Because he can't get a job, so he feels bad.

12. Even though he is well qualified, but he can't find a job.

13. After he checked all the windows and locked the front and back doors Bob went to bed.

14. He's saving his money for buy a new car.

15. Because her bad health, she had to quit her job.

16. He's working at the same job since he came to the U.S.

17. When I will go back to my country, I will visit my relatives.

18. Even she can't speak English well, she has a good job.

19. In spite of she can't speak English well, she has a good job.

20. Before you go home today, I will tell you about the test.

21. He was so tired, that he didn't even change into his pajamas before going to bed.

22. The weather won't stop me. I'll drive to New York even it snows.

23. Before prepare dinner, she washed her hands.

Part 2   Fill in each blank to give a reason or purpose.

EXAMPLE: I come to this school in order to *learn English.* _____

1. I come to this school for _____

2. I want to learn English so that _____

3. People sometimes don't understand me because of _____

4. Since _____ _____, English is not easy for me.

Part 3   Fill in each blank with *so (that), because, because of, since, for,* or *(in order) to.*

EXAMPLE: He came to the U.S. *because of* _____ a war in his country.

1. He came to the U.S. _____ he could learn English.

2. He came to the U.S. _____ find a better job.

3. He came to the U.S. _____ the opportunities.

4. He came to the U.S. _____ he wanted to have a better life.

Part 4   Complete each statement.

1. In spite of the fact that my English teacher doesn't speak my language,

   _____

2. _____ even though I don't like to do it.

3. In spite of _____, Americans still understand me.

4. Even though _____, I like this school.

Part 5   Fill in each blank with an appropriate time word: *when, whenever, while, for, during, since, until.*

> EXAMPLE: They were talking *during*_____ the whole movie. Everyone
>   around them was annoyed.

1. They talk _____ they go to the movies. This happens every time.

2. They were talking _____ everyone else was trying to watch the movie.

3. They started talking _____ they sat down at the beginning of the movie.

4. They had been talking _____ they entered the theater.

5. They had been talking _____ two hours.

6. They stopped talking _____ the movie was over. Then they left.

7. They didn't stop talking _____ they left.

8. I haven't seen them _____ we went to the movies last week.

Part 6   Complete each sentence.

> EXAMPLES: He's had his driver's license for *three years.*_____
>
>   He's had his driver's license since *1992.*_____

1. He didn't get a driver's license until _____

2. He practiced driving during _____

3. Until he bought a car, _____

4. Whenever he drives his car, _____

5. While _____, he had an accident.

6. He bought his car when _____

Part 7   Fill in each blank with *if, unless,* or *even if.*

1. Only people 21 years old or older can enter a bar. You can't enter a bar

    _____ you're at least 21 years old.

2. _____ you're under 21 years old, you can't enter.

3. Everyone must show identification. _____ you're 90 years old, you
    must show identification!

Part 8   Fill in each blank with *so, so much/many,* or *such (a/an)* along with a result.

EXAMPLE: I had _*such a*_____ good time at the party _*that I didn't want to leave.*_

1. There were _____ people at the party _____

   _____

2. The food at the party was _____ good _____

   _____

3. There was _____ food at the party _____

   _____

4. The music at the party was _____ loud _____

   _____

5. One man told _____ funny story _____

   _____

LESSON TEN

GRAMMAR

Noun Clauses

CONTEXT

Impressions of the United States
Iceman
A Folk Tale
The Cuban Missile Crisis

Lesson Focus Noun Clauses

A noun clause functions as a noun in a sentence. Compare sentences with a simple object and sentences with a noun clause as the object:

Subject	Verb	Connecting Word	Simple Object/Noun Clause Object
I	believe		him.
I	believe	(that)	he's telling the truth.
He	asked		a question.
He	asked	if	I would call him later.
You	know		my address.
You	know	where	I live.

A noun clause is used:

- After verbs and adjectives of mental state.
    I believe *that all people are good.*
    He's sorry *that he left his country.*

- To include a question in a statement.
    I don't know *what time it is.*

- To repeat someone's exact words.
    He said, *"I will go to the U.S."*

- To report what someone has said or asked.
    He said *that he would go to the U.S.*
    He asked *me what he should take* to the U.S.

. . . .

**R
E
A
D
I
N
G**

Before you read:

You probably saw American movies in your country. What impression did you get about the U.S. from these movies?

Read the following conversation between a foreigner (F) and an American (A). Pay special attention to noun clauses after verbs and adjectives.

IMPRESSIONS OF THE UNITED STATES

A. What surprises you in the U.S.?

F. I'm surprised **that so many people are homeless.** As I walk down the street, I'm amazed **that there are so many beggars.**

A. Aren't you also amazed **that the subways of New York are so dirty?**

F. Not really. I saw many American movies in my country, so I'm not surprised.

A. Is there anything else that surprises you?

F. I know **that Americans have the best health care in the world.** However, I'm angry **that it's so expensive and that doctors are so rich.** In my country, health care isn't so advanced, but it's free for everyone.

A. Are you sorry **you came to the U.S.?**

F. No. I'm happy **I came here,** but I'm disappointed **that life isn't as easy as I had thought.**

A. What did you think?

F. I thought **that it would be easy to find a job,** but it isn't true. I've been here for six months, and I haven't found a job yet.

A. Do you think **your life in the U.S. will improve?**

F. I hope so. I'm sure **that I will get used to it little by little.**

10.1 Noun Clauses After Verbs and Adjectives

A noun clause can follow a verb of mental state.

Subject	Verb		Noun Clause
I	hope	(that)	I will find a job soon.
I	believe	(that)	the U.S. is a great country.

A noun clause can be the complement of the sentence after an adjective.

Subject	Verb	Adjective		Noun Clause Complement
I	am	surprised	(that)	there are so many poor people.
It	is	obvious	(that)	not everyone is rich.

Language Notes

1. The following are verbs of mental state:

believe	feel*	know	pretend	show
complain	find out	learn	realize	suppose
decide	forget	notice	regret	think
dream	hope	predict	remember	understand
expect				

*NOTE: *Feel* followed by a noun clause means "believe" or "think."

2. Noun clauses can be replaced by *so* after *think, hope, believe, suppose, expect,* and *know.*

A. I hope (that) you will find a job soon.
B. I hope *so* too.

A. Do you think that English grammar is difficult?
B. I know *so.*

3. Use *would,* not *will,* if the main verb is in the past tense. Use *was/were going to,* not *is/am/are going to,* if the main verb is in the past tense.

I thought (that) I *would* find a job right away.
I knew (that) you *would* be happy in the U.S.
She realized (that) life *wasn't going to* be easy.

4. In conversation, *that* is often omitted.

EXERCISE 1   Respond to each statement by using "I know," "I'm surprised," or "I'm not surprised."

EXAMPLES: Russia is closer to the U.S. than Cuba is.
I'm surprised that Russia is closer than Cuba is.

The biggest state in the U.S. is Alaska.
I know that the biggest state in the U.S. is Alaska.

The majority of American families have a VCR.[1]
I'm not surprised that the majority of American families have a VCR.

1. The U.S. has more crime than Japan.
2. Life expectancy in Japan is higher than in the U.S.
3. Over 60% of Americans own a home.
4. Over 50% of American women work for pay.
5. Over 50% of American households have a pet.
6. Fourteen percent of the American population is considered poor.
7. Some states have no state income tax.
8. Students at some private colleges pay more than $20,000 a year for tuition.
9. More Canadians go to college than Americans.
10. Twenty-four percent of American households have just one person.

---

[1]*VCR* means *videocassette recorder.*

11. Only 2% of American families live on farms.
12. One-third of the American population is over 65.

EXERCISE 2 Fill in each blank to talk about your knowledge and impressions of the U.S. Form a small group and discuss your answers.

EXAMPLES: **I know that** *there are fifty states in the U.S.*

I'm surprised that *there is unemployment in the U.S.*

1. I think (that) _____

2. I'm disappointed (that) _____

3. I hope (that) _____

4. I'm afraid (that) _____

5. It's unfortunate (that) _____

6. I'm surprised (that) _____

7. I've noticed (that) _____

8. Americans think (that) _____

EXERCISE 3 Fill in each blank and discuss your answers.

1. Before I came to the U.S., I thought that _____, but it wasn't true.

2. Before I came to the U.S., I didn't know that _____

3. In my country, people often say that _____

10.2 Noun Clauses After a Passive Verb

A noun clause can be used with certain verbs in the passive voice to show a general belief.

> People think that love is a necessary ingredient in life.
> *It is thought* that love is a necessary ingredient in life.
>
> People assume that there is no life on Mars.
> *It is assumed* that there is no life on Mars.

EXERCISE 4   Change to a passive construction to show a general belief.

>   EXAMPLE: **At one time, people thought that the earth was the center of the universe.**
>
>   **At one time, it was thought that the earth was the center of the universe.**

1. People say that love is blind.
2. People know that women live longer than men.
3. People have said that money is the root of all evil.
4. People have concluded that smoking is dangerous.
5. People often say that business and friendship don't mix.
6. People often say that necessity is the mother of invention.

• •

R
E
A
D
I
N
G

Before you read:

Have you ever visited a museum of natural history? What kinds of exhibits do you like to see in a museum? Why do you like to see these things?

Read the following article. Pay special attention to noun clauses.

ICEMAN

In 1991 a German tourist found something interesting on a hiking trip in the Alps. He didn't know **what it was.** At first, he thought it was a doll's head. However, the tourist's find turned out to be the head of a man whose body had been preserved by the ice of a glacier for over 5,000 years.

"Iceman," as this prehistoric man is called, was between 25 and 35 years old and was in good physical condition when he died. He had several tattoos on his body and was wearing a fur robe covered by a grass cape. He had a copper axe and a bow and arrows with him.

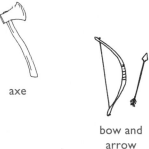

axe

bow and
arrow

This was a very important scientific discovery. Scientists had never before had the opportunity to study the body of a person who had lived so long ago. By studying Iceman, scientists can find out **what kind of tools people used 5,000 years ago, what kind of clothes they wore,** and **how they lived.**

Nobody knows **what Iceman was doing on the mountain, why he was alone,** or **how he died.** We do know that Iceman will provide us with a lot of information about life 5,000 years ago.

Learning about Iceman will not be cheap. It costs $10,000 a month to study and take care of him.

• •

10.3 Noun Clauses as Embedded Questions

Sometimes a noun clause is used to include a question in a statement or another question.

Main Clause	Embedded Question (Noun Clause)
Nobody knows	how Iceman died.
Do you know	if Iceman was alone?

Statement word order is used for an embedded question. Study the change from a direct question to an embedded question.

Yes/No Questions: Introduce the embedded question with *if* or *whether.* You can add *or not* at the end.

	Direct Question	Embedded Question
Questions with *Be* or Auxiliary Verb	Was Iceman a hunter? Have scientists studied Iceman? Could scientists determine his age?	I wonder if he was a hunter. I'm not sure if they have studied Iceman or not. I don't know whether scientists could determine his age.
Questions that Have *Do, Does, or Did*	Did the tourist call the police? Do people know about Iceman?	I dont know if the tourist called the police. I wonder if people know about Iceman.

Wh- Questions: Introduce the embedded question with the question word.

	Direct Question	Embedded Question
Questions with *Be* or Auxiliary Verb	Where was Iceman going? What can we learn from Iceman?	Do you know where Iceman was going? I don't know what we can learn from Iceman.
Questions that Have *Do, Does, or Did*	How did Iceman die? What do scientists want to learn?	Nobody knows how he died. Can you tell me what scientists want to learn?
Questions with *Wh-* Word As Subject	Who found Iceman? What happened to him?	I don't know who found Iceman. I wonder what happened to him.

Language
Notes

1. An embedded question is used after phrases like these:

I don't know	I can't understand	I have no idea
Do you know	Can you tell me	I wonder
I'm not sure	I can't tell you	I don't remember
Nobody knows	Please tell me	Do you remember

2. Use a period if the main clause is a statement. Use a question mark if the main clause is a question.

I don't know what time it is.
Do you know what time it is?

3. An embedded question is often used to make a question more polite, especially when asking for information from strangers. COMPARE:

Where is the post office?
MORE POLITE: Can you tell me *where the post office is?*

EXERCISE 5   Use "I don't know . . ." to respond to these questions. (These are *yes/no* questions with *be* or an auxiliary verb.)

EXAMPLE: **Have scientists studied Iceman?**
          I don't know if scientists have studied Iceman.

1. Are scientists happy with this   3 Is his age known?
   discovery?   4. Was he looking for food?
2. Was Iceman a hunter?   5. Have scientists studied his clothes?

EXERCISE 6   Change these direct questions to embedded questions with "Do you know . . ". (These are *yes/no* questions with *do, does,* or *did.*)

EXAMPLE: **Did Iceman live in the mountains?**
          Do you know if Iceman lived in the mountains?

1. Did Iceman have tools with him?   4. Did Iceman get lost?
2. Do scientists know his age?   5. Did the tourist go to the police?
3. Does Iceman's body have tattoos?

EXERCISE 7   Use "I don't know . . ." to respond to these questions. (These are *wh-* questions with *be* or an auxiliary verb.)

EXAMPLE: **Where was he found?**
          I don't know where he was found.

1. Where is Iceman now?   4. Where was Iceman found?
2. What are scientists studying?   5. What have scientists learned?
3. Where can we get more information?

EXERCISE 8   Change these direct questions to embedded questions with "Can you tell me . . .". (These are *wh-* questions with *do, does,* or *did.*)

> EXAMPLE: **What did the tourist do?**
> **Can you tell me what the tourist did?**

1. Where did Iceman live?
2. How did he die?
3. What does "glacier" mean?
4. What kind of tools did people use 5,000 years ago?
5. How much does it cost to take care of Iceman?

EXERCISE 9   Use "I don't know . . . " to respond to these questions. (These are questions about the subject.)

> EXAMPLE: **Who found Iceman?**
> **I don't know who found Iceman.**

1. How many people are studying Iceman?
2. What happened after Iceman was found?
3. Who saw him first?
4. Who is taking care of Iceman now?
5. What preserved Iceman's body for so many years?

EXERCISE 10   You probably have some questions for the teacher about this college or this city. Write questions to ask your teacher, beginning with "Can you tell me . . .?"

> EXAMPLES: **Can you tell me when the semester will end?**
> **Can you tell me where I can buy used clothes?**
> **Can you tell me if I can register for college English next semester?**

1. _____
2. _____
3. _____

EXERCISE 11   Write what you know or don't know about the teacher. Use "I know that . . ." or "I don't know. . . ."

> EXAMPLES: **I know that you majored in linguistics.**
> **I don't know where you went to college.**
> **I don't know whether you speak another language or not.**

1. _____
2. _____
3. _____

10.4 Question Words Followed by an Infinitive

An infinitive can be used to embed certain questions.

Question	Main Clause	Question Word	Infinitive
What should I do?	I don't know	what	to do.
How can I register?	Please tell me	how	to register.
Should I buy or rent a new car?	I can't decide	whether	to buy or rent a new car.

Language Notes

1. An infinitive is sometimes used to shorten an included question with modals *can, could,* or *should*. In order to do so, the understood subject of the infinitive must be the same as the subject of the main verb.

Different subjects—an infinitive cannot be used:
   I don't know what *he* should do.

Same subject—change to infinitive:
   I don't know what *I* should do. = I don't know what *to do*.

2. When *whether* introduces an infinitive, the choices are connected with *or*.

   I don't know *whether* to go to a two-year college *or* a four-year college.
   She doesn't know *whether* to fix her car *or* buy a new one.

EXERCISE 12   Complete each statement with an infinitive phrase.

EXAMPLE: I can't decide whether _to buy a new or used computer._

1. I need to buy used textbooks. Do you know where _____

2. Have you decided where _____ on your vacation?

3. A car buyer has to decide whether _____ or a foreign car.

4. I often look up a word in the dictionary and find four or five English

   translations. I don't know which word _____

EXERCISE 13   Complete each statement with an infinitive phrase. Discuss your sentences in a small group or with the entire class.

      EXAMPLES: I can't decide . . .
                  I can't decide whether to stay in this city or move to another city.
                  I can't decide what kind of car to buy.

1. When I came to the U.S., I didn't know how . . .
2. I can't decide . . .
3. When I came to the U.S., I had to decide . . .
4. A new student at this college needs to know where . . .
5. There are so many choices of products in the stores. Sometimes I can't decide . . .

EXERCISE 14   Two students are talking. Fill in each blank to complete the embedded questions. Use correct punctuation (period or question mark).

A. Hi. Where are you going in such a hurry?

B. I need to get to the library before it closes. What time does it close?

A. I'm not sure what time _it closes._

B. What time is it now?

A. I don't have my watch, so I don't know what time _____. But I'm
                                                                 (1)

    sure it must be after six. Why do you need to use the library?

B. The teacher told us to write a paper. She told us to choose a topic. I don't

    know what topic _____
                                   (2)

A. Why don't you write about Iceman? That's an interesting topic. There were a lot of articles written about him when he was found.

B. Do you remember when _____
                                       (3)

A. No. I can't remember _____ in 1991 or 1990. But you can get
                                      (4)

    that information from the computer in the library.

B. But I don't know how _____ the computer.
                                      (5)

A. It's easy.

B. In fact, I don't even know where _____
                                        (6)

A. It's on the first floor. Come on. I'll show you.

(Later)

B. Uh-oh. The library is closed. I wonder what time _____
                                                                    (7)
tomorrow.

A. The sign says, "Open 9–6."

B. Can you meet me at the library at 10 o'clock?

A. I'm not sure _____ or not. I have an appointment at 9:30, and I
                              (8)

don't know ___ _____ by 10 o'clock or not. But don't worry. The
                    (9)

librarian can show you how _____ _____ the computer.
                                                 (10)

• •

R
E
A
D
I
N
G

Before you read:

Did you ever lose a valuable object or an important document? Did you ever find it?

Nasreddin is a character in many Middle Eastern folk tales. Read the following story. Pay special attention to the exact quotations.

A FOLK TALE

One day a neighbor passed Nasreddin's house and saw him outside his barn on his hands and knees. He appeared to be looking for something. "What are you doing?" the neighbor asked.

"I'm looking for something," answered Nasreddin.

"What are you looking for?" the neighbor asked.

"I'm looking for my ring. It's very valuable," Nasreddin replied.

"I'll help you," said his neighbor. The neighbor got down on his hands and knees and started to help Nasreddin look for his ring. After searching for several hours, the neighbor finally asked, "Do you remember where you were when you lost it?"

"Of course," replied Nasreddin. "I was in the barn milking my cow."

"If you lost your ring inside the barn, then why are we looking for it outside the barn?" asked the neighbor.

"Don't be a fool," said Nasreddin. "It's too dark in the barn. But out here we have light."

• •

10.5 Exact Quotations

A noun clause is often used in a sentence to report what someone has said. When exact words are written, these words are called a quotation or quote. They are written inside quotation marks:". . ."

Main Clause	Exact Quote (Noun Clause)
He asked,	"What are you looking for?"
He said,	"I'm looking for my ring."

Language Notes

1. *Said* or *asked* can come at the beginning or the end of a quotation. Notice the punctuation used. Also note that the first letter of an exact quotation is a capital.

He said, "It's dark in the barn."
    ↑ ↑   ↑↑

"It's dark in the barn," he said.
↑   ↑↑   ↑

He asked, "What are you doing?"
    ↑↑   ↑↑

"What are you doing?" he asked.
↑   ↑↑   ↑

2. Sometimes the subject and verb are inverted when they follow the exact quotation.
"What are you doing?" *asked the neighbor.*

EXERCISE 15   Punctuate the following sentences. Put in capital letters where they are needed.

EXAMPLE: *"What are you doing?" asked the neighbor.*

1. I'm looking for my ring answered Nasreddin

2. Nasreddin said my ring is very valuable

3. His neighbor asked where did you lose it

4. I'll help you said the neighbor

5. Why are you looking outside his neighbor asked

6. Nasreddin replied it's too dark inside

R
E
A
D
I
N
G

Before you read:

Has your country been at war with another country recently? What started the war?

Read the following article. Pay special attention to noun clauses used to report what someone has said.

missles

THE CUBAN MISSILE CRISIS

In October 1962 the United States and the Soviet Union came close to war.

The U.S. discovered that the Soviet Union was beginning to send missiles to Cuba, which is only about 90 miles from Florida. From these missile bases in Cuba, the Soviet Union could attack any country in the Western Hemisphere.

The U.S. President, John F. Kennedy, met with Congressional leaders about the possibility of war. After several days of talking to his advisers, he said, **"We have decided to take action."** On October 22 he announced **that he would send out the U.S. Navy** to block Soviet ships from delivering weapons to Cuba. Kennedy told the Soviet Premier, Nikita Khrushchev, to recall all weapons. At first, Khrushchev said **that there were no Soviet missiles in Cuba.** But the United States had spy photos to prove that there were. The U.S. prepared for war.

Finally, on October 28, Khrushchev told Kennedy that **he would stop building military bases in Cuba** and that **the missiles already in Cuba would be returned to the Soviet Union.** In exchange, the U.S. agreed not to invade Cuba.

10.6 Exact Quotations and Reported Speech

We often use reported speech to report what someone has said. Compare an exact quotation with reported speech.

Kennedy said, "We have decided to take action."
Kennedy said that they had decided to take action.

Kennedy said, "I will send out the Navy."
Kennedy said that he would send out the Navy.

When we use reported speech, we usually follow the rule of sequence of tenses: when the main verb is in the past tense (for example, *said*), the tense of the verb in the noun clause moves back.

Notice the difference in verb tenses in the following sentences.

Exact Quotation	Reported Speech
He said, "I *know* you." (present)	He said (that) he *knew* me. (simple past)
He said, "I *am studying.*" (present continuous)	He said (that) he *was studying.* (past continuous)
He said, "She *saw* me yesterday." (simple past)	He said (that) she *had seen* him the day before. (past perfect)
He said, "She *was helping* me." (past continuous)	He said (that) she *had been helping* him. (past perfect continuous)
He said, "I *have taken* the test." (present perfect)	He said (that) he *had taken* the test. (past perfect)
He said, "I *had* never *done* that." (past perfect)	He said (that) he *had* never *done* that. (past perfect)

Modals	
He said, "I *can* help you tomorrow."	He said (that) he *could* help me the next day.
He said, "She *may* leave early." (*may* = possibility)	He said (that) she *might* leave early.
He said, "You *may* go." (*may* = permission)	He said (that) I *could* go.
He said, "I *must* go."	He said (that) he *had to* go.
He said, "I *will* stay."	He said (that) he *would* stay.

Modals That Do Not Change Their Form in Reported Speech	
He said, "You *should* leave."	He said (that) I *should* leave.
He said, "You *should have* left this morning."	He said (that) I *should have* left that morning.
He said, "You *could have* come."	He said (that) I *could have* come.
He said "You *must have* known."	He said (that) I *must have* known.

Language Notes

1. Besides changing tenses, the following changes are also made:

- The pronouns and possessive forms are changed in reported speech.

   She said, "*You* took *my* pen."
   She said that *I* had taken *her* pen.

- Quotation marks are not used.
- A comma is not used after *said*.

- Some time words are changed:

   today → that day
   yesterday → the day before
   tomorrow → the next day
   this morning → that morning

2. The word *that* can be used to introduce reported speech, or it can be omitted.

EXERCISE 16   Change each sentence to reported speech. Follow the rule of sequence of tenses.

      EXAMPLE: **The teacher said, "I have been teaching English for many years."**

          The teacher said *that he had been teaching English for many years.*

  1. The teacher said, "You must do all your homework."

     The teacher said _____

  2. The teacher said, "I'll repeat the explanation if you don't understand it."

     The teacher said _____

  3. The teacher said, "All of you passed the last test."

     The teacher said _____

  4. The teacher said, "I'm pleased with your progress."

     The teacher said _____

  5. The teacher said, "I'm planning a test on noun clauses."

     The teacher said _____

  6. The teacher said, "The test will be on Friday."

     The teacher said _____

  7. The teacher said, "You can stay after class if you have any questions."

     The teacher said _____

  8. The teacher said, "I have been teaching at this school for two years."

     The teacher said _____

  9. The teacher said, "I had never taught composition before."

     The teacher said _____

 10. The teacher said, "I hope you will enjoy your vacation."

     The teacher said _____

 11. The teacher said, "You can use your dictionary to write a composition."

     The teacher said _____

10.7 *Say* vs. *Tell*

For direct speech, we usually follow these patterns:

> Subject *said*, ". . . ."
>
> Khrushchev said, "There are no Soviet missiles in Cuba."
>
> Subject *said to* someone, ". . . ."
>
> Khrushchev said to Kennedy, "There are no missiles in Cuba."

For reported speech, we usually follow these patterns:

Subject	*Told*	Someone	(*That*)	. . . .
He	told	him	(that)	there were no missiles in Cuba.

Subject	*Said*	(*That*)	. . . .
He	said	(that)	there were no missiles in Cuba.

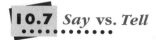

1. We *say* something. We *tell* someone some-thing. *Tell* is usually followed by an indirect object.

2. *Tell* is not usually used with an exact quotation.

EXERCISE 17   Susan bought a car from her cousin John. Change these exact quotations to reported speech. Follow the rule of sequence of tenses. Use an object after *told*.

EXAMPLES: **John said, "My car is three years old."**

He said *(that) his car was three years old.*

John said to her, "It has a new battery."

He told *her (that) it had a new battery.*

1. John said, "It's running very well."

   He told _____

2. He said, "It has only 35,000 miles on it."

   He said _____

3. He said, "I bought the car new from a dealer."

   He told _____

4. He said, "I have been getting good gas mileage."

   He said _____

5. He said, "It has a stick shift."

   He told _____

6. Susan said, "I like driving a stick shift."

   She told _____

7. John said, "I want to sell it because I need some money."

   He told _____

8. He said, "I had a tune-up in November."

   He said _____

9. He said, "I have to transfer the title to your name."

   He told _____

10. Susan said, "I must get insurance."

    She said _____

11. She said "I will call several insurance companies."

    She told _____

12. She said, "I hope the insurance won't be too expensive."

    She said _____

1. When the main verb is in the present tense, the rule of sequence of tenses is not applied.

> He always *says,* "I*'m* right."
> He always *says* that he *is* right.

2. In reporting a general truth, the rule of sequence of tenses is often not applied.

> He *said,* "The sun *is* larger than the moon."
> He *said* that the sun *is* larger than the moon.

3. In reporting a habitual activity, the rule of sequence of tenses is often not applied if the statement is still true and still present. COMPARE:

> Yesterday my brother *said,* "I *work* hard every day."
> My brother *said* that he *works* hard every day.
> In 1935 my grandfather *said,* "I *work* hard every day."
> In 1935 my grandfather *said* that he *worked* hard every day.

4. When reporting speech soon after it was said, often the rule of sequence of tenses is not applied.

> He *just said,* "I *lost* my pen."
> He *said* that he *lost* his pen.

5. In reporting a verb in the future tense, we can use *will* if the future action has not happened yet. If it has already passed, we must use *would.*

> He said, "I *will* marry you in the year 2010."
> He said that he *will* (or *would*) marry me in the year 2010.

> Kennedy said, "I *will* send out the Navy."
> Kennedy said that he *would* send out the Navy.

10.8 Reporting an Imperative

To report an imperative, an infinitive is used.

Imperative	Reported Imperative		
	Subject *Tell/Ask* Object	*(Not)*	Infinitive
Remove all weapons.	Kennedy told Khrushchev		to remove all weapons.
Sit down.	The secretary asked me		to sit down.
Don't be late.	The teacher told me	not	to be late.

1. *Ask* sounds less demanding than *tell.* It is more of an invitation than a demand.

2. *Say* is not used to report an imperative.

3. An object must follow *tell* or *ask.*

> WRONG: He told to sit down.
> RIGHT: He told *me* to sit down.

EXERCISE 18 Change these imperatives to reported speech. Use *asked* or *told* + object.

EXAMPLES: The candidate said, "Vote for me."

The candidate *asked us to vote for her.*

The father said to his daughter, "Don't come home late."

The father *told his daughter not to come home late.*

1. The thief said, "Give me your money."

   The thief _____

2. The teacher said, "Don't be late for class."

   The teacher _____

3. The teacher said, "Don't cheat on the test."

   The teacher _____

4. The teacher said, "Do your homework."

   The teacher _____

5. The doctor said to the man, "Take two aspirins and go to bed."

   The doctor _____

6. The dentist said to the girl, "Brush your teeth after every meal."

   The dentist _____

7. The mother said to her children, "Wash your hands before eating."

   The mother _____

8. The father said to his son, "Don't watch so much television."

   The father _____

9. The wife said to her husband, "Don't open my mail."

   The wife _____

10.9 Reported Questions

An exact question can be changed to a reported question.

Exact Question	Reported Question
He asked, "Is she a teacher?"	He asked if she was a teacher.
He asked, "Have they left?"	He asked if they had left.
He asked, "What will they do?"	He asked what they would do.
He asked, "Does he know?"	He asked whether he knew (or not).
He asked, "Did they go home?"	He asked if they had gone home.
He asked, "Where does she live?"	He asked where she lived.
He asked, "Who knows the answer?"	He asked who knew the answer.
He asked, "What happened?"	He asked what had happened.

1. Follow the rule of sequence of tenses if the main verb is in the past tense *(asked)*.

2. Use statement word order in reported questions.

3. An object can be added after *ask:* "He *asked me* where I was going."

4. A reported question ends in a period, not a question mark.

EXERCISE 19   Jim went to see an apartment for rent. The landlady asked him the following questions. Report these questions. Follow the rule of sequence of tenses.

   EXAMPLE: **Do you have a pet?**

   She asked him *if he had a pet.*

1. Are you married?

   She asked him _____

2. Do both you and your wife work?

   She asked him _____

3. How many children do you have?

   She asked him _____

4. How long have you lived at your present address?

   She asked him _____

5. Do you have a major credit card?

   She asked him _____

6. Where did you see the ad for this apartment?

   She asked him _____

7. Are you interested in a one-bedroom or a two-bedroom apartment?

   She asked him _____

8. When do you plan to move?

   She asked him _____

EXERCISE 20   Jim asked the landlady a lot of questions. What were the exact words Jim used?

   EXAMPLE: He asked her if there were laundry facilities in the building.

   He asked, *"Are there laundry facilities in the building?"*

1. He asked her why she hadn't installed smoke detectors.

   He asked, _____

2. He asked her if the tenant had to pay the utilities.[2]

   He asked, _____

3. He asked her if she would have the apartment painted before he moved in.

   He asked, _____

4. He asked her if she had cleaned the apartment.

   He asked, _____

5. He asked her if she lived in the building.

   He asked, _____

6. He asked her if he could install a new lock.

   He asked, _____

_____
[2]*Utilities* are the services you use: gas, electricity, water.

7. He asked her when he had to pay the rent.

He asked, _____

8. He asked her how many closets the apartment had.

He asked, _____

9. He asked her if there was a janitor in the building.

He asked, _____

10. He asked her when the present tenant was moving out.

He asked, _____

11. He asked her when he could move in.

He asked, _____

12. He asked her if there was a parking space for the tenant.

He asked, _____

EXPANSION ACTIVITIES

DISCUSSIONS   1. You probably see and hear things in the U.S. that are unfamiliar to you. Maybe you wonder about these strange customs. Express your questions with "I wonder. . . ." Share your sentences with the class.

EXAMPLES: I wonder why so many marriages end in divorce.
I wonder where Americans like to go for vacation.
I wonder if Americans like soccer.

A. _____

B. _____

C. _____

2. Tell what you know or don't know about another student and his or her country. Use "I know that . . ." or "I don't know. . . ." Share your sentences with this student.

EXAMPLES: I know that you come from Pakistan.
I don't know what the capital of Pakistan is.
I don't know whether you studied English in Pakistan or not.

A. _____

B. _____

C. _____

3. What advice did your parents or other people give you when you were younger? Write three sentences. Share them with the class.

EXAMPLES: My mother told me to be honest.
My grandfather told me to study hard and get a good education.

A. _____

B. _____

C. _____

4. What advice or information did your teacher tell you at the beginning of this semester? Work in a small group and write three sentences to report what the teacher said.

EXAMPLES: She told us that we had to do all the homework.
She told us to buy *Grammar in Context.*
She said that she would give a final exam.

A. _____

B. _____

C. _____

WRITING 1. Write a paragraph about an interesting conversation or argument that you had or heard recently.

EXAMPLE: Last week I had a conversation with my best friend about having children. I told her that I didn't want to have children. She asked me why I was against having children. I told her that people had children for all the wrong reasons. I explained that I had seen many parents use their children to satisfy their own needs. . . .

2. Write about an unpopular belief that you have. Explain why you have this belief.

EXAMPLES: I believe that there is life on other planets.
I believe that people shouldn't get married.
I believe that everyone should own a gun.
I believe that marijuana should be legal.
I believe that God does not exist.

3. Write about a belief that you used to have that you no longer have. Explain what this belief was and why you no longer believe it to be true.

EXAMPLES: I used to believe that communism was the best form of government.
I used to believe that parents should be very strict with their children.
I used to believe that marriage made people happy.
I used to believe that the U.S. was the best country in the world.

4. Write about a general belief that people in your country have. Explain what this belief means. Do you agree with it?

EXAMPLES: In my country, it is often said that a whole community raises a child.
In my country, it is believed that wisdom comes with age.

5. Write a short fable that you remember. Use quotations. Use correct punctuation and capitalization.

OUTSIDE ACTIVITIES

1. Go to the library. Ask the reference librarian to help you do a periodical search to find out more about Iceman. Find the latest article you can. Bring to class updated information about Iceman.

2. Ask an older American if he or she remembers the Cuban missile crisis. Ask if he or she was worried about war at that time. Tell the class his or her answer.

EDITING ADVICE

1. Use *that* (or nothing) to introduce an included statement.

   I know ~~what~~ *(that)* she likes to swim.

2. Use statement word order in an indirect question.

   I don't know what time ~~is it~~ *it is*.

3. Use a period in an indirect question.

   I don't know what time it is~~?~~ .

4. We say *something*. We tell *someone* something.

   He ~~said~~ *told* me that he wants to be a doctor.

   He ~~told~~ *said*, "I want to be a doctor."

5. Don't use a comma before a noun clause.

   I know ~~,~~ that he speaks English well.

6. Use *not* + infinitive to report an imperative.

   He told me ~~don't~~ *not to* come in.

7. Notice where we put quotation marks in English.

   WRONG: He said, I love you.

   WRONG: He said «I love you.»

   WRONG: He said, „I love you."

   RIGHT: He said, "I love you."

8. Use *if* or *whether* to introduce an indirect yes/no question.

   I can't decide ^*if* I should buy a car or not.

9. Use *would*, not *will*, to report something that is past.

   My father said that he ~~will~~ *would* come to the U.S. in 1989.

10. Don't use *so* before a noun clause.

    He thinks ~~so~~ the U.S. is a beautiful country.

SUMMARY OF LESSON TEN

Uses of Noun Clauses

Direct Statement or Question	Sentence with Noun Clause	Use of Noun Clause
She has a car.	I'm sure *(that) she has a car.* I know *(that) she has a car.*	After certain adjectives and verbs of mental state
He stole the money.	It is believed *that he stole the money.*	After certain passive verbs.
Is he married?	I don't know *if he's married (or not).*	With an embedded question
Where does he live?	Do you know *where he lives?*	
What should I do?	I don't know *what I should do.* OR I don't know *what to do.*	(An infinitive can sometimes be used.)
I will leave.	He said, *"I will leave."* He said *that he would leave.*	To report a statement
Did you see the movie?	He asked, *"Did you see the movie?"* He asked me *if I had seen the movie.*	To report a question
Sit down. Don't be late.	He told me *to sit down.* He asked me *not to be late.*	To report an imperative, an infinitive is used. A noun clause is not used.

LESSON TEN TEST/REVIEW

Part 1   Find the mistakes and correct them. Not every sentence has a mistake. If the sentence is correct, write *C*.

EXAMPLES: I don't know~~x~~where he lives.

"Where do you live?" asked the child.   *C*

1. She wants to know where do you live.

2. She is happy what her daughter got married.

3. He said me, "You are right."

4. The President said, "There will be no new taxes."

5. I don't know what time it is?

6. I don't know what to do.

7. I told you not to leave the room.

8. Last week, the weatherman said that we will have rain on Sunday, but we didn't.

9. Do you think so it's going to rain?

10. Do you think I'm intelligent?

11. I don't know she understands English or not.

12. She said, «Come here.»

13. He asked me where do I live.

14. He told that he wanted to speak to me.

15. I know, that she likes to dance.

Part 2   Fill in each blank with an embedded question.

EXAMPLE: How old is the President?

Do you know *how old the President is?*

1.   Where does Jack live?

I don't know _____

2.   Did she go home?

I don't know _____

3. Why were they late?

Nobody knows _____

4. Who ate the cake?

I don't know _____

5. What does "liberty" mean?

I don't know _____

6. Are they working now?

Can you tell me _____

7. Where was the dictionary found?

I don't know _____

8. Has she ever gone to France?

I'm not sure _____

9. Can we use our books during the test?

Do you know _____

10. What should I do?

I don't know _____

Part 3   Change the following sentences to reported speech. Follow the rule of sequence of tenses.

EXAMPLE: **He said, "She is late."**

He said that she was late.

1. He said, "Give me the money."

_____

2. She said, "I can help you."

_____

3. He said, "Don't go away."

_____

4. He said, "My mother left yesterday."

   _____

5. She said, "I'm learning a lot."

   _____

6. He said, "I've never heard of Iceman."

   _____

7. They said to me, "We finished the job."

   _____

8. He said to us, "You may need some help."

   _____

9. He said to her, "We were studying."

   _____

10. He said to her, "I have your book."

    _____

11. He said to us, "You should have called me."

    _____

12. He said to his wife, "I will call you."

    _____

13. He asked me, "Do you have any children?"

    _____

14. He asked me, "Where are you from?"

    _____

15. He asked me, "What's your name?"

    _____

16. He asked me, "Did your father come home?"

_____

17. He asked me, "Where have you been?"

_____

18. He asked me, "What will you do tomorrow?"

_____

19. He asked me, "Where do you live?"

_____

20. He asked me, "Are you a student?"

_____

LESSON ELEVEN

GRAMMAR
Unreal Conditions
Wishes

CONTEXT
The Drug Problem
Agent Orange
Regrets

Lesson Focus Unreal Conditions; Wishes

In Lesson Nine, we studied real conditions. A real condition shows that there is a real possibility that something will happen if the condition is met.

> If I find a good job, I will buy a house.
> She will call you if she needs you.

- An unreal condition is used to talk about a situation that is not real. It is used for hypothetical or imaginary situations.[1]

Reality:	Hypothesis:
I don't have a lot of money.	If I had a lot of money, I would travel.

Reality:	Imagination:
I'm not a bird.	If I were a bird, I'd feel free.

- Unreal situations can also be expressed after the word *wish.*

Reality:	Wish:
I'm not rich.	I wish I were rich.

Reality:	Wish:
I have to work hard.	I wish I didn't have to work so hard.

· ·

R
E
A
D
I
N
G

Before you read:

Do you think drugs like marijuana and cocaine should be legalized? Why or why not?

Read the following article. Pay special attention to unreal conditions.

THE DRUG PROBLEM

Drug abuse has been going down in the United States since the 1970s, when it was at its highest. However, drugs still remain a problem in the U.S. Over 50% of high school seniors[2] today say that they have tried an illegal drug at least once. Marijuana is the drug of choice among young people. Teenagers are often pressured by their friends to try drugs. Also, many rock and rap musicians glorify drug use in the words of their songs.

There have been many suggestions on how to control or eliminate the drug problem. Some experts think that the way to control drugs is through better education of young people. They believe that **if** youngsters **understood** the dangers of drugs and addiction, they **would not start** to use them. Others believe that to eliminate the drug problem,

---

[1]Unreal conditions are sometimes called *contrary-to-fact* clauses.

[2]A *senior* is a student in the last (fourth) year of high school or college. The other years are as follows: 1 = freshman, 2 = sophomore, 3 = junior.

conditions of poverty and family life must be improved. More social services for poor people **would help. If** children **came** from loving homes or **had** better social services, they **would not use** drugs. Others believe that the way to solve the drug problem is to punish drug traffickers more severely. They reason that **if** drugs **were** not so readily available, people **wouldn't be able to** buy them. Some people suggest that the government legalize drugs. **If** drugs **were** legal, they **might not be** so desirable. In addition, the crimes associated with drug traffic **would stop.**

There are no easy solutions to this serious problem.

11.1 Unreal Conditions—Present

For an unreal condition in the present, a past form is used in the condition clause. *Would/might/could* + base form is used in the main clause.

If + Subject + Past Form ,	*Would* Subject + *Might* + Base Form *Could*
If youngsters *understood* the dangers, If you *didn't smoke,* If drugs *were* legal, If you *used* drugs,	they *wouldn't use* drugs. your health *would improve.* they *might* not *be* so desirable. you *could ruin* your health.

Language Notes

1. For the verb *be, were* is the correct form in the condition clause for all subjects. However, you will often hear people use *was* with *I, he, she,* and *it.*

   If I *were* a judge, I'd send drug dealers to jail for life.
   If it *were* up to me, I'd legalize drugs.

2. We often give advice with the expression "If I were you, . . ."

   If I *were* you, I'd quit smoking.
   If I *were* you, I'd buy a new car.

3. To talk about a present continuous situation, use *were* + verb + *-ing* in the condition clause. We can use *would be* + verb + *ing* in the main clause.

   If I *were living* in my country, I'd be with my relatives.
   If I *weren't studying* English this semester, I *wouldn't be learning* about conditionals.

4. All pronouns except *it* can be contracted with *would:*

   I'd   you'd   he'd   she'd   we'd   they'd

EXERCISE 1   Complete each statement.

 EXAMPLE: **If I studied harder, . . .**
                      If I studied harder, I would get better grades.

   1. If I were the leader of my country, . . .
   2. If I were in my native country now, . . .
   3. If I didn't come to class every day, . . .
   4. If I weren't studying English this semester, . . .
   5. If I could live to be 200 years old, . . .
   6. If I could predict the future, . . .
   7. If I were rich, . . .
   8. If I could be a child again, . . .
   9. If I were the teacher, . . .
  10. Even if someone paid me a million dollars, . . .
  11. If drugs were legalized, . . .

EXERCISE 2   Complete each statement.

 EXAMPLE: **The teacher would be surprised if . . .**
                      The teacher would be surprised if everyone got an A on the test.

   1. I'd be much happier if . . .   6. I'd be very unhappy if . . .
   2. I wouldn't be in the U.S. if . . .   7. I wouldn't return to my country
   3. I'd be learning English faster if . . .   unless . . .
   4. I'd study more if . . .   8. I wouldn't tell a lie unless . . .
   5. I'd travel a lot if . . .   9. I wouldn't kill anyone unless . . .

EXERCISE 3   Answer each question with *yes* or *no.* Then make a statement with an unreal
condition.

 EXAMPLES: **Are you a movie star?**

                      No. If I were a movie star, I'd be rich.

                      Do you have the textbook?

                      Yes. If I didn't have the textbook, I wouldn't be able to do this exercise.

   1. Are you an American?

   _____

   2. Can you go back to your country?

   _____

3. Can you sleep late in the morning?

_____

4. Do all the students in this class speak the same language?

_____

5. Does the teacher speak your language?

_____

6. Are you taking other courses this semester?

_____

7. Do you have a car?

_____

8. Do you have children?

_____

9. Do you exercise regularly?

_____

10. Do you feel OK now?

_____

11. Do you have a job?

_____

EXERCISE 4   Make a list of things you would do if you had more free time. Share your sentences in a small group or with the entire class.

> EXAMPLES: **If I had more free time, I'd read more novels.**
>   **If I had more free time, I'd visit my grandmother more often.**

1. _____

2. _____

3. _____

EXERCISE 5   Make a list of things you would do differently if you spoke English fluently. Share your sentences in a small group or with the entire class.

> EXAMPLES: **If I spoke English fluently, I wouldn't come to this class.**
> **If I spoke English fluently, I'd have more American friends.**

1. _____

2. _____

3. _____

EXERCISE 6   Fill in each blank. Share your sentences in a small group or with the entire class.

1. If I could change one thing about myself (or my life), I'd change _____

   _____

2. If I lost my _____, I'd be very upset.

3. People in my country would be happier if _____

• •

R
E
A
D
I
N
G

Before you read:

1. Has the government of your country ever done anything that put people in danger?
2. Has there ever been a danger in your country that the government kept secret from the people?

Read the following article. Pay special attention to past conditions.

AGENT ORANGE

During the war in Vietnam, the American military sprayed an herbicide[3] from airplanes to kill the vegetation in the jungles of Vietnam. This chemical is called Agent Orange. Many American military personnel came in contact with Agent Orange by being present at the time of the spraying, by handling the spraying equipment, or by marching through a sprayed jungle. Most of the spraying occurred in 1967 and 1968.

Years later, some Vietnam veterans started to complain about a number of diseases, from depression to cancer, that they believed resulted from contact with Agent Orange. Tests done with laboratory animals showed that this chemical is highly toxic. Veterans wanted to sue the company that manufactured this chemical as well as the U.S. govern-

_____

[3]An *herbicide* is a chemical used to kill plants.

ment for putting them in danger. Many claimed that **if** they **had not been exposed** to Agent Orange, they **would not have developed** cancer. However, the U.S. government continued to insist that there was no link[4] between Agent Orange and cancer. In addition, because the military did not keep clear records as to who was actually exposed to Agent Orange, the U.S. government said that veterans could not prove that they had been exposed. Angry veterans who remembered coming into contact with this chemical said that if the military **had kept** better records, they **would have been able to** prove the connection between their diseases and Agent Orange. Families of veterans who had already died of some kinds of cancer claimed that their relatives **would not have died** if they **had not been exposed.**

Finally, in 1991 the U.S. Congress passed the "Agent Orange Act," compensating some victims and their families for the diseases they suffered.

11.2 Unreal Conditions—Past

To talk about an unreal condition in the past, the past perfect is used in the condition clause. *Would/might/could have* + past participle is used in the main clause.

If + Subject + Past Perfect ,	Subject + *Would* *Might* + *Have* + Past Participle *Could*
If the government *had kept* better records,	the connection between Agent Orange and cancer *would have been* easier to prove.
If soldiers *had not been exposed* to Agent Orange,	they *might not have developed* cancer and they *could have had* healthier lives.

Language Notes

1. *Could* is changed to *had been able to* in the condition clause. Compare:

She *couldn't* finish the test on time. She didn't pass it.
If she *had been able to* finish the test on time, she would have passed it.

2. In informal speech, *have* is often pronounced like *of* or /ə/ after a modal. Listen to your teacher pronounce the sentences in the box above with fast, informal pronunciation.

---

[4]A *link* is a connection.

EXERCISE 7   Fill in each blank to complete the unreal condition.

   EXAMPLE: **I yelled at my boss. I lost my job.**

   If I _hadn't yelled_ at my boss, I _wouldn't have lost_ my job.

1. He went to a party. He met his future wife.

   If he _____, he _____.

2. Mary didn't study for the test. She failed it.

   If she _____, she _____.

3. He didn't know she was an alcoholic. He married her.

   He _____ her if he _____
   she was an alcoholic.

4. He told her his secret. He didn't know she was going to tell everyone.

   He _____his secret if he _____
   she was going to tell everyone.

5. Their parents approved of their marriage. They got married.

   They _____ married if their parents

   _____ of the marriage.

6. He left his country. He couldn't find a job there.

   If he _____ a job in his country, he

   _____.

7. I found a lost wallet. I couldn't return it because there was no name in it.

   I _____ the wallet if _____ a
   name or phone number in it.

8. I didn't know my friends were coming over. I didn't prepare any food.

   If I _____ they were coming over, I

   _____ some food.

9. The child told a lie. His mother punished him.

   She _____ him if he _____ a lie.

10. She didn't know she was going to come to the U.S. She didn't study English.

   She _____ English if she _____ she was going to come to the U.S.

Language Notes

1. A past condition can have a present or present continuous result.

   If he *hadn't been exposed* to Agent Orange, he *might be* alive today.
      past condition   present result

   If I *hadn't come* to the U.S., I *would be living* with my parents.
      past condition   present continuous
                                        result

2. A present condition can have a past result.

   If I *were* a Vietnam veteran, I *would have sued* the government.
      present condition   past result

   If I *were* you, I *wouldn't have left* my country.
      present   past result
      condition

EXERCISE 8   Fill in each blank with the correct form of a verb. These sentences have mixed tenses.

   EXAMPLE: I wasn't born in the U.S. I don't speak English perfectly.

      If I _had been born_ in the U.S., I _would speak_ English perfectly.

1. He bought a winning lottery ticket. He's now rich.

   If he _____ that lottery ticket, he _____ rich.

2. She didn't marry Edward. She's happy.

   If she _____ Edward, she _____ happy.

3. I passed the last course. I'm in this course.

   I _____ in this course if I _____ the last course.

4. I'm not you. I didn't buy that car.

   If I _____ you, I _____ that car.

5. She didn't see the accident. She can't tell you what happened.

She _____ you what happened if she _____ the accident.

6. You didn't come to class yesterday. You don't understand the teacher's explanation today.

You _____ the teacher's explanation today if you _____ to class yesterday.

7. I don't know how to speak Portuguese. I didn't help you translate the letter.

If I _____ how to speak Portuguese, I _____ you translate the letter.

8. He's not living in his native country. He didn't graduate from college there.

He _____ from college by now if he _____ in his native country.

9. She doesn't have a car. She didn't drive you to the hospital.

If she _____ a car, she _____ you to the hospital.

EXERCISE 9   Complete each statement with a past or present result.

EXAMPLES: **If I hadn't known some English, . . .**
            **If I hadn't known some English, I wouldn't have been able to
               take this course.**

            If I had lived in Spain as a child, . . .
            **If I had lived in Spain as a child, I would know how to speak
               Spanish.**

1. If I had been born in the U.S., . . .
2. If I'd come to the U.S. (fifteen) years ago, . . .
3. If I hadn't come to the U.S., . . .
4. If I hadn't taken beginning English, . . .
5. If I hadn't come to class today, . . .
6. If I hadn't studied for the last test, . . .
7. If I hadn't paid last month's rent, . . .
8. If I had been born 200 years ago, . . .

EXERCISE 10 Complete each statement with a past or present condition.

EXAMPLES: **I would have stayed in my country if . . .**
I would have stayed in my country if my family had stayed.
OR
**I would have stayed in my country if the political situation
were better.**

1. I would have stayed after class yesterday if . . .
2. I would have stayed home today if . . .
3. I would have done better/worse on the last test if . . .
4. I would have taken an easier/harder course if . . .
5. I would have studied (more) English in my country if . . .
6. The teacher would have explained the last lesson again if . . .
7. I would have stayed in my country if . . .
8. My parents would have been disappointed in me if . . .

EXERCISE 11 Fill in each blank with the correct form of a verb. Some sentences have mixed tenses.

EXAMPLE: **I took a wrong turn on the highway. I arrived at the meeting one
hour late.**

If I __*hadn't taken*__ a wrong turn on the highway, I __*would*__ _____

__*have arrived*_____ at the meeting on time.

1. I forgot to set my alarm clock, so I didn't wake up on time.

   I _____ on time if I _____ my alarm clock.

2. She didn't pass the final exam, so she didn't pass the course.

   If she _____ the final exam, she _____ the course.

3. I didn't see the movie, so I can't give you any information about it.

   If _____ the movie, I _____ some information about it.

4. I don't like potatoes, so I didn't eat the potato salad.

   I _____ the potato salad if I _____ potatoes.

5. He loves her, so he married her.

   If _____ her, he _____ her.

6. She didn't hear the phone ring, so she didn't answer it.

   She _____ the phone if she _____ it ring.

7. He left his keys at the office, so he couldn't get into the house.

   If he _____ his keys at the office, he _____ into the house.

8. I don't have much money, so I didn't buy a new coat.

   I _____ a new coat if I _____ more money.

9. He didn't take the medicine, so his condition didn't improve.

   If he _____ the medicine, his condition _____.

10. I didn't have my credit card with me, so I didn't buy the stereo.

    I _____ the stereo if I _____ my credit card with me.

EXERCISE 12   Write a conditional statement based on these facts, which are from articles you have read in this book.

> EXAMPLE: **Many Mexicans couldn't find a good job in Mexico. They came to the U.S.**
>
> *If they had been able to find a good job in Mexico, they wouldn't have come to the U.S.*

1. Columbus discovered America. Europeans came to America.

   _____

   _____

2. Europeans came to America. The native people got diseases.

   _____

   _____

3. Columbus got money for his trip. He was able to come to America.

   _____

   _____

4. Oswald was killed after the assassination of President Kennedy. This made the investigation more difficult.

_____

_____

5. Arlena Twigg took a blood test. The Twiggs found out that Arlena wasn't their real daughter.

_____

_____

6. The babies were switched at birth. The Twiggs didn't go home with a healthy daughter.

_____

_____

7. A tourist was walking in the Alps. Iceman was found.

_____

_____

8. We have used a lot of chemicals (CFCs). The ozone layer has a hole. (Change *a lot of* to *so many.*)

_____

_____

9. The U.S. won the Spanish-American war. Puerto Rico became a territory of the U.S.

_____

_____

EXERCISE 13   Fill in each blank with the correct form of the verb in parentheses ( ).
Both real conditions and unreal conditions are used.

EXAMPLES: If I _____*were*_____ you, I _____*would buy*_____ a new car.
                                (be)   (buy)

I'll buy a new car if I _____*get*_____ a raise this year.
                                      (get)

1. If I _____ in my country now, I _____ a political
                (be)   (be)
    prisoner.

2. A. Will Linda marry Paul?

    B. She _____ him even if he _____ the last man on
                (not/marry)   (be)
       earth.

3. My mother may visit me next week. If my mother _____ here, I
                                                              (come)
    _____ absent from class for a few days.
         (be)

4. Everybody who ate the fish got sick. I didn't eat any fish. If I

    _____ the fish, I _____ sick.
          (eat)   (get)

5. I left my country six years ago. If I _____, I _____
                                                (stay)   (finish)
    my degree by now.

6. She loves her dog. She _____ her dog even if you
                                  (not/sell)
    _____ her a million dollars.
         (pay)

7. My boss will probably call. If he _____, tell him I'm not home.
                                            (call)

8. He didn't know she was dishonest. If he _____ how dishonest
                                                   (know)
    she was, he _____ her with his money.
                     (never/trust)

9. I can't speak French. If I _____, I _____ to France
                                    (can/speak)   (go)
    for my vacation.

10. She may get some money from her parents. If her parents _____
    (send)

    her some money, she _____ some new clothes.
    (buy)

11. My family lives in Minneapolis. It's so cold there in the winter. If it

    _____ so cold there, I _____ there to be with my
    (be/not)   (move)

    family.

12. It's raining now. If it _____, we _____ roller
    (not/rain)   (can/go)

    skating.

13. My friend likes to parachute out of airplanes. I _____ it even if
    (not/do)

    you _____ me a million dollars.
    (pay)

14. She was sleeping when the burglar entered the house. If she

    _____, she _____ the burglar.
    (not/sleep)   (hear)

15. We weren't born in the U.S. If we _____ born in the U.S., we
    (be)

    _____ in this class.
    (not/be)

. . . .

R
E
A
D
I
N
G

Before you read:

Sometimes we make a decision in our lives and then wait too long to take action. Other times, we act too quickly and regret our decision. Has there been a decision that you acted on too quickly or not quickly enough?

Read the following conversation. Pay special attention to the verb forms used after *wish*.

REGRETS

A. Are you happy you came to the U.S.?

B. Well, I'm glad I'm here. But **I wish I had come** here when my brother came 15 years ago.

A. Why?

B. Well, now I'm 40 years old, and it's harder to learn English and find a good job. My brother already speaks English well, has a small business, and owns a house in the suburbs. If I had come here with him, I would already be successful in this country. **I wish I didn't have to start** so many new things at my age. Also, **I wish my parents would come** here, but they think they're too old.

A. There are a lot of things **I wish were** different in my life too.

B. What, for example?

A. **I wish I hadn't gotten** married so young. I never had a chance to enjoy my freedom. My first son was born when I was 19 years old. **I wish I had waited.** I would have been a better parent if I had been older.

B. **I wish I could go back and start** my life again. There are a lot of things I would do differently.

11.3 Wishes

We often wish for things that are not real or true.

Time	Real Situation	Wish Statement
Present	My life *is* not easy.	I wish my life *were* different.
	I *can't* start my life again.	I wish I *could* start my life again.
	I'*m not working.*	I wish I *were working.*
Past	I *got* married young.	I wish I *hadn't gotten* married so young.
	I *couldn't come* to the U.S. with my brother.	I wish I *could have come* with him.

1. The verb in a *wish* clause is like the verb in a clause of an unreal condition. COMPARE:

If my parents *were* here, I'd be happy.
I wish my parents *were* here.

If I *hadn't gotten married* so young, my life would have been better.
I wish I *hadn't gotten married* so young.

2. Clauses after *wish* are noun clauses. *That* can introduce the clause, but it is usually omitted.

I wish (that) my parents were here.

3. With *be*, *were* is the correct form for all subjects. In conversation, however, you will often hear people use *was* with *I*, *he*, *she*, and *it*.

FORMAL: I wish he *were* here.
INFORMAL: I wish he *was* here.

EXERCISE 14   Fill in each blank to make a wish about the present.

EXAMPLE: **Today isn't Friday. I wish it** _were_____ **Friday.**

1. You're not here with me. I wish you _____ here.

2. I have to work 60 hours a week. I wish I _____ so much.

3. I can't speak English perfectly. I wish I _____ English perfectly.

4. I don't have a car. I wish I _____ a car.

5. You're going on vacation to Hawaii? I can't go. I wish I _____ with you.

6. I'm not rich. I wish I _____ rich.

7. I have a lot of responsibilities. I wish I _____ so many responsibilities.

EXERCISE 15   Fill in each blank to make a wish about the past.

EXAMPLE: **I didn't come to the U.S. as a child. I wish I** _had come_ __ **to the U.S. as a child.**

1. I didn't know it was your birthday. I wish I _____. I would have baked a cake.

2. I had a baby when I was 17. I was too young. I wish I _____.

3. I couldn't attend your graduation. I wish I _____.

4. I didn't see the parade. I wish I _____ it.

5. I studied German in my country. I wish I _____ English in my country.

6. I didn't see his face when he opened the present. I wish I _____ his face.

7. I lost my favorite ring. I was wearing it at the party. I wish _____.

8. I told Larry my secret, and he told all his friends. I wish _____.

EXERCISE 16   Name something. Discuss your answers in a small group or with the entire class.

EXAMPLE: **Name something you wish had never happened.**

I wish the war in Vietnam had never happened.

1. Name something you wish you had done as a child.
2. Name something you wish you had studied when you were younger.
3. Name something your family wishes you had done differently.
4. Name something you wish you had known before you came to the U.S.
5. Name something you wish you had done before coming to the U.S.

6. Name something you wish you had brought to the U.S. but couldn't.
7. Name something you wish you had never done.
8. Name something you wish your parents had done or told you.

1. *Wish + would* is often used to make a request or show a desire that someone do something differently.

   My neighbors play their music loud late at night. I wish they *would turn down* their stereo.

   Your hair is too long. I wish you *would cut* it.

2. Compare these sentences with *wish*.

   I wish my parents *would* come to the U.S. (I would like them to come to the U.S.)

   I wish my parents *were* here. (I'm unhappy that they're not here.)

EXERCISE 17   Fill in each blank to show a desire that someone do something differently.

   EXAMPLE: **My parents are going back to my country. I wish they**

   would stay here.

1. Are you leaving so soon? I wish you _____ for a few more hours.

2. My son doesn't want to clean his room. I wish he _____ his room.

3. My apartment is too cold. I wish the landlord _____ more heat.

4. Some students are talking loudly in the library. I wish they _____.

5. The teacher gives a lot of homework. I wish she _____.

6. Will the teacher review this lesson? I wish she _____ because it's so difficult.

7. The teacher often tells Max to write more clearly. She wishes he

   _____ more legibly.[5]

8. The teacher speaks English too fast. I wish _____.

---

[5]To write *legibly* means to write so that other people can read your writing.

EXERCISE 18   Complete each statement. Share your sentences with the class.

    EXAMPLE: **I wish I had . . .**
                      I wish I had more money.

1. I wish I were . . .
2. I wish I knew (how to) . . .
3. I wish I didn't have to . . .
4. I wish I had . . .
5. I wish I could . . .

EXERCISE 19   Complete each statement. Share your sentences with the class.

    EXAMPLE: **I wish the class . . .**
                      I wish the class didn't have so many students.

1. I wish my family . . .
2. I wish the teacher . . .
3. I wish Americans . . .
4. I wish the world . . .
5. I wish more people . . .
6. I wish my apartment . . .
7. I wish my country . . .

EXERCISE 20   Fill in each blank to complete this conversation. Two men are talking about a problem that one of them is having.

A. I have a problem. I need your advice.

B. What is it?

A. My wife's mother is going to come to visit for a month. A week's OK, but a month is too much.

B. If I __ _were_ ___ you, I _____ tell her that she can visit, but only for
                                  (1)

    one week.

A. I wish I _____ tell her that, but my wife, Brenda, insists that she stay
                    (2)

    for a month.

B. What's so terrible about her?

A. Well, when she babysits for our kids, she tells them the opposite of what my wife and I tell them. For example, we tell the kids to go to bed at 9 o'clock. But she tells them that they can stay up as late as they like. I wish she

    _____ follow the same rules we do.
        (3)

B. At least you get a free babysitter. I wish my children _____ a grand-
   (4 have)

mother to babysit for them. But their grandparents live in Vietnam.

A. I wish my mother-in-law _____ in Vietnam. Unfortunately, she lives in
   (5)

Minneapolis and visits twice a year.

B. I think you're making too much of the problem.

A. But there's more. The last time she was here, she gave the kids an expensive
   video game.

B. What's so bad about that?

A. We told the kids that they couldn't play video games. If she _____ us
   (6 ask)

before giving them the game, we _____ her that we don't allow video
   (7 tell)

games in our house. But she never asked us. The kids think that we're mean
and that Grandma is nice.

B. Maybe she has nothing to do. If she _____ a life of her own, maybe
   (8)

she _____ you so often.
   (9)

A. The problem is that she isn't interested in anything, except interfering in our
   lives.

B. Can't she stay at a hotel while she's visiting?

A. Hotels are expensive. If I _____ a lot of money, I _____
   (10)   (11)

definitely put her in a hotel.

B. I wish I _____ help you, but I can't.
   (12)

A. I know. I just needed to talk to someone about it. If I _____ that
   (13 know)

Brenda's mother was such a busybody,[6] I _____ Brenda.
   (14 not/marry)

B. I'm sure you don't mean that.

_____
[6]A *busybody* is a person who interferes in other people's lives.

EXPANSION ACTIVITIES

PROVERBS
1. The following proverb contains an unreal condition. Discuss the meaning of this proverb. Do you have a similar proverb in your language?

   If wishes were horses, then beggars would ride.

2. The following proverb expresses the importance of being careful before you do something. Do you have a similar proverb in your language?

   Look before you leap.

3. The following proverb expresses the importance of doing something when the moment is right. Do you have a similar proverb in your language?

   Strike while the iron is hot.

DISCUSSIONS
1. With a partner or in a small group, talk about your job, your school, your apartment, or your family. What do you wish were different?

   EXAMPLE: my job
   I have to work on Saturdays.
   I wish I didn't have to work on Saturdays.
   I get $7 an hour.
   I wish my boss would give me a raise.

2. Fill in the blank with an age, and discuss your answers in a small group or with the entire class.

   I wish I were _____ years old.

3. Complete this sentence in three different ways. Discuss your sentences in a small group or with the entire class.

   The world would be a better place if . . .

   A. _____

   B. _____

   C. _____

4. In your opinion, what would solve the drug problem?
   Is there a drug problem in your country?

5. Write three sentences to complain about members of your family. What do you wish they would do differently? Share your sentences with the class.

   EXAMPLES: **My husband smokes a lot. I wish he would quit smoking.**
   My son watches TV all day. I wish he would play with his friends more.

   A. _____

   B. _____

   C. _____

WRITING

1. Write about an event in history. Tell what the result would/might have been if this event hadn't happened.

2. Write about how your life would have been different if you had stayed in your country.

3. Write about a regret you have about something you have done or not done. Explain how your life has been affected.

4. Write about how your life would have been different if a major event had (or had not) happened.

   EXAMPLES: **getting married when you were young**
   the death of someone important
   dropping out of high school

5. If you could travel to the past or the future, which direction would you go? Why? What would you see or do? Write a composition to explain your choice.

6. Write about some things in your present life that you are not happy about. How would you like to change your life?

OUTSIDE ACTIVITIES

1. Ask an American to finish this sentence:

   The world would be a better place if . . .
   Report to the class what the American said.

2. Interview an American.

   A. Ask for his or her opinion on the drug problem in the U.S. Ask: "Do you think drugs should be legalized in the U.S.?"
   B. Ask for his or her opinion on other controversial subjects: abortion, prayer in the schools, gun control.

SUMMARY OF LESSON ELEVEN

1. Unreal Conditions

   PRESENT: If I *were* you, I'*d go* to medical school.
                If I *were living* in Paris, I'*d be* with my family.

   PAST: If I *had seen* the accident, I *would have reported* it.

   MIXED: If she *had married* him, she'*d be* very unhappy now.

   MIXED: If she *were* rich, she *would have sent* her children to an expensive college.

2. Wishes

   PRESENT: I wish I *had* a car.
                I wish I *could* fly.

   PAST: I wish you *had called* me.

   COMPLAINT: I wish he *wouldn't smoke* so much.

LESSON ELEVEN TEST/REVIEW

Part 1   Fill in each blank with the correct form of the verb in parentheses ( ). Both real conditions and unreal conditions are used.

EXAMPLES: If I _____*were*_____ you, I ___*would buy*___ a new car.
       (be)   (buy)

      I'll buy a new car if I _____*get*_____ a raise this year.
              (get)

1. Maybe my mother will come to visit me. If she _____, I
                (come)
 _____ her to see the art museum.
  (take)

2. He can't go back to his country. If he _____ back, he _____
              (can)   (visit)
 his father.

3. It's raining now. The children _____ to the park if it _____.
             (go)   (not/rain)

4. She didn't find a job. If she _____ a job, she _____ a car last
          (find)   (buy)
 month.

5. If I _____ a child, I _____ with video games all day.
   (be)   (play)

6. She never expected to come to the U.S. If she _____ she was going
               (know)
 to be in the U.S., she _____ more English in her country.
        (study)

7. They weren't prepared to take the test last year, so they didn't take it. If they
 _____ it at that time, they _____.
  (take)   (fail)

8. She applied to medical school because she wants to become a doctor. If she
 _____ a doctor, she _____ in a small town.
  (become)   (work)

9. I wasn't born in the U.S. If I _____ in the U.S., I _____ in
 this class now.   (be/born)   (not/be)

10. If I _____ you, I _____ to the U.S. ten years ago.
   (be)   (come)

Part 2   Complete each sentence.

EXAMPLE: **If I had a million dollars,** *I would travel around the world.*

1. People would live longer if _____

   _____

2. If I had lived in the U.S. as a child, _____

   _____

3. The teacher would have skipped this lesson if _____

   _____

4. I wouldn't have come to the U.S. if _____

   _____

5. If we had had a test on this lesson last week, _____

   _____

Part 3   Complete each sentence.

EXAMPLES: **I'm not fluent in English. I wish I** *were fluent in English.*

   I didn't prepare for the test. I wish I *had prepared for the test.*

1. I don't have a car. I wish I _____ a car.

2. I have to work 60 hours a week. I wish I _____ so many hours.

3. I ate the fish and got sick. I wish I _____ the fish.

4. I didn't have the opportunity to come to the U.S. when I was younger. I wish

   I _____ the opportunity to come here when I was younger.

5. I'm in the U.S. My sister is in Poland. I wish we _____ together.

6. I can't type. I wish I _____ type.

7. She couldn't attend the concert last night. I wish she _____ the
   concert.

8. I didn't know you ten years ago. I wish I _____ you ten years ago.

9. I didn't study English as a child. I wish I _____ English when I was young.

10. The children are making a lot of noise. I wish they _____ quiet.

Appendix A

Noncount Nouns

The following groups of words are classified as noncount nouns.

Group A. Nouns that have no distinct, separate parts. We look at the whole:

air	coffee	oil	tea
blood	electricity	paper	thunder
bread	lightning	pork	water
butter	meat	poultry	wine
cholesterol	milk	soup	yogurt

Group B. Nouns that have parts that are too small or insignificant to count:

corn	popcorn	sand
grass	rice	snow
hair	salt	sugar

NOTE: Count and noncount nouns are grammatical terms, but they are not always logical. *Rice* is very small and is a noncount noun. *Beans* and *peas* are also very small but are count nouns.

Group C. Nouns that are classes or categories of things:

food (vegetables, meat, spaghetti)
furniture (chairs, tables, beds)
clothing (sweaters, pants, dresses)
mail (letters, packages, postcards, fliers)
fruit (cherries, apples, grapes)
makeup (lipstick, rouge, eye shadow)
homework (compositions, exercises, reading)
jewelry (necklaces, bracelets, rings)
housework (washing dishes, dusting, cooking)
money or cash (nickels, dimes, dollars)

Group D. Nouns that are abstractions:

advice	fun	life	patience
art	happiness	love	pollution
beauty	health	luck	time
crime	help	music	trouble
education	information	nature	truth
energy	intelligence	noise	unemployment
experience	knowledge	nutrition	work

Group E. Subjects of study:

biology	geometry	history
chemistry	grammar	math (mathematics)*

*NOTE: Even though *mathematics* ends with *s*, it is not plural.

Notice the quantity words used with count and noncount nouns.

Singular Count	Plural Count	Noncount
a tomato	tomatoes	coffee
one tomato	two tomatoes	two cups of coffee
	some tomatoes	some coffee
no tomato	no tomatoes	no coffee
	any tomatoes	any coffee (with questions and negatives)
	a lot of tomatoes	a lot of coffee
	many tomatoes	much coffee
	(with questions and negatives)	
	a few tomatoes	a little coffee
	several tomatoes	
	How many tomatoes?	How much coffee?

The following words can be used as either count nouns or noncount nouns. However, the meaning changes according to the way the nouns are used.

Count	Noncount
Oranges and grapefruit are *fruits* that contain a lot of vitamin C.	I bought some *fruit* at the fruit store.
Ice cream and butter are *foods* that contain cholesterol.	We don't need to go shopping today. We have a lot of *food* at home.
He wrote a *paper* about hypnosis.	I need some *paper* to write my composition.
He committed three *crimes* last year.	There is a lot of *crime* in a big city.
I have 200 *chickens* on my farm.	We ate some *chicken* for dinner.
I don't want to bore you with all my *troubles*.	I have some *trouble* with my car.
She went to Puerto Rico three *times*.	She spent a lot of *time* on her project.
She drank three *glasses* of water.	The window is made of bulletproof *glass*.
I had a bad *experience* during my trip to Paris.	She has some *experience* with computer programming.
I don't know much about the *lives* of my grandparents.	*Life* is sometimes happy, sometimes sad.
I heard *a noise* outside my window.	Those children are making a lot of *noise*.

Appendix B

Uses of Articles

Overview of Articles

Articles tell us if a noun is definite or indefinite.

	Count		Noncount
	Singular	Plural	
Definite	the book	the books	the coffee
Indefinite	a book	(some/any) books	(some/any) coffee

Part A: Uses of the Indefinite Article

1. To classify a subject
2. To make a generalization
3. To introduce an indefinite noun into a conversation

To Classify the Subject

1. We use *a/an* after the verb *be* to classify, define, or identify a singular subject:

What's Chicago?[1]	It's *a city.*
What's Illinois?	It's *a state.*
Who was Abraham Lincoln?	He was *an American President.*
What's this? ☆	It's *a star.*

2. We use no article after *be* to classify a plural subject:

What are Poland and Russia?	They're *countries.*
What are these? ❤ ❤	They're *hearts.*
Who were Lincoln and Washington?	They were *American Presidents.*

To Make a Generalization

To say that something is true of all members of a group:

1. With a count noun, use *a(n)* + singular form or no article + plural form:

A dog has sharp teeth.	*An elephant* has big ears.
OR	OR
Dogs have sharp teeth.	*Elephants* have big ears.

---

[1]Proper nouns (names) do not usually use articles.

2. With a noncount noun, use no article:

   Coffee contains caffeine.
   Milk is white.
   Love makes people happy.
   Time passes quickly when you're having fun.
   Money can't buy *happiness.*

To Introduce an Indefinite Noun into a Conversation

When we introduce a new noun into a conversation, the noun is indefinite. The speaker may or may not have something specific in mind, but the listener does not.

1. Use the indefinite article *a(n)* with singular count nouns. With plural nouns, you can use *some* or *any* to show an indefinite quantity.

   I had *a dog* when I was a child.
   I had *(some) turtles* when I was a child.
   Do you have *(any) questions* about this lesson?

2. You can use the indefinite quantity words *some/any* with noncount nouns.

   I have *(some) money* in my pocket.
   Do you want *(any) milk* with your lunch?

3. *There* + a form of *be* can introduce an indefinite noun into a conversation.

   Is there *an elevator* in this building?
   Are there *(any) public telephones* in this building?
   There is *(some) money* on the table.

NOTE: *Some* or *any* can be omitted before an indefinite noun.

Part B: Uses of the Definite Article

1. To refer to a previously introduced noun
2. When the speaker and the listener have the same reference
3. With certain familiar places
4. To make a formal, general statement

To Refer to a Previously Introduced Noun

After an indefinite noun comes into the conversation, the speaker talks about it again by using the definite article.

1. COUNT NOUNS:

   I had a dog when I was a child. My father gave me *the dog* for Christmas.
   I had some turtles when I was a child. I kept *the turtles* in my room.

2. NONCOUNT:

   I need some sugar. I need *the sugar* to bake a cake.
   Did you buy any coffee? Yes. *The coffee* is in the cabinet.

When the Speaker and the Listener Have the Same Reference

The definite article shows that the speaker and listener have the same person(s) or object(s) in mind.

1. The object is present:

    COUNT: *The dog* has big ears.
                    The cats are sleeping.
    NONCOUNT: *The milk* is sour. Don't drink it.

2. There is only one:

    The sun is not very bright in the winter.
    There are many problems in *the world*.
    Write your name on *the top* of the page. (The page has only one top.)
    Sign your name on *the back* of the check. (The check has only one back.)
    The Amazon is *the longest river* in the world.
    December is *the last month* of the year.

3. The speaker and listener share a common experience:

    Students in the same class talk about *the teacher, the textbook, the homework, the black-
        board*, etc.
    Did you do *the homework* last night?
    People who live together talk about *the house, the door, the windows, the light switch*, etc.
        When you leave *the house*, please turn off *the lights*.
    People who live in the same country talk about *the President, the government, the Congress*,
    etc.
    Did you see *the President* on TV last night?

4. The speaker defines or specifies exactly which one:

    The house on the corner is beautiful.
    I spent *the money you gave me*.

Uses of *The* with Places

1. We often use *the* with certain familiar places and people—*the bank, the zoo, the park, the store,
    the movies, the beach, the post office, the bus/train, the doctor*—when we refer to one that we
    habitually visit or use.

    I'm going to *the store* after work. Do you need anything?
    The bank is closed. I'll go tomorrow.

2. We omit *the* with some places after a preposition *(to, at, in)*.

    He's *in church*.
    I'm going *to school*.
    They're *at work*.
    I'm going *to bed*.

3. We say *go home* and *go downtown* without the article or the preposition.

    I'm going *home* now.
    Are you going *downtown* after class?

4. When we say *go to college* or *be in college,* this means to be a student at a college or university.

   Is your son in high school?
   No. He *goes to college* now.
   OR
   No. He's *in college* now.

Use of *the* to Make a Formal, General Statement

1. We can use *the* with singular, count nouns to make a formal, general statement. We do this with the following categories:

   A. SPECIES:
      The shark is the oldest and most primitive fish.
      The bat is a nocturnal animal. It hunts for food at night.

      shark   bat

   B. Inventions:
      The computer has changed the way Americans deal with information.
      Bell invented *the telephone.*

   C. Organs of the body:
      The heart is a muscle that has four chambers.
      The ear has three parts: outer, middle, and inner.

   D. In certain proverbs and sayings:
      The pen is mightier than *the sword.*
      The hand is quicker than *the eye.*
      Which came first, *the chicken* or *the egg*?

2. For informal generalizations, use *a* + singular noun or no article with a plural noun. Compare:

   The computer has changed the ways Americans deal with information.
   Computers are expensive.
   A computer is expensive.

Part C: Special Uses of Articles

No Article	Article

Personal names:
    John Kennedy
    Michael Jackson
	The whole family:
	    the Kennedys
	    the Jacksons

Title and name:
    Queen Elizabeth
    Pope John Paul
	Title without name:
	    the Queen
	    the Pope

Cities, states, countries, continents:
    Cleveland
    Ohio
    Mexico
    South America
	Places that are considered a union:
	    the United States
	    the former Soviet Union
	    the United Kingdom
	Place names: the _____ of _____
	    the Republic of China
	    the District of Columbia

No Article	Article
Mountains	Mountain ranges:
Mount Everest	the Himalayas
Mount McKinley	the Rocky Mountains
Islands:	Collectives of islands:
Coney Island	the Hawaiian Islands
Staten Island	the Virgin Islands
	the Philippines
Lakes:	Collectives of lakes:
Lake Superior	the Great Lakes
Lake Michigan	the Finger Lakes
Beaches:	Rivers, oceans, seas, canals:
Palm Beach	the Mississippi River
Pebble Beach	the Atlantic Ocean
	the Dead Sea
	the Panama Canal
Streets and avenues:	Well-known buildings:
Madison Avenue	the Sears Tower
Wall Street	the World Trade Center
Parks:	Zoos:
Central Park	the San Diego Zoo
Hyde Park	the Milwaukee Zoo
Seasons:	Deserts:
summer fall	the Mojave Desert
spring winter	the Sahara Desert
Summer is my favorite season.	
NOTE: After a preposition, *the* may be used.	
In (the) winter, my car runs badly.	
Directions:	Sections of a piece of land:
north south	the Southwest (of the U.S.)
east west	the West Side (of New York)
School subjects:	Unique geographical points:
history	the North Pole
math	the Vatican
Name + *college* or *university:*	The University (College) of ___
Northwestern University	the University of Michigan
Bradford College	the College of DuPage County
Magazines:	Newspapers:
Time	the *Tribune*
Sports Illustrated	the *Wall Street Journal*

No Article	Article

Months and days:
    September
    Monday
	Ships:
	    the *Titanic*
	    the *Queen Elizabeth*

Holidays:
    Thanksgiving
    Mother's Day
	Holiday exception:
	    the Fourth of July

Diseases:
    cancer
    polio
    AIDS
    malaria
	Ailments:
	    a cold
	    a headache
	    a toothache
	    the flu

Games and sports:
    poker
    soccer
	Musical instruments, after *play:*
	    the drums
	    the piano
	NOTE: Sometimes *the* is omitted.
	    She plays (the) drums.

Languages:
    French
    English
	The _____ language:
	    the French language
	    the English language

Last month, year, week, etc. = the one before this one:
    I forgot to pay my rent last month.
    The teacher gave us a test last week.
	The last month, the last year, the last week, etc.
	    = the last in a series:
	    December is the last month of the year.
	    Summer vacation begins the last week in May.

In office = in an elected position:
    The president is in office for four years.
	In the office = in a specific room:
	    The teacher is in the office.

In back/front:
 	
    She's in back of the car.
	In the back/the front:
	
	    He's in the back of the bus.

Appendix C

The Verb *GET*

Get has many meanings. Here is a list of the most common ones:

- get something = receive
  I got a letter from my father.

- get + (to) place = arrive
  I got home at six. What time did you get to school?

- get + object + infinitive = persuade
  She got him to wash the dishes.

- get + past participle = become

get accustomed to	get hurt
get acquainted	get lost
get bored	get married
get confused	get scared
get divorced	get tired
get dressed	get used to
get drunk	get worried
get engaged	

  They got married in 1989.

- get + adjective – become

get angry	get old
get dark	get rich
get fat	get sleepy
get hungry	get upset
get nervous	get well

  It gets dark at 6:30.

- get an illness = catch
  While I was traveling, I got malaria.

- get a joke or an idea = understand
  Everybody except Tom laughed at the joke. He didn't get it.
  The boss explained the project to us, but I didn't get it.

- get ahead = advance
  He works very hard because he wants to get ahead in his job.

- get along (well) (with someone) = to have a good relationship
  She doesn't get along with her mother-in-law.
  Do you and your roommate get along well?

•get around to something = find the time to do something

   I wanted to write my brother a letter yesterday, but I didn't get around to it.

•get away = escape

   The police chased the thief, but he got away.

•get away with something = escape punishment

   He cheated on his taxes and got away with it.

•get back = return

   He got back from his vacation last Saturday.

•get back at someone = get revenge

   My brother wants to get back at me for stealing his girlfriend.

•get back to someone = communicate with someone at a later time

   I can't talk to you today. Can I get back to you tomorrow?

•get by = have just enough but nothing more

   On her salary, she's just getting by. She can't afford a car or a vacation.

•get in trouble = be caught and punished for doing something wrong

   They got in trouble for cheating on the test.

•get in(to) = enter a car

   She got in the car and drove away quickly.

•get out (of) = leave a car

   When the taxi arrived at the theater, everyone got out.

•get on = to seat yourself on a bicycle, motorcycle, horse, etc.

   She got on the motorcycle and left.

•get on = enter a train, bus, airplane, boat, etc.

   She got on the bus and took a seat in the back.

•get off = leave a bicycle, motorcycle, horse, train, bus, airplane

   They will get off the train at the next stop.

•get out of something = escape responsibility

   My boss wants me to help him on Saturday, but I'm going to try to get out of it.

•get over something = recover from an illness or disappointment

   She has the flu this week. I hope she gets over it soon.

•get rid of someone or something = free oneself of someone or something undesirable

   My apartment has roaches, and I can't get rid of them.

•get through (to someone) = to communicate, often by telephone

   She tried to explain the dangers of drugs to her son, but she couldn't get through to
      him.

   I tried to call her many times, but her line was busy. I couldn't get through.

•get through with something = finish

   I can meet you after I get through with my homework.

•get together = to meet with another person

   I'd like to see you again. When can we get together?

•get up = to arise from bed

   He woke up at 6 o'clock, but he didn't get up until 6:30.

Appendix D

Gerund and Infinitive Patterns

1. VERB + INFINITIVE:

> They need *to leave.*
> I learned *to speak* English.

agree	consent	need	tend
appear	decide	offer	threaten
arrange	demand	plan	try
ask	expect	prepare	volunteer
be able	fail	pretend	want
beg	forget	promise	wish
can afford	hope	refuse	would like
care	know how	remember	
choose	learn	seem	
claim	manage	swear	

2. VERB + NOUN/OBJECT PRONOUN + INFINITIVE:

> I want you *to leave.*
> He expects me *to call* him.

advise	convince	hire	require
allow	dare	instruct	select
appoint	enable	invite	teach
ask	encourage	need	tell
beg	expect	order	urge
cause	forbid	permit	want
challenge	force	persuade	warn
choose	get	remind	would like
command	help*		

*NOTE: After *help*, *to* is often omitted: "He helped me (to) move."

3. ADJECTIVE + INFINITIVE:

> They're happy *to be* here.
> We're willing *to help* you.

afraid	disturbed	lucky	shocked
ashamed	eager	pleased	sorry
amazed	foolish	prepared	surprised
careful	fortunate	proud	upset
content	free	ready	willing
delighted	glad	reluctant	wrong
determined	happy	sad	
disappointed	likely		

337

4. VERB + GERUND

> I enjoy *dancing.*
> They don't permit *drinking.*

admit	detest	miss	resent
advise	discuss	permit	resist
anticipate	dislike	postpone	risk
appreciate	enjoy	practice	stop
avoid	finish	put off	suggest
can't help	forbid	quit	tolerate
complete	imagine	recall	understand
consider	keep (on)	recommend	
delay	mention	regret	
deny	mind	remember	

5. EXPRESSIONS WITH GO + GERUND:

> He *goes fishing* every Saturday.
> They *went shopping* yesterday

go boating	go hiking	go skating
go bowling	go hunting	go skiing
go camping	go jogging	go swimming
go dancing	go sailing	
go fishing	go shopping	

6. PREPOSITION + GERUND:

> Verb + Preposition + Gerund
> We talked about *moving.*
> I look forward to *having* my own apartment.

argue about	talk about	succeed in	insist on
care about	think about	feel like	plan on
complain about	worry about	(dis)approve of	adjust to
dream about	refrain from	concentrate on	look forward to
forget about	believe in	depend on	object to

> Adjective + Preposition + Gerund
> I'm fond of *traveling.*
> She's not accustomed to *eating* alone.

concerned about	good at	suitable for	guilty of
excited about	surprised at	interested in	proud of
lazy about	appropriate for	afraid of	sure of
sorry about	famous for	ashamed of	tired of
upset about	grateful to . . . for	(in)capable of	accustomed to
worried about	responsible for	fond of	used to

> Verb + Object + Preposition + Gerund
> I thanked him for *helping* me.
> I apologized to him for *forgetting* his birthday.

warn . . . about	blame . . . for	accuse . . . of
prevent . . . from	forgive . . . for	suspect . . . of
apologize to . . . for	thank . . . for	devote . . . to

> **Gerund After Preposition in Certain Expressions**
> Who's in charge of *collecting* the papers?
> What is your reason for *coming* late?

need for	technique for	in charge of	in the middle of
reason for	interest in	in danger of	the point of
requirement for	impression of	in favor of	

> **Gerund After Preposition in Adverbial Phrases**
> I can't read English without *using* a dictionary
> Instead of *going* to work, he went to a baseball game.

after	in addition to
before	in return for
by	in place of
without	instead of

7. NOUN + GERUND

> He has difficulty *speaking* English.
> She had a problem *finding* a job.
> She spent three weeks *looking* for an apartment.

Use a gerund after the noun in these expressions:

have a difficult time	have a hard time
have difficulty	have a problem
have experience	have trouble
have fun	spend time
have a good time	there's no use

8. VERB + GERUND OR INFINITIVE (With little or no difference in meaning).

> They like *to sing*.   I started *to read*.
> They like *singing*.   I started *reading*.

attempt	intend
begin	like
can't stand	love
continue	neglect
deserve	prefer
hate	start
hesitate	

Appendix E

Prepositions

Verb + Preposition		
adjust to	disapprove of	prevent . . . from*
agree with	dream about/of	rely on
apologize to . . . for*	feel like	speak about
approve of	forget about	succeed in
argue about	forgive . . . for*	suspect . . . of*
believe in	hear about	take care of
blame . . . for*	hear of	talk about
care about	insist on	thank . . . for*
complain about	listen to	think about
concentrate on	look at	wait for
consist of	look for	warn . . . about*
deal with	look forward to	worry about
decide on	object to	
depend on	plan on	

Adjective + Preposition		
accustomed to	fond of	responsible for
afraid of	glad about	sad about
amazed at/by	good at	satisfied with
angry about	grateful to . . . for*	sick of
angry at	guilty of	sorry about
ashamed of	happy about	sorry for
aware of	incapable of	sure of
bored with/by	interested in	surprised at
capable of	lazy about	tired of
concerned about	mad about	upset about
different from	mad at	used to
excited about	opposed to	worried about
famous for	proud of	

*NOTE: The dots indicate that an object is needed: "He accused the boy of taking the money."

Appendix F

Direct and Indirect Objects

1. The order of direct and indirect objects depends on the verb you use.

         IO   DO
He told his friend the answer.
              DO   IO
He explained the answer to his friend.

2. The order of the objects sometimes depends on whether you use a noun or a pronoun object.

    S V IO   DO
He gave the woman the keys.
    S V DO IO
He gave them to her.

3. In some cases, the connecting preposition is *to;* in some cases *for.* In some cases, there is no connecting preposition.

    She'll serve lunch *to* her guests.
    She reserved a seat *for* you.
    I asked him a question.

Each of the following groups of words follows a specific pattern of word order and preposition choice.

Group I (Pronouns affect word order.)

Patterns: He gave a present to his wife.
           He gave his wife a present.
           He gave it to his wife.
           He gave her a present.
           He gave it to her.

Verbs:

bring	lend	pass	sell	show	teach
give	offer	pay	send	sing	tell
hand	owe	read	serve	take	write

Group II (Pronouns affect word order.)

Patterns: He bought a car for his daughter.
He bought his daughter a car.
He bought it for his daughter.
He bought her a car.
He bought it for her.

Verbs:

bake	buy	draw	get	make
build	do	find	knit	reserve

Group III (Pronouns don't affect word order.)

Patterns: He explained the problem to his friend.
He explained it to her.

Verbs:

admit	introduce	recommend	say
announce	mention	repeat	speak
describe	prove	report	suggest
explain			

Group IV (Pronouns don't affect word order.)

Patterns: He cashed a check for his friend.
He cashed it for her.

Verbs:

answer	change	design	open	prescribe
cash	close	fix	prepare	pronounce

Group V (Pronouns don't affect word order.)

Patterns: She asked the teacher a question.
She asked him a question.
It took me five minutes to answer the question.

Verbs:

ask	charge	cost	wish	take (with time)

Appendix G

Spelling and Pronunciation

Spelling of the -S Form

The chart below shows the spelling of the -s form.

Rule	Verbs	-S Form
Add *s* to most verbs to make the -s form.	hope	hopes
	eat	eats
When the base form ends in *s, z, sh, ch,* or *x,* add *es* and pronounce an extra syllable, /ɪz/.	miss	misses
	buzz	buzzes
	wash	washes
	catch	catches
	tax	taxes
When the base form ends in a consonant + *y,* change the *y* to *i* and add *es.*	carry	carries
	worry	worries
When the base form ends in a vowel + *y,* do not change the *y.*	pay	pays
	obey	obeys
Add *es* to *go* and *do.*	go	goes
	do	does

Pronunciation of the -S Form

A. We pronounce /s/ if the verb ends in a voiceless sound: /p t k f/.

hope—hopes	pick—picks
eat—eats	laugh—laughs

B. We pronounce /z/ if the verb ends in a voiced sound.

live—lives	read—reads	sing—sings
grab—grabs	run—runs	borrow—borrows

C. When the base form ends in *s, z, sh, ch, x, se, ge,* or *ce,* we pronounce an extra syllable, /ɪz/.

miss—misses	watch—watches	change—changes
buzz—buzzes	fix—fixes	dance—dances
wash—washes	use—uses	

D. These verbs have a change in the vowel sound.

do /**du**/—does /**d** ʌ **z**/
say /**sei**/—says /**s** ɛ **z**/

Spelling of the -*ing* Form

The chart below shows the spelling of the -*ing* form.

Rule	Verbs	-*ing* Form
Add *ing* to most verbs.	eat go study	eating going studying
For a one-syllable verb that ends in a consonant + vowel + consonant (CVC), double the final consonant and add *ing*.	p l a n │ │ │ C V C s t o p │ │ │ C V C s i t │ │ │ C V C	planning stopping sitting
Do not double final *w, x,* or *y*.	show mix stay	showing mixing staying
For a two-syllable word that ends in CVC, double the final consonant only if the last syllable is stressed.	refér admít begín	referring admitting beginning
When the last syllable of a two-syllable word is not stressed, do not double the final consonant.	lísten ópen óffer	listening opening offering
If the word ends in a consonant + *e,* drop the *e* before adding *ing*.	live take write	living taking writing

Spelling of the Past Tense of Regular Verbs

The chart below shows the spelling of the -*ed* form.

Rule	Verbs	-*ed* Form
Add *ed* to the base form to make the past tense of most regular verbs.	start kick	started kicked
When the base form ends in *e*, add *d* only.	die live	died lived
When the base form ends in a consonant + *y*, change the *y* to *i* and add *ed*.	carry worry	carried worried
When the base form ends in a vowel + *y*, do not change the *y*.	destroy stay	destroyed stayed
For a one-syllable word that ends in a consonant + vowel + consonant (CVC), double the final consonant and add *ed*.	s t o p | | | C V C p l u g | | | C V C	stopped plugged
Do not double final *w* or *x*.	sew fix	sewed fixed
For a two-syllable word that ends in CVC, double the final consonant only if the last syllable is stressed.	occúr permít	occurred permitted
When the last syllable of a two-syllable word is not stressed, do not double the final consonant.	ópen háppen	opened happened

Pronunciation of Past Forms That End in -*ed*

The past tense with -*ed* has three pronunciations. Listen to your teacher's pronunciation.

A. We pronounce a /t/ if the base form ends in a voiceless sound: /p, k, f, s, š, č/.

jump—jumped	cough—coughed	wash—washed
cook—cooked	kiss—kissed	watch—watched

B. We pronounce a /d/ if the base form ends in a voiced sound.

rub—rubbed	charge—charged	bang—banged
drag—dragged	glue—glued	call—called
love—loved	massage—massaged	fear—feared
bathe—bathed	name—named	free—freed
use—used	learn—learned	

C. We pronounce an extra syllable /**Id**/ if the base form ends in a /**t**/ or /**d**/ sound.

wait—waited   want—wanted   need—needed
hate—hated   add—added   decide—decided

Spelling of Short Comparative and Superlative Adjectives and Adverbs

A. For most short adjectives and adverbs, we add *er* to make the comparative form and -*est* to make the superlative form.

old—older—oldest

tall—taller—tallest

fast—faster—fastest

B. If the word ends in -*e*, just add *r* or *st*.

nice—nicer—nicest

fine—finer—finest

C. For adjectives that end in -*y*, change *y* to *i* before adding *er* or *est*.

happy—happier—happiest

healthy—healthier—healthiest

sunny—sunnier—sunniest

NOTE: Do not add *er* or *est* to an -*ly* adverb.

quickly—more quickly—most quickly

D. For one-syllable words that end in consonant-vowel-consonant, we double the final consonant before adding *er* or *est*.

big—bigger—biggest

sad—sadder—saddest

hot—hotter—hottest

EXCEPTION: Do not double final *w*.

new—newer—newest

Spelling Rules for Adverbs Ending in -*ly*

1. Most adverbs of manner are formed by putting -*ly* at the end of an adjective.

Adjective	Adverb
careful	carefully
quiet	quietly
illegal	illegally

2. For adjectives that end in -*y*, we change *y* to *i*, then add -*ly*.

easy—easily

happy—happily

lucky—luckily

3. For adjectives that end in *-e*, we keep the *e* and add *-ly*.

    nice—nicely

    free—freely

EXCEPTION:

    true—truly

4. For adjectives that end in a consonant + *-le*, we drop the *e* and add *-ly*.

    simple—simply

    comfortable—comfortably

    double—doubly

5. For adjectives that end in *-ic*, add *-ally*.

    basic—basically

    enthusiastic—enthusiastically

EXCEPTION:

    public—publicly

Appendix H

Irregular Verbs—Past and Past Participle

Base Form	Past Form	Past Participle	Base Form	Past Form	Past Participle
arise	arose	arisen	drink	drank	drunk
be	was/were	been	drive	drove	driven
bear	bore	born OR borne	eat	ate	eaten
beat	beat	beaten	fall	fell	fallen
become	became	become	feed	fed	fed
begin	began	begun	feel	felt	felt
bend	bent	bent	fight	fought	fought
bet	bet	bet	find	found	found
bind	bound	bound	fit	fit	fit
bite	bit	bitten	flee	fled	fled
bleed	bled	bled	fly	flew	flown
blow	blew	blown	forbid	forbade	forbidden
break	broke	broken	forget	forgot	forgotten
breed	bred	bred	forgive	forgave	forgiven
bring	brought	brought	freeze	froze	frozen
broadcast	broadcast	broadcast	get	got	gotten
build	built	built	give	gave	given
burst	burst	burst	go	went	gone
buy	bought	bought	grind	ground	ground
cast	cast	cast	grow	grew	grown
catch	caught	caught	hang	hung	hung[1]
choose	chose	chosen	have	had	had
cling	clung	clung	hear	heard	heard
come	came	come	hide	hid	hidden
cost	cost	cost	hit	hit	hit
creep	crept	crept	hold	held	held
cut	cut	cut	hurt	hurt	hurt
deal	dealt	dealt	keep	kept	kept
dig	dug	dug	know	knew	known
do	did	done	lay	laid	laid
draw	drew	drawn	lead	led	led

---

[1]*Hanged* is used as the past form to refer to punishment by death.

Base Form	Past Form	Past Participle	Base Form	Past Form	Past Participle
leave	left	left	split	split	split
lend	loaned/lent	loaned/lent	spread	spread	spread
let	let	let	spring	sprang	sprung
lie	lay	lain	stand	stood	stood
light	lit OR lighted	lit OR lighted	steal	stole	stolen
lose	lost	lost	stick	stuck	stuck
make	made	made	sting	stung	stung
mean	meant	meant	stink	stank	stunk
meet	met	met	strike	struck	struck OR stricken
mistake	mistook	mistaken	strive	strove	striven
pay	paid	paid	swear	swore	sworn
prove	proved	proven OR proved	sweep	swept	swept
put	put	put	swim	swam	swum
quit	quit	quit	swing	swung	swung
read	read	read	take	took	taken
ride	rode	ridden	teach	taught	taught
ring	rang	rung	tear	tore	torn
rise	rose	risen	tell	told	told
run	ran	run	think	thought	thought
say	said	said	throw	threw	thrown
see	saw	seen	understand	understood	understood
seek	sought	sought	upset	upset	upset
sell	sold	sold	wake	woke	woken
send	sent	sent	wear	wore	worn
set	set	set	weave	wove	woven
shake	shook	shaken	weep	wept	wept
shed	shed	shed	win	won	won
shine	shone	shone	wind	wound	wound
shoot	shot	shot	withdraw	withdrew	withdrawn
show	showed	shown OR showed	wring	wrung	wrung
shrink	shrank	shrunk	write	wrote	written
shut	shut	shut			
sing	sang	sung			
sink	sank	sunk			
sit	sat	sat			
sleep	slept	slept			
slide	slid	slid			
slit	slit	slit			
speak	spoke	spoken			
speed	sped	sped			
spend	spent	spent			
spin	spun	spun			
spit	spit	spit			

The past and past participle of some verbs can end in *-ed* or *-t*. Americans generally prefer the *-ed* form:

burn	burned or burnt
dream	dreamed or dreamt
kneel	kneeled or knelt
learn	learned or learnt
spill	spilled or spilt
spoil	spoiled or spoilt

Appendix I

Modals and Related Expressions

Degrees of Expectation and Certainty	
Examples	**Explanation**
Present:	
My teacher lived in Japan when she was a child. She *must speak* Japanese.	I think this is probably true based on the evidence or information that I have.
She *may/might/could speak* other languages.	Maybe she speaks other languages. This is possible, but I really don't know for sure.
Future:	
I don't have time to help you today. I *should have* more time tomorrow.	I will probably have more time tomorrow.
Express mail *is supposed to arrive* the next day.	We are told to expect this.
Overpopulation *could/may/might cause* starvation.	This is a possible result of overpopulation.
Past:	
President Kennedy was killed. The investigation committee decided that Oswald *must have killed* him.	The evidence led the committee to this conclusion.
Oswald *may/might/could have been* the agent of another government.	We don't know. There are other possibilities as well.
The package *was supposed to arrive* yesterday, but there was a snow storm.	This was expected, but it didn't happen.

Necessity/Obligation

Present/Future:

You *have to/must be* 18 years old to apply for citizenship.	It is the law.
I *have to/have got to go* to the dentist next week.	It is necessary for me.
I'*m supposed to see* my counselor once a week.	This is expected of me.
You *are allowed to/are permitted to/may/ can vote* if you are 18 or older.	You have legal permission to vote.

Past:

I *had to leave* my country because of the war.	It was necessary or urgent for me to leave.
She *was permitted to/was allowed to/could apply* for a visa.	This was permitted.
I *was supposed to see* my counselor last week, but I was sick.	This was expected, but it didn't happen.

Advice

Present/Future:

When you leave a party, you *should thank* the host or hostess for a good time.	This is advice.
You'*d better drive* carefully in the rain, or you might have an accident	This is a warning. There are negative consequences.
What *can* I *wear* to the party? You *could wear* your blue dress or your red suit.	These are suggestions.
You don't have to send a "thank-you" note to the hostess, but you *can*.	This is acceptable behavior, but not required.

Past:

Susan didn't say thank you when she left the party. She *should have said* thank you.	This advice comes too late. It describes a past mistake.

Ability/Possibility

Present:

Pharmacists *know how to/are able to/can read* Latin.

They have this ability.

Future:

The pharmacist *will be able to/can fill* your prescription later.

This will be possible.

Past:

The pharmacist *was able to reach* my doctor.

She was successful.

I *could* read Latin when I was in high school, but I can't now.

I had this ability.

Kennedy *could have used* a closed car, but he preferred an open car.

He had this opportunity, but he didn't do it.

A. I voted for Kennedy in 1964.
B. What? You *couldn't have voted* for him in 1964! He died in 1963.

The first statement is not true because it is absolutely impossible.

Polite Requests

Would you mind opening the window?
Could/Would you open the window?
Can/Will you open the window?

These expressions are more polite than the imperative, "Open the window."

Would you *mind* if I used your pen?
Do you *mind* if I use your pen?
May
Could } I use your pen?
Can

These expressions are more polite than the imperative, "Give me your pen."

I'd *like* a glass of water.

I want a glass of water.

Would you *like* a glass of water?

Do you want a glass of water?

Preference

Would you *rather* go out or stay home?
I'd *rather* stay home than go out.
Would you *prefer* to go out or stay home?
I'd *prefer* to stay home.

Which one do you prefer?

Appendix J

Comparative, Superlative, Equality

The chart below shows comparative and superlative forms.

	Simple	Comparative	Superlative
One-syllable adjectives and adverbs	tall	taller	the tallest
	fast	faster	the fastest
EXCEPTIONS:	bored	more bored	the most bored
	tired	more tired	the most tired
Two-syllable adjectives that end in -y	easy	easier	the easiest
	happy	happier	the happiest
	pretty	prettier	the prettiest
Other two-syllable adjectives	frequent	more frequent	the most frequent
	active	more active	the most active
Some two-syllable adjectives have two forms.	simple	simpler	the simplest
		more simple	the most simple
	common	commoner	the commonest
		more common	the most common

NOTE: These two-syllable adjectives have two forms: *handsome, quiet, gentle, narrow, clever, friendly, angry.*

	Simple	Comparative	Superlative
Adjectives with three or more syllables	important	more important	the most important
	difficult	more difficult	the most difficult
-ly adverbs	quickly	more quickly	the most quickly
	brightly	more brightly	the most brightly
Irregular adjectives and adverbs	good/well	better	the best
	bad/badly	worse	the worst
	far	farther/further*	the farthest/furthest
	little	less	the least
	a lot	more	the most

*NOTE: *Farther* is for distances. *Further* is for ideas.

The Superlative Form

Subject	Verb	Superlative Form + Noun	Prepositional Phrase
Alaska	is	the biggest state	in the U.S.
California	is	the most populated state	in the U.S.

The Comparative Form:

Subject	Linking Verb[1]	Comparative Adjective	*Than*	Noun/Pronoun
She	is	taller	than	her sister (is).
She	seems	more intelligent	than	her sister.

Subject	Verb Phrase	Comparative Adverb	*Than*	Noun/Pronoun
I	speak English	more fluently	than	my sister (does).
I	sleep	less	than	you (do).

Comparisons with Nouns:

X	Verb	Comparative Word + Noun	*Than*	Y
I	work	fewer hours	than	you (do).
I	have	more time	than	you (do).

Equatives with Adjectives and Adverbs:

Subject	Linking Verb	*As*	Adjective	*As*	Noun
She	isn't	as	old	as	her husband (is).
She	looks	as	pretty	as	a picture.

Subject	Verb Phrase	*As*	Adverb	*As*	Noun
She	speaks English	as	fluently	as	her husband (does).
He	doesn't work	as	hard	as	his wife (does).

---

[1]The linking verbs are *be, look, seem, feel, taste, sound, seem.*

Equatives with Quantities:

Subject	Verb	As Many/ Much	Noun	As	Noun
She	works	as many	hours	as	her husband (does).
Milk	doesn't have	as much	fat	as	cream (does).

Subject	Verb	As Much As	Noun		
Chicken	doesn't cost	as much as	meat (does).		
I	don't drive	as much as	you (do).		

Equatives with Nouns:

		Pattern A			
Subject	Verb	The Same	Noun	As	Noun/Pronoun
She	wears	the same	size	as	her mother (does).
She	isn't	the same	height	as	her brother (is).

		Pattern B			
Subject & Subject	Verb	The Same	Noun		
She and her mother	wear	the same	size.		
She and her brother	aren't	the same	height.		

Similarities using *Like:*

	Pattern A		
X	Linking Verb	Like	Y
Pepsi	looks	like	Coke.
Regular coffee	tastes	like	decaf.

	Pattern B		
X and Y	Linking Verb	Alike	
Pepsi and Coke	look	alike.	
Regular coffee and decaf	taste	alike.	

Appendix K

Question Word Order

Questions with a Main Verb Only.

(*Wh-* Word)	*Do/Does/Did(n't)*	Subject	Verb (base form)	Complement
	Did	you	eat	a sandwich?
What	did	you	eat?	
	Doesn't	Jack	have	a car?
Why	doesn't	Jack	have	a car?
How	do	you	spell	"occasion"?
What	does	"occasion"	mean?	
How much	did	your car	cost?	
How	do	you	say	"good-bye" in Spanish?

Questions with *Be:*

(*Wh-* Word)	*Be (n't)*	Subject	Complement
	Is	your wife	from Peru?
Where	is	she	from?
	Were	you	in class yesterday?
Why	weren't	you	in class yesterday?

Questions with Auxiliary Verbs—Modals and *Have* + Past Participle:

(*Wh-* Word)	Aux. *(n't)*	Subject	Verb	Complement
	Will	they	come	back?
When	will	they	come	back?
	Can	I	help	you?
How	can	I	help	you?
	Have	they	seen	the movie?
Why	haven't	they	seen	the movie?

Questions about the Subject:

Wh- Subject	Verb	Complement
Who	knows	the answer?
How many people	took	the test?
Which students	came	late?
How many students	are	absent?
Who	will begin?	

Appendix L

Pronouns and Possessive Forms

Subject Pronoun	Object Pronoun	Possessive Adjective	Possessive Pronoun	Reflexive Pronoun
I	me	my	mine	myself
you	you	your	yours	yourself
he	him	his	his	himself
she	her	her	hers	herself
it	it	its	—	itself
we	us	our	ours	ourselves
you	you	your	yours	yourselves
they	them	their	theirs	themselves
who	whom	whose	whose	—

INDEX

The United States of America

AL	Alabama	IN	Indiana	NE	Nebraska	SC	South Carolina
AK	Alaska	IA	Iowa	NV	Nevada	SD	South Dakota
AZ	Arizona	KS	Kansas	NH	New Hampshire	TN	Tennessee
AR	Arkansas	KY	Kentucky	NJ	New Jersey	TX	Texas
CA	California	LA	Louisiana	NM	New Mexico	UT	Utah
CO	Colorado	ME	Maine	NY	New York	VT	Vermont
CT	Connecticut	MD	Maryland	NC	North Carolina	VA	Virginia
DE	Delaware	MA	Massachusetts	ND	North Dakota	WA	Washington
FL	Florida	MI	Michigan	OH	Ohio	WV	West Virginia
GA	Georgia	MN	Minnesota	OK	Oklahoma	WI	Wisconsin
HI	Hawaii	MS	Mississippi	OR	Oregon	WY	Wyoming
ID	Idaho	MO	Missouri	PA	Pennsylvania	DC*	District of Columbia
IL	Illinois	MT	Montana	RI	Rhode Island		

*The District of Columbia is not a state. Washington D.C. is the capital of the United States. Note: Washington D.C. and Washington state are not the same.

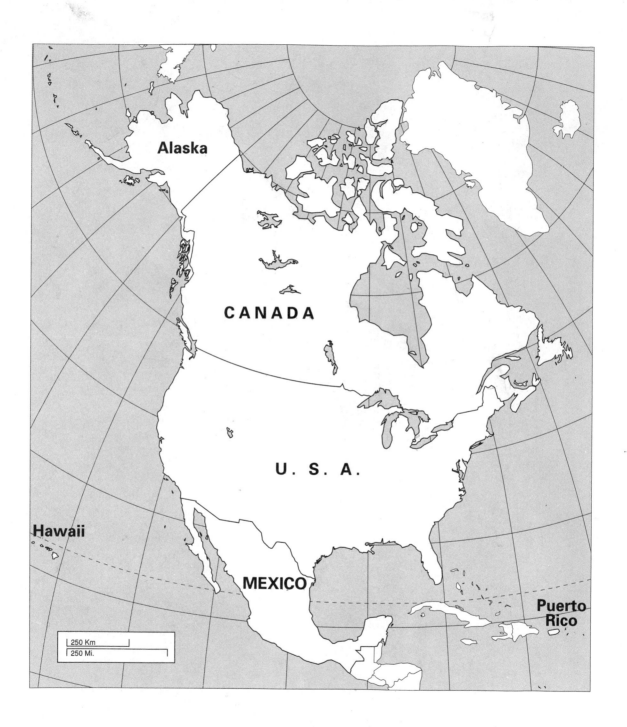

Alaska

CANADA

U. S. A.

Hawaii

MEXICO

Puerto
Rico

250 Km
250 Mi.